A contested landscape

A contested landscape

International perspectives on diversity
in mass higher education

Edited by
Jim Gallacher
and
Michael Osborne

niace
promoting adult learning

Published by the National Institute of Adult Continuing Education
(England and Wales)
21 De Montfort Street
Leicester
LE1 7GE
Company registration no. 2603322
Charity registration no. 1002775

First published 2005

NIACE has a broad remit to promote lifelong learning
opportunities for adults. NIACE works to develop
increased participation in education and training,
particularly for those who do not have easy access
because of class, gender, age, race, language and culture,
learning difficulties or disabilities, or insufficient
financial resources.

You can find NIACE online at www.niace.org.uk

Cataloguing in Publication Data
A CIP record of this title is available from the British Library

ISBN: 1 86201 233 4

Designed and typeset by Avon DataSet Ltd, Bidford on Avon, B50 4JH
Printed and bound in the UK by Antony Rowe Limited, Chippenham

Contents

Introduction

Michael Osborne

Access to higher education (HE) in most OECD countries is no longer the preserve of a small elite, and in most societies there has been a rapid expansion of participation with an emphasis in much of the policy rhetoric directed towards greater equity. In order to achieve the desired growth of systems, a range of initiatives have been put into place (see Osborne, 2003a and b), and it is inescapably the case that greater funding and more efficient use of existing resources are both needed. As the OECD (2001a) has commented:

> *Because of the wide range of activities encompassed by even modest lifelong learning scenarios, and the size of the participation and expenditure gaps that would have to closed in order to realise them, it is almost self-evident that full implementation of the lifelong learning concept will require additional resources.*
>
> *It will be vital that maximum efforts are made to ensure that both existing and new public expenditure on lifelong learning are effective.* (OECD, 2001a, p. 113)

In that context a focus on shorter cycle higher education is of interest, since this form of offer provides a route to expansion that has the potential to be economically viable for both individuals and governments. Moreover, evidence is emerging in some countries that programmes with a shorter duration of study encourage disproportionate participation from those groups who do not traditionally access HE, thereby combating social exclusion, a policy imperative in many societies. It is also the case that those countries where non-university HE (normally short-cycle) is important relative to university education provide more years of tertiary education as a whole (OECD, 2001a, p. 77). The USA is among the leaders in the provision of non-university education as a proportion of the total offer, and it is interesting to note that 'only in the US have participation rates of the low socio-economic groups grown faster than the average rate' (OECD, 2001a, p. 78).

However, relatively little has been published that compares the various models of short-cycle HE provision around the world, and the forms and efficacy of articulation from short-cycle HE to other study. In this book we consider the features of a range of models, their effectiveness as agents of widening participation and the outcomes of this form of HE both in terms of progression to further HE and to the labour market.

The area of vocational education and training (VET) as a provider of short-cycle HE is a particular focus within a number of chapters that follow. Articulation between VET and university-level HE through progression from sub-degree to degree-level education and training is a field of particular policy significance internationally. In Europe, within the UK in particular,[1] there is a major role for institutional providers of HE that are not formally defined as higher education institutions (HEIs). This is also the case elsewhere in the world, particularly in North America and Australasia, where short-cycle HE outside the university sector is an important feature of increasing participation and widening access (OECD, 2001b). The key features of their offer fit well with the precepts of creating a universal HE system, and to a certain extent an equitable one. Whether it is community colleges (CCs) in the USA and Canada, technical and further education (TAFE) in Australia or further education (FE) in the UK, the sector is one of the most significant contributors to these goals. The short cycle of provision, typically two years full time equivalent, the flexibility of the curriculum in terms of its modularity, timing, and location are all features that encourage participation by traditionally excluded groups, including those from lower socio-economic classes, minority ethnic groups, women and those with disabilities. Not only do these institutions play a role in combating social injustice, they also play a role in promoting economic development, the two objectives of course not being mutually exclusive, and this is manifested in the regional dimensions of their work. Despite this role, the work of these institutions has largely been overlooked, and they have been described as the 'Cinderellas' of post-compulsory education (PCE).

In terms of international coverage the main focus of this book is a set of English-speaking countries with a variety of systems of PCE (namely the USA, the UK, Ireland, Canada, Australia, and New Zealand). Some of these countries are characterised by having systems within which a VET sector serves multiple purposes, one of which is to provide short-cycle HE that articulates to varying degrees with university-level education (the

USA, the UK, Canada, and Australia). In other systems based on the Anglo-Saxon tradition, there is a less obvious VET sector, and less differentiation in terms of provider status by level of activity at undergraduate level (Ireland and New Zealand). Another focus will be a system with a binary (and emerging partial trinary) system of advanced HE, namely Germany, where VET and HE have few, if any, points of contact. This book will provide a comparison of these forms of national systems (with strong and weak roles for VET), exploring the historical and cultural factors that have led to these different forms of development.

At the national level, fields of categorisation for each review will focus on the following issues: organisational links, including franchise arrangements; curriculum articulation; approaches to assessment; credit accumulation; teaching and learning approaches; student support systems in both FE and HE, and to support transition; retention; institutional incentivisation; and labour market outcomes.

In this opening chapter the particular role of the VET sector in the provision of HE is initially examined and there follows an exploration of structures of post-compulsory provision more generally. This analysis is undertaken across a range of different national settings, including those beyond the specific countries highlighted in particular chapters that follow.

The role of the VET sector

Vocational education and training refers to provision that relates to the requirements of particular occupational areas, with vocational education normally relating to formal programmes of study that lead to an academic award and vocational training to provision that is short term and focused on the development of specific skills. However, these distinctions are not absolute and, as in many areas of educational endeavour, there is much blurring.

Provision that is defined within the VET category varies from basic skills training through to Masters level training of the International Standard Classification of Education (ISCED) type B form described in more detail later. Providers are necessarily varied as well and include institutions that specialise in offering non-advanced courses at pre-HE level, as well as HEIs and private providers.[2]

In many countries there exist institutions that occupy a distinct position within a hierarchy, offering only ISCED level IV, post-secondary, non-tertiary education. However, in most instances there also exist institutions that offer provision that covers level IV and extends to the next level, V, the first stage of tertiary education. So taking Spain as one example among many, specific employment and training programmes are offered in a variety of forms at level IV within *Escuelas Taller* (workshop schools), *Casa de Oficios* (craft centres) and *Talleres de Empleo* (employment workshops) (EURYDICE, 2003). In parallel, in certain cases there is a separate vocational branch of post-compulsory secondary education offered by secondary education schools (*Institutos de Educación Secundaria*), providing initial vocational training to school pupils. However, there also exist schools devoted exclusively to specific vocational training at both initial and higher levels to both school-leavers and adults, and thus there is an overlap in levels of offer between initial vocational education and HE. It is this phase of higher-level vocational education that concerns much of this book, and in particular the degree to which this paralleling of offer leads to an interface that allows transfer. This crossover role of institutions with a vocational mission into HE is extensive throughout the world, though it occurs in a variety of institutional forms. So, for example, in the USA, CCs offer vocational education at the 'non-baccalaureate post-secondary level', primarily focusing on occupationally specific preparation as well as post-secondary level occupational (*career*) and academic (*collegiate*) programmes. In Australia, TAFE colleges not only offer initial vocational educational, but also diplomas and higher diplomas, that within the Australian Qualifications Framework are designated as HE level. Very similar arrangements exist within the UK within FECs.

Structures of post-compulsory education – providers and provision

Much has been written about the structural forms of the HE component of PCE. Scott (1995, p. 35) suggests that systems can be classified as *dual*, *binary*, *unified* and *stratified*. Both dual and binary systems contain alternative forms of HE providers, usually offering comparable but distinguishable forms of provision; in the case of the binary systems, alternative institutions have been set up to complement and rival existing traditional structures. In unified systems, there is no formal differentiation of institutions, and in stratified systems institutions are allocated a role within a total system.

A second useful form of distinction when describing systems concerns their *tiering*. A two-cycle system, for example, is one in which study up to Masters level is divided into two sections (undergraduate/postgraduate); this contrasts with a one-cycle system of the same period of duration.

A third distinction is the orientation of provision. In most countries in Europe, for example, HE provision at undergraduate level can be divided into academic programmes of a largely theoretical nature (defined by *ISCED 1997* (UNESCO, 1997) as level V, type A) and those with an occupational orientation (ISCED level V, type B). Generally this distinction parallels institutional differentiation between universities and other types of HE provider, and type B qualifications do not provide access to doctoral studies.

There are of course many exceptions to this generalised description of structures and for Europe these are best described in a recent EURYDICE (2003) publication. Some ways in which exceptions demonstrate themselves are outlined as follows:

- In some countries, such as Greece, Finland, Norway and Malta, all courses of HE are defined as being type A irrespective of provider.
- In most European countries it is only type A qualifications that are divided into two cycles. Courses with a vocational orientation are normally only available as short-cycle type B awards.
- In some countries, most particularly the UK and in North America, the duration of such awards can be less than three years, and there are in effect three cycles up to Masters, with the first cycle variously known as Foundation Degree (England), Higher National Certificate or Diploma (UK as a whole) or Associate Degree (US and Canada).
- In other countries, including Estonia, the Netherlands, Poland and Slovenia, two cycles up to Masters are available in both type A and type B form, and in some of these (Estonia and Poland) even if the first cycle is type B the second cycle is type A.
- Transfer may occur in the very early stages of type B provision to type A. For instance in the Netherlands, higher professional education (HBO – *Hoger Beroeps Onderwijs*) at *Hogescholen* has expanded considerably since the 1970s and it is possible to enter university study (*Wetenschappelijk Onderwijs*) with the HBO propaedeutic (i.e. first year of HE) certificate. A similar situation pertains in relation to the Higher National Certificate in the UK, particularly in Scotland.

Distinctions amongst providers

These ways in which providers of HE are distinguished are best understood by considering some concrete examples. At one end of the unified/stratified continuum lies Sweden, a country that presents a highly unified structure, where, at least formally, there is no distinction between types of institutions, whether they be universities or university colleges. All HE is pursued on a modular credit basis with courses either taken independently or chosen in such a way as to form one of the three general degrees in undergraduate education as follows:

- The Higher Education Diploma (*Högskoleexamen* – two years of full time equivalent (FTE) study).
- The Bachelor's degree (*Kandidatexamen* – at least three years of FTE study).
- The Master's degree (*Magisterexamen* – four years of FTE study).

Germany's binary system of both universities and *Fachhochschulen* is perhaps the most well known of its type internationally. In the university sector the *Diplom, Magister or Staatsexamen* last from four to six years' study including a thesis with a duration of a half to one year, with the titles differentiated by their degree of concentration on main subjects, and their relationship to regulated professions. *Fachhochschulen* (universities of applied sciences) offer primarily professionally oriented courses in engineering, economics, social professions, administration, and design, and students are granted the title *Diplom (FH)*. Historically the system has been described as a one-cycle structure, although there are a number of different degree titles. However, as in many other parts of Europe, the Bologna process,[3] which seeks to provide *inter alia*, a common two-cycle system across the continent is having an impact. As Kirstein (1999) reports, the amended University Act of 1998 provides for the national introduction of first and second degrees leading to Bachelor's degrees (three to four years) followed by Master's degrees (one to two years).

The difficulty in describing systems is reflected not only in their complexity but also in their propensity for modification. So not only is the historic single cycle of the German HE system breaking down, but also to describe it as a simple binary structure is inaccurate. Furthermore, a regional dimension has to be taken into account because of the decentralisation of responsibilities in education. In certain states within Germany (*Länder*), *Berufsakademien* (professional academies) form part of the tertiary sector and combine academic training at a *Studienakademie* (study institution) with practical professional training in the workplace, thus constituting an 'academic' version of the dual system (*duales System*) of vocational education (described in detail by Deissinger in this volume). The *Berufsakademien* are not strictly simply vocational schools and should in reality be classified as a third arm of HE with a vocational orientation.

Very clear binary systems exist in many other European countries. So, for example, in Finland there exist universities and *ammattikorkeakoulu* (polytechnics), in Norway universities and *statslige høgskoler* (state colleges), and in the Netherlands universities and *hogescholen (HBO)* (universities of professional education offering professionally oriented programmes). It should be noted that binary divisions are not necessarily characterised as a distinction between the academic and the vocational. In France, for example, there is a clear division between universities and specialist institutions such as the *Grandes Ecoles* offering high-level professional training for elite professions. Divides are found in other parts of the world; Haas (1999), for example, provides useful descriptions of the systems of a number of Asian countries, including Indonesia where universities, institutes and tertiary schools provide undergraduate-level courses. In this case, and that of a number of countries with a market-led economy, institutions tend to compete rather than complement each other. In Indonesia, where public resources for education are constrained, it is not entirely surprising that of 1339 post-secondary institutions, 1159 are private (Haas, 1999, p. 16). As is evident in further discussions of articulation the public/private divide also has a considerable influence on the level and degree of co-operation across sectors.

In other countries, such as the UK and Australia, binary divides have formally been removed, and in others, such as South Africa, there has been considerable realignment. In the former two countries the arm of HE within the binary/dual divide concerned with vocationally orientated HE is no longer formally distinguishable following processes of re-designation and merger. There the divide between universities and organisations respectively known as polytechnics and colleges of advanced education in these countries does not exist.[4] However, the vestigial effect of their former status almost certainly manifests itself in informal divides. So, for example, there is a clear inverse link between the former status of being a polytechnic in the UK and the amount of government funding for research, and the funding gulf is so great that new binary lines are emerging.

New binary lines have emerged in other ways in the UK. The disappearance of the polytechnics has coincided with the expansion of the further education colleges (FECs) as providers of HE. These institutions and their role will be described in two later chapters concerned with England and Scotland. In both countries these institutions provide a range of vocationally oriented awards from basic skills through to postgraduate level. A significant emphasis within the chapters on England and Scotland in this book (see Parry and Gallacher's respective contributions) is placed on the role of FECs in offering short-cycle HE. This largely occurs through the Higher National Certificate and Diploma (HNC/D), once the staple of the former polytechnic sector. These qualifications were historically designed as qualifications to meet particular labour market needs, but increasingly are being positioned as qualifications that allow progression with credit to further HE. Such has been the growth of this area of work in the UK that many FECs have taken on at least in part the characteristics of an emerging second sector of HE, and this is particularly the case in Scotland.

However, FECs can be viewed as part of a stratified system of HE, with different institutions playing particular roles in an overall system. This role of providing the first and second year of HE followed by articulation inside a credit accumulation and transfer system (CATS) is a key element of government policy in the UK. However, it cannot yet be aid to be a fully accepted or systemised element of the HE offer as is evident later in this volume. More well-established and longstanding models of stratification are observed in North America. Bonham, later in this volume, describes the community colleges (CCs) that provide in many cases a two-year Associate degree route to four-year degree level studies at universities or colleges. However these two-year programmes are not simply routes to further study: in addition to this *collegiate* route, the Associate degrees at community colleges also take the form of directly vocationally relevant awards, the so-called *career* route (Cohen and Brawser, 1989). While this distinction between the purposes of these routes is important it has become blurred in the US and elsewhere. Much that was designed for a vocational purpose is used as an entry route with credit to Bachelor's courses of type A form.

Analogous stratified systems exist elsewhere, for example in Canada and Japan. Canada too has a set of CCs[5] with the multiple missions of their US counterparts. However, a clear role in providing transfer with credit to HE is prevalent in only a minority of provinces, including British Columbia, Alberta and Québec. But where the route exists, the purpose of short-cycle HE is more clear-cut; and, as Burtch reports later in this volume, they act as *commuter institutions*, facilitating eventual entrance to university studies for those who are not taking strictly vocational/technical programmes. It should be noted that considerable variation exists between provincial jurisdictions in Canada, even where transfer is well organised. In British Columbia, for example, there is extensive transfer into year three of four-year university degrees, whereas in Québec the *Collèges d'enseignement général et professional* (CEGEP) are the mandated route for school leavers wishing to enter universities. In Québec a school leaver obtains a two-year *diplôme d'études collégiale* at a CEGEP in order to enter a three-year undergraduate degree.

In Japan both junior colleges and technical colleges offer two-year programmes. The junior colleges are a direct legacy of the period of occupation of the country by the US following World War II and are largely attended by women (Yamamoto *et al.*, 2000); in a society where there still isn't a general expectancy for anything other than short-term careers for women, progression to university isn't common. The technical colleges produce technicians with high-level skills and some ten per cent progress to higher-level study with quotas in place at certain universities.

The tiers of HE

In Europe, increasingly two cycles of study have become the norm for HE as new legislation has been introduced to secure conformity to the precepts of the *Bologna Declaration* of 1999. In certain countries, such as Cyprus, France, Greece, Iceland, Ireland, Malta, Portugal, and the UK, two cycles have a long history and have been largely based on a three-year + two-year model (equivalent to a Bachelor's degree followed by a Master's degree). In other countries, such as Denmark and Finland, this structure has been in place for some time, but not applied to all fields until recently. Many countries in Central and Eastern Europe and the Baltic region, such as Bulgaria, the Czech Republic, Latvia, Lithuania, Poland, and Slovakia, began to adopt the two-tier structure during the period of reform of educational systems during the 1990s.

However, it is the Bologna Declaration that has caused a step-wise change in structures. The premises of the Bologna Process are based on the *Paris-La Sorbonne Declaration* of 1988 in which the education ministers of France, Germany, Italy and the UK signalled their intentions 'to improve the international transparency of courses and the recognition of qualifications by means of gradual convergence towards a common framework of qualifications and cycles of study' (EURYDICE, 2003, p.9). Overall, the Declaration's object was to move towards the harmonisation of qualifications in what now is described as the *European Higher Education Area*. Among the six specific principles of the subsequent Bologna Declaration was the implementation of a system of HE based on two main cycles. According to the European Universities Association (EUA, 2003) some 80 per cent of countries have already achieved two-tier structures or are in the process of doing so with the remaining 20 per cent preparing the necessary legislative structures. Thus any vestiges of a one-cycle system are likely to have disappeared in most European countries before long, apart from in medicine and fields associated with this discipline.

However, as Haug (1999) has commented in documents produced as part of the Bologna Process, there is 'extreme complexity and diversity of curricular and degree structures in European countries' and 'in countries with a binary system, the line of divide between the university and non-university sectors (and their degree structure) is become increasingly blurred'.

Blurring of provision and providers

Two other interesting features of providers are worthy of mention at this point, and these pertain firstly to the ways in which the funding and location of particular levels of post-compulsory provision may not necessary be based on institutional status. A clear example of this approach by government is found in New Zealand. Unlike in most countries, there is huge fluidity between the types of programmes offered by the various types of providers. The key factor underpinning provision is the ability of institutions to offer programmes to required quality standards, rather than organisational type. Thus, while most Bachelors' provision is found within universities, some degree programmes are also available at most institutes of technology, polytechnics, *Wānanga* (specialist centres offering provision for the Māori population), and colleges of education, and at some private training establishments. Thus the focus in New Zealand is on articulation within rather than between institutions and, as a consequence, intersectoral work tends to be a lower priority (see chapter by Anderson later in this volume). Secondly, there are countries where the boundaries between institutional forms have broken down. Tertiary education in Australia has developed three types or models of institutional arrangements for articulation in tertiary education: single-sector; stand-alone HE and VET institutions with various links and relations between the sectors; 'dual-sector' universities; and 'co-located' institutions. Wheelahan and Moodie describe later in this volume the operation of dual sector institutions that have both VET and HE elements. While these providers have been established in this form to improve articulation arrangements and have comprehensive policies to do so (Haas, 1999), the unified status does not assure transfer, since a range of internal barriers to collaboration between the two arms of these institutions appear to emerge (Chapman *et al.*, 2000).

Within other countries, the types of structural arrangements found in Australia and a number of other forms and variants exist, making global comparisons complex. For example, in England four broad multilateral partnership arrangements exist between FECs and HEIs: associate college agreements; regional or sub-regional networks; multi-agency partnerships; and multi-college partnerships.⁶ Furthermore, in England, at least to a limited extent, attempts have been made to create institutions of similar form to the Australian dual sector universities by linking FECs with universities, as has been the case in Bradford. By comparison, in the US, for example, five types of arrangements exist between CCs and universities: articulation and co-ordination agreements; on-site upper division course offerings; on-site degree programmes; satellite campus; and satellite university/university college.

It is clear that a range of models of collaboration that involve cross-sectoral links of various degrees of cohesion and complexity exist elsewhere, and perhaps are best described and understood in the typology created by Woodrow and Thomas (2002) based on studies from Australia, Ireland, the Netherlands, and the US. Their four-fold classification describes forms as being *vertical*, *longitudinal*, *all-embracing*, or *integrated*. Not all necessarily involve a VET sector or a HEI, but nonetheless their model encompasses the two sectors that are one of the concerns of this book, and illustrate that these sectors do not necessarily collaborate with each other in isolation from other sectors.

The vertical model refers to those approaches that are concerned with direct links between sectors, as is exemplified in the links between the VET sector and universities that take the form of arrangements to provide access and articulation. The longitudinal model relates to the provision of a continuum of cross-sector learning opportunities (Woodrow and Thomas, 2002, p. 13). This model is illustrated by Eggink (2002), who describes a regional strategy of this form in Holland to tackle the low participation rates of minority groups that is based on co-operation between three sectors around Utrecht where the *Regional Opleidengen Centrum Utrecht*, the *Hogeschool van Utrecht* and the *Universiteit van Utrecht* have created the 'Utrecht Bridge' to improve the educational infrastructure. The all-embracing model is distinguished from the vertical and longitudinal models by the breadth of partnership and the extent of the involvement of all stakeholders, and is exemplified by regional strategy in Ireland. Integration refers to those models where institutional barriers have formally been dissolved, as in the Australian dual sector institutions.

In considering the vertical model in more detail, the most common of links that provides access and articulation, it is quite evident that there are a number of gradations within its development. In the UK context, such links have been described by Morgan-Klein and Murphy (2001) as *outreach*, and there are many examples internationally of the VET sector simply providing an alternative access route to HE provision. Vertical transfer with credit is also common but, as is already evident from a comparison of the US and Canadian arrangements for transfer from CCs, a number of forms exist. At one extreme, articulation is a feature of educational planning and embedded in arrangements between institutions. This is exemplified in structures that guarantee progression from one institution to another and to a lesser extent by quotas that select a proportion of successful candidates from a VET institution. At the other extreme, short-cycle HE is an end in itself and there is no vertical movement at all. Between these extremes there are arrangements that create a certain ambiguity. For example, in a number of societies, particularly in Europe and Australasia, qualifications are credit-rated within a framework that gives a measurable value of each element of an award, which are designed to facilitate inter-institutional transfer.

In some European countries this is an emerging phenomenon reflecting the pressure of Bologna to harmonise provision. In Portugal, for example, *Cursos de Especialização Tecnológica* (CETs) at ISCED level IV are offered at *Escolas Tecnológicas*, some of which have protocols with some universities.[7] Credits obtained in some of the CETs, therefore, can be transferred to specific HE programmes of study, at those universities with whom protocols have been signed. It is not surprising that in developing systems there will be variability in practice, but the systematic differentiation of transfer opportunities in more mature systems points to systems that are designed with in-built inequalities. However, for example, in Scotland more often than not, despite the existence of a national system of credit transfer, credit ratings are largely symbolic and are not respected, especially by elite institutions. Transfer from FECs is clearly skewed to particular types of HEIs and, as a consequence, it is likely that certain types of individuals, particularly those from lower socio-economic groups, and adults are denied entry to certain more exclusive professional areas of work (see Osborne and Maclaurin, 2002).

Diversification and equity

In conclusion, this account, which aims to overview the diversity of provision and providers that constitute HE today, suggests that the increasing importance of short-cycle HE is linked to the perception by governments around the world that greater numbers of their populations should benefit from HE. Furthermore, policies in many nations direct that a more representative proportion of the population should participate than historically has been the case. Short-cycle HE, particularly that offered within VET institutions, is one approach that is perceived to both meet supply and cater for diverse demand. In Scotland, for example, the emphasis put upon routes from and through FECs is the accessibility of these institutions to traditionally non-participant groups, notably within present policy initiatives to those from lower socio-economic classes (Raab and Davidson, 1999). By comparison to HEIs, FECs are perceived to offer relatively greater ease of entry to their provision, closer geographical proximity to their potential student body, and a more diverse and flexible curriculum. Furthermore, because the cost of widening participation is slowing the growth of HE, and there are dangers that the UK government falls short of its target of 50 per cent participation of people aged between 18 and 30 by the year 2010, cheaper short cycle may also be a financial imperative. Thus, throughout the UK, stress has been placed by the government funding councils on HE within FE, and on partnerships between FECs and HEIs, to enhance progression opportunities (see, for example, HEFCE (2001a) and SHEFC (1999)). Thereby, intra-sectoral and cross-sectoral partnership at both a sub-regional and regional level are central to much of current development in England and are described within the Partnerships for Progression funding policy framework introduced in 2002–03.

The agenda of widening participation, while having a strong focus on social justice should not, as I suggested earlier in this introduction, be divorced from the economics of participation. This applies both at an individual level, and as part of regional and national economic development. In this respect the geographical diversification of HE provision has and continues to play a strong role in policy making that pertains to economic development. Bélanger and Lyck (1995) have reported the belief of policy makers that the higher the level of educational attainment of a region, the lower its unemployment levels; though, as Phelps (1998) suggests, while rural areas may benefit from local initiatives, there is some empirical evidence that a nation as a whole benefits more in income and employment growth by placing universities in it largest urban areas. There is little doubt, nonetheless, that economic and equity considerations underpin moves to massification around the world, and these are linked to diversification in both a geographical sense and in relation to institutional type and form of provision. Clearly, amongst the armoury of nations to envelop these compatible rather than conflicting agendas is the flexibility afforded by short-cycle HE offered by VET providers. Lest we be too sanguine, there are also dangers, however, that this provision offers little more than an instrument of social control, directing a proportion of the population through an easily accessible, but ultimately less rewarding path. There certainly is evidence that expansion of educational opportunity in itself may not reduce inequality by social class in educational achievement (Raftery and Hout, 1993; Shavit *et al.*, 2004). Furthermore, it has been argued that within stratified systems, as the less selective part of the HE sector expands its numbers, there is skewing of participation by social class (Lucas, 2001). In short, in a universal system those from lower socio-economic classes participate in greater numbers, but do so with greatest frequency in less elite institutions, and at the same time elite HEIs become more selective. These thoughts may be a stimulus to read on.

Notes

[1] Apart from the UK, perhaps it is Denmark that provides the extensive use of an articulating system. Since reforms of 2000, short-cycle, medium-cycle and long-cycle education (namely, *Videregående voksenuddannelse (VVU)* (Advanced Adult Education); *Diplomuddannelse* (Diploma programmes); *Masteruddannelse* (Master's programmes) offered through vocational colleges, centres for medium-cycle education and universities, respectively) have been linked into a common framework for open adult education (Undervisnings Ministeriet, 2002).

[2] For information on private providers see Anderson (1994, 1995), Barnett and Wilson (1995), European Training Foundation (1996), Fiske and Ladd (2000), Osborne and Turner (2002), Roussel and Murphy (2000), Todd (1996), UNESCO (1998).

[3] See http://www.sgroup.be/ga2001/Bolognaprocessinfodocl.pdf for a summary of the Bologna Declaration of 1999, the Salamanca Convention of European Higher Education in 2001, and the Prague meeting of Ministers of Education of 2001.

[4] In Australia, the 1988 White Paper, *Higher Education: A Policy Statement* (Dawkins, 1988), classified all institutions offering HE provision as universities utilising amalgamations where necessary to achieve a necessary minimum of 2000 full-time equivalent students. Postle and Sturman (2003) provide further details. For comparison of the UK and Australia in this regard see Gallacher *et al.* (1996)

[5] Burtch, in this volume, notes the term 'community college' is not used in all Canadian jurisdictions. In Alberta, for example, such institutions are known as 'public colleges', in Saskatchewan as 'regional colleges' and in Québec as 'Collèges d'enseignement général et professional (CEGEP)'.

[6] There are many examples of these models, and these are described in HEFCE's (2001b) guide to good practice in widening participation. For a specific example of associate college arrangements see the work of Sheffield Hallam University online at: http://extra.shu.ac.uk/acn/introduction.html

[7] Personal communication with Ana Ramalho Correia, Universidade Nova de Lisboa, 9 October 2004.

References

Anderson, D. (1994) *Blurring the Boundaries: TAFE and Commercial Colleges in the Open Training Market*. Adelaide: National Centre for Vocational Education Research.

Anderson, D. (1995) 'Blurring the boundaries', *Australian TAFE Teacher*, 29(2), pp. 49–56.

Barnett, K. and Wilson, S. (1995) *Separate Responsibilities: A Comparative, Equity-Focused Study of Commercial and Community Training Providers*. Canberra: Australian Government Publishing Service.

Bélanger, C.H. and Lyck, L. (1995) 'Outlying universities and the Swiss army pocket knife', *Higher Education Management*, 7(2), pp. 221–8.

Chapman, B., Doughney, L. and Watson, L. (2000) *Towards a Cross-Sectoral Funding System for Education and Training*, Discussion Paper No. 2. Canberra: Lifelong Learning Network, University of Canberra.

Cohen, A. and Brawer, F. (1989) *The American Community College*, 2nd edn. San Francisco: Jossey-Bass.

Dawkins, J.S. (1988) *Higher Education: A Policy Statement*, Higher Education White Paper. Canberra: Australian Government Publishing Service.

Eggink, B. (2002) 'The Bridge – Spanning the sectors in the Netherlands', in: M. Woodrow, *Pyramids or Spiders? Cross-Sector Collaboration to Widen Participation: Learning from International Experience*. Edinburgh: Scottish Funding Councils.

European Training Foundation (1996) *Continuing Training: The Roles and Responsibilities of Key Players Within Continuing Training (Including Management Training). Executive Summary and Recommendations.* Advisory Forum meeting, 10–12 June, Turin: European Training Foundation. Online at: http://www.etf.eu.int/etfweb.nsf/pages/downloadcontinuingtraining

Eurydice (2003) *Information Network Database of Education Systems in Europe.* Thessalonniki: EURYDICE.

Fiske, E.B. and Ladd, H.F. (2000) *When Schools Compete.* Washington, DC: The Brookings Institution Press.

Gallacher, J., Osborne, M., and Postle, G. (1996) 'Increasing and widening access to higher education: a comparative study of policy and provision in Scotland and Australia', *International Journal of Lifelong Education*, 15(6), pp. 418–37.

Haas, A.R. (1999) *Trends in Articulation Arrangements for Technical and Vocational Education in the South East Asian Region.* Melbourne: UNESCO UNEVOC/RMIT University.

Haug, G. (1999) 'Main Trends and Issues in Higher Education Structures in Europe'. Project Report of the Trends in Learning Structures in Higher Education to Bologna Process Committee. Online at: http://www.esib.org

Higher Education Funding Council for England (HEFCE) (2001a) *Partnerships for Progression: Proposals by the HEFCE and the Learning and Skills Council*, Report 01/73. Bristol: HEFCE.

Higher Education Funding Council for England (HEFCE) (2001b) *Strategies for Widening Participation in Higher Education: A Guide to Good Practice*, Report 01/36. Bristol: HEFCE.

Kirstein, J. (1999) 'Information on Learning Structures in Higher Education in the EU/EEA countries'. Project report of the Trends in Learning Structures in Higher Education to Bologna Process Committee. Online at: http://www.esib.org

Lucas, S.R. (2001) 'Effectively maintained inequality: Education transitions, track mobility, and social background effects', *American Journal of Sociology*, 106, pp. 1642–90.

Morgan-Klein, B. and Murphy, M. (2001) 'Access and Recruitment: Institutional policy in widening participation', in: P. Trowler (ed.) *Higher Education Policy and Institutional Change*. Buckingham: SRHE and Open University Press.

OECD (2001a) *Economics and Finance of Lifelong Learning.* Paris: OECD.

OECD (2001b) *Education at a Glance.* Paris: OECD.

Osborne, M (2003a) 'A European comparative analysis of policy and practice in widening participation to lifelong learning', *European Journal of Education*, 38(1), pp. 5–24.

Osborne, M. (2003b) 'Policy and practice in widening participation: A six country comparative study', *International Journal of Lifelong Education*, 22(1), pp. 45–58.

Osborne, M. and Maclaurin, I. (2002) 'Data on FE/HE transfer in Scotland', in: M. Osborne, M. Murphy and J. Gallacher, *A Research Review of FE/HE Links: Report to Scottish Executive.* Stirling: Centre for Research in Lifelong Learning/Scottish Executive). Online at: http://www.scotland.gov.uk/about/ELLD/HESP/00016640/annexE.aspx

Osborne, M. and Turner, E. (2002) 'Private training providers in Scotland', *Journal of Vocational Education and Training*, 54(2), pp. 267–93.

Phelps, R.P. (1998) 'The effect of the university host community on state growth', *Economics of Education Review*, 17(2): 149–58.

Postle, G. and Sturman, A. (2003) 'Widening access to higher education – an Australian case study', *Journal of Adult and Continuing Education*, 8(2), pp. 195–212.

Raab, G. and Davidson K. (1999) *Distribution of FE Provision in Scotland*. Edinburgh: SOEID.

Raftery, A.E. and Hout, M. (1993) 'Maximally maintained inequality: Expansion, reform and opportunity in Irish education, 1921–75', *Sociology of Education*, 66, pp. 41–62.

Roussel, S. and Murphy, T. (2000) *Public and Private Provision of Post-Secondary Education and Training: 1993 and 1997 Compared*. Canberra: DETYA.

Scott, P. (1995) *The Meanings of Mass Higher Education*. Buckingham: SRHE/OU.

Scottish Higher Education Funding Council (SHEFC) (1999) *Wider Access Development Funding. Letter to Principals/Directors of HEIs funded by SHEFC*, Circular Letter 21/99. Edinburgh: SHEFC.

Shavit, Y., Arum, R. and Gamoran, A. (2004) *Expansion, Differentiation and Stratification in Higher Education: A Comparative Study of 15 Countries*. Paper presented at the International Sociological Association, Research Committee on Social Stratification and Mobility (RC28), 7–9 May 2004. Online at: http://www.sidos.ch/method/RC28/abstracts/Yossi%20Shavit.pdf

Todd, E. (1996) *Survey of Private Providers in Tasmania*. Hobart: Department of Vocational Education and Training.

Undervisnings Ministeriet (2002) *The Danish Higher Education System*. Online at: http://eng.uvm.dk/publications/factsheets/fact7.htm

UNESCO (1997) *International Standard of Classification of Education: ISCED 1997*. Paris: UNESCO. Online at:
http://www.uis.unesco.org/TEMPLATE/pdf/isced/ISCED_A.pdf

UNESCO (1998) *International Project on Technical and Vocational Education – Vocational Education and Training in Europe on the Threshold of the 21st Century*. UNESCO-OEEK Symposium on Vocational Education and Training in Europe on the Threshold of the 21st Century, Crete, Greece, 23–26 September 1998. Online at: http://www.unevoc.de/publications/pdf/iug018e.pdf

Woodrow, M. and Thomas, E. (2002) 'Pyramids or spiders? Cross-sector collaboration to widen participation: Learning from international experience – A comparative study to identify the most effective ways for post compulsory institutions to work together to widen participation', in: E. Thomas, M. Cooper and J. Quinn (eds), *Collaboration to Widen Participation in Higher Education*. Stoke-on-Trent: Trentham Books.

Yamamoto, S., Fujitsuka, T. and Honda-Okitsu, Y. (2000) 'From traditional higher education to lifelong learning: Changes in higher education in Japan', in: H.G. Schuetze and M. Slowey (eds) *Higher Education and Lifelong Learners*. London: Routledge.

Separate post-compulsory education sectors within a liberal market economy: Interesting models generated by the Australian anomaly

Leesa Wheelahan and Gavin Moodie

Introduction

OECD member countries follow two broad patterns in structuring their post-compulsory education (PCE). One pattern, which is most associated with continental Europe, is to separate vocational education from HE in organisation, curriculum and student groups. The other pattern, which is most associated with Anglophone countries, is to have a gradual merging and much greater overlap of vocational education and HE (Clark, 1983; Furth, 1973).

These patterns in PCE coincide with two patterns for structuring economies and their relationship with PCE. Continental Europe tends to have market economies which are co-ordinated by their social partners: government, business and labour. Vocational and higher education students might be placed on quite separate PCE tracks, but the co-ordinated market economy matches graduates and job vacancies for most. The market economies of the Anglophone countries are rather freer, relying more on the market to sort and match graduates and employment. In the unpredictable liberal market economy students need more general PCE and greater mobility between vocational and higher education to match their education with employment opportunities (Hall and Soskice, 2001).

Australia is distinctive in formally distinguishing its post-compulsory education and training sectors as deeply as many continental European countries, but it does so within a liberal market economy which in other Anglophone countries is associated with merged vocational and HE sectors. This inconsistency in Australia's organisation of its economy and PCE is illustrated in Table 1.

This chapter opens by outlining the structure and institutions of Australian PCE. The most consistent and pervasive organising element of Australian PCE is qualification level, and the Australian qualifications framework is described, with particular attention to the 'crossover' qualifications of diplomas and advanced diplomas. Patterns of student access to and transfer between institutions and sectors are described, and the transfer of credit following transfer between sectors is considered. Following this description of standard arrangements we consider various measures to improve student access and mobility. These include dual-sector and co-located institutions, the latter often involving multiple partners. Australia has also experimented with course links of various types: pathways, credit transfer, and dual-sector awards and nested awards. The chapter concludes by anticipating future relations between the sectors and other developments.

Structure and composition of Australian post-compulsory education

Australia is a federation of approximately 20 million people, with power shared between the national Commonwealth government and eight state and territory governments. There are four sectors of post-compulsory education and training: senior secondary school, adult and community education (ACE), vocational education and training (VET) and higher education (HE). While education is a state responsibility under the Constitution, the Commonwealth has varying levels of responsibility largely related to its share of government funding. HE is directly funded

Table 1. Patterns of organisation of the economy and post-compulsory education.

Market economy	Post-compulsory education sectors	
	Merged	Separate
Liberal	Anglo	Australia
Co-ordinated		Euro

by and accountable to the Commonwealth government, whereas the states have primary but not exclusive responsibility for the VET, school and ACE sectors. While there is some national co-ordination through joint Commonwealth-state ministerial councils, considerable diversity remains between the state and territories' VET, ACE and senior schooling systems.

Governments' continuous reform from the late 1980s has sought to make the VET and HE sectors more 'responsive' to industry, to the 'needs' of the economy, and to align the activity of the sectors more closely with government economic policy objectives. Reforms introduced market relations within each sector, although these have been more far-reaching in VET than in HE (Marginson, 1997).

A unified national system of HE was created in 1988, with the amalgamation of colleges of advanced education (the sector equivalent to polytechnics) into 37 publicly funded universities in Australia, all of which are self-accrediting. The introduction of income-contingent loans,[1] pressure on universities to run full-fee graduate programmes and other income-generating and fee-for-service activities, means that the Commonwealth government directly contributes only 45 per cent of the recurrent income of universities (derived from Department of Education, Science and Training (DEST), 2002, Table 1).

VET consists of publicly funded institutes of technical and further education (TAFE), private providers, and community based, not-for-profit providers. However, TAFE is the largest component, constituting just over 78 per cent of all enrolments and almost 88 per cent of delivery (National Centre for Vocational Education Research (NCVER), 2003, p. 5). The Commonwealth government uses its 36 per cent share of government funding towards VET provision (with the remainder coming from the states) as a policy lever to drive its reforms (DEST, 2002, Table 1). However, there are significant differences between the states' VET systems, in location of portfolio, funding, governance and institutional autonomy (Keating, 2000; Wheelahan, 2000). A national VET system was constituted in 1994, when the Commonwealth and state governments agreed to jointly establish the Australian National Training Authority (ANTA). All VET systems are required, as a result of national agreements, to implement nationally endorsed training packages based on competency-based training (CBT). These are similar to the National Vocational Qualifications in England. There are no equivalents to the English General National Vocational Qualifications.

The ACE sector is the least funded and most diffuse of the four sectors of post-compulsory education and training, with varying levels of government support (Golding *et al.*, 2001). ACE offers a range of programmes, which include accredited VET qualifications. It consists of small and dispersed community-based, not-for-profit providers. In spite of this, it is of central importance in re-introducing adults to study and in providing pathways to further study, although it has not yet been mapped into pathways frameworks in any meaningful way. It is the 'Cinderella' of post-compulsory education and training (Golding *et al.*, 2001; Senate, 1991).

Learning environments in TAFE and HE and pass rates

The learning environment in TAFE is quite different to that in HE: classes are generally smaller, contact hours higher, teaching is more supportive, and curriculum and assessment is competency-based. Also, TAFE teachers are more likely than HE teachers to be formally qualified as *teachers*, as well as in their industry or discipline.

Smith (2001), and Fuller and Chalmers (1999) found in their respective studies that there were some differences between TAFE and HE students in approaches to study (deep, surface, achieving, and so on)[2] and in their learning preferences, but that overall the two groups of students were similar in many respects, and that these similarities were more important than the differences.

The pass rates for TAFE articulators in HE are comparable to other groups of students, particularly school-leavers, demonstrating that they are able to cope with study at this level. National comparative data showed mixed results with TAFE students in some states experiencing lower pass rates, but overall the rates were comparable (Dobson *et al.*, 1998). Institutionally based research also demonstrates that TAFE articulators achieve results comparable to other groups of students (Ramsay *et al.*, 1998; Wheelahan, 2001).

There is no data comparing the labour market outcomes of TAFE articulators who graduate from HE with other HE graduates. Broad conclusions can be drawn however, and these are that the labour market outcomes depend on the university that the student attended and the course they completed. TAFE students find it more difficult to enter the elite universities and HE courses with highly competitive entry. It is access to these courses that results in higher graduate employment and starting salaries (Department of Education Training and Youth Affairs (DETYA), 1998).

Australian Qualifications Framework

The Australian Qualifications Framework (AQF) was created in 1995 (see Table 2). The AQF is the only systemic framework that spans post-compulsory education and training in Australia.[3] Unlike the qualifications frameworks in England and Scotland, the AQF has no accreditation or recognition functions, or quality assurance functions (Keating, 2000). The AQF designates which qualifications are offered in each sector and the descriptors that accompany each (Australian Qualifications Framework Advisory Board (AQFAB), 2002).[4] It does not *prohibit* one sector from offering a qualification that is generally offered by the other, provided the sector is able to adhere to the accreditation and other requirements that accompany the issuing of the qualification. Generally, however, institutions do not receive public funding for any qualification they may offer outside their sector.

The AQF has – based on agreement between the peak bodies in both sectors – promulgated credit transfer guidelines, and has developed recognition of prior learning principles and operational guidelines which are currently progressing through the ministerial endorsement process. However, while these guidelines are valuable, at most they can be regarded as recommendations (particularly for self-accrediting universities) and it remains to be seen whether these initiatives, while important, will contribute to seamlessness.

The AQF was established, in part, to facilitate learning pathways between and within sectors. However, the AQF Handbook (AQFAB, 2002, p. 1) states that:

> ... *there are no standardised rankings or equivalences between different qualifications issued in different sectors, as these qualifications recognise different types of learning reflecting the distinctive educational responsibilities of each sector. Where the same qualifications are issued in more than one sector but authorised differently by each sector (i.e. Diploma, Advanced Diploma) they are equivalent qualifications, although sector-differentiated.*

Table 2. Australian Qualifications Framework

Schools sector	Vocational education and training sector	Higher education sector
		Doctoral degrees
		Masters degrees
		Graduate diploma
		Graduate certificate
		Bachelor degrees
	Advanced diploma	Advanced diploma/ Associate degrees
	Diploma	Diploma
	Certificate IV	
	Certificate III	
Senior Secondary	Certificate II	
Certificates of Education	Certificate I	

Source: AQFAB, 2002

This insistence on sectoral differentiation of qualifications contributes to the deep divide between the sectors, and the problems that students experience in moving between them – it fuels arguments that the learning and certification of learning in each sector is incommensurable. So rather than promoting seamlessness, it can be argued that until now the AQF has contributed to entrenching the differences between the sectors. Moreover, seamlessness has been difficult to achieve 'as articulation arrangements all remain state and institutionally based. As well, the multitude of credit transfer and advanced standing agreements may well be observed more frequently in their breach than in their implementation' (Keating, 2000). The AQF has been most effective in underpinning the national scaffolding of qualification levels within the VET sector, and this is an important national achievement, as previous state-based arrangements meant qualifications awarded in one state were not always recognised in another (Keating, 2003; Wheelahan, 2003b).

At a system-wide level the AQF has also (until recently) been relatively effective in helping to maintain the boundaries between the sectors, and thereby sectoral peace, although arguably this has been at the cost of facilitating the seamless movement of students and credit between sectors.

The basis of the precarious sectoral peace is contested: on the one hand there are arguments that the sectors have different missions and serve the nation's interests in different ways; on the other, there are arguments that there is no fundamental difference in what each sector does and that the peak bodies insist on sectoral difference out of a self-interested justification of their continuing existence.

Regardless of which view seems more credible, the sectoral peace came unstuck in 2002 and 2003: unseemly brawling broke out between the sectors over the addition to the AQF of a new qualification, the two-year 'associate degree,' which is similar in conception to England's foundation degree. The Australian Vice-Chancellors' Committee (AVCC) argued that associate degrees should be solely HE awards, while the Australian National Training Authority (ANTA) argued the awards should be duplicated in each sector, as are the existing diplomas and advanced diplomas (Wheelahan, 2003a). The AVCC has won this battle – for now.[5] The AVCC is now arguing for diplomas and advanced diplomas to become VET-only awards (AVCC, 2002), thus making the AQF *entirely* segregated by sector, with no crossover qualifications. ANTA, on the other hand, wants to retain both advanced diplomas and diplomas as duplicated qualifications (ANTA, 2002).

Diplomas and advanced diplomas: Ambiguously situated

Australian universities offered undergraduate diplomas as a considerable part of their student load from their foundation in the middle of the nineteenth century until the creation of colleges of advanced education in the 1960s, which then assumed this role. Since the creation of the unified national system of HE in 1988, HE has all but relinquished this role (focusing instead on graduate certificates and diplomas) and over the last 15 years diplomas and advanced diplomas came to be predominantly offered in the VET sector (Moodie, 2003b). VET diplomas and advanced diplomas are based on training packages, and consequently on competency-based training models of curriculum.

However, diplomas and advanced diplomas are dual-sector awards under the AQF, and the characteristics of learning outcomes and distinguishing features of both HE and VET diplomas and advanced diplomas are identical; where they differ is in the accreditation and jurisdiction descriptors. Moodie (2003b, p. 46) explains that 'diplomas and advanced diplomas ... are located ambiguously within Australian tertiary education to buy a peace, however uneasy and temporary, in the sectoral contest over the qualifications.'

Approximately 12 per cent of VET students were undertaking diplomas or advanced diplomas in 2002 (NCVER, 2003, p. 10), whereas only approximately two per cent of HE students were enrolled in HE AQF diplomas or advanced diplomas in 2000 (DETYA, 2001, p. 6). It is possible, consequently, to argue that diplomas and advanced diplomas are substantively VET qualifications, despite the fact that they are dual-sector awards in the AQF. However, Moodie (2003a) and Karmel and Nguyen (2003) argue that these are 'crossover awards'. Moodie (2003b, p. 52) has calculated that if diplomas and advanced diplomas are regarded as short-cycle HE awards, then they are approximately 15 per cent of HE provision, almost all of which is offered in VET/TAFE. Karmel and Nguyen (2003, p. 11) explain that '... the diploma qualification is a sort of "cross-over" qualification with around 10 per cent of persons with a VET qualification (non-diploma) having a diploma and over 20 per cent, for some age groups, of persons with a degree also having a diploma.' Diplomas and advanced diplomas are therefore potentially an important access mechanism for disadvantaged students to short-cycle HE and a pathway to degree and higher-level awards in universities. However, the evidence does not show this.

The demographic characteristics of the VET and HE sectors are quite different: VET students are more broadly representative of the whole community, whereas HE students are more likely to come from relatively privileged backgrounds (Karmel and Nguyen, 2003). However, demographic characteristics of VET diploma and advanced diploma students are more similar to HE students than to the rest of the VET student population. They are younger, more urban, are more likely to have completed secondary school and to study full time, are less likely to come from low socio-economic status backgrounds or to be of Aboriginal or Torres Strait Islander background. They are also more than twice as likely to proceed to HE: 52.8 per cent and 74.2 per cent of diploma and advanced diploma graduates proceeding to further study respectively enrolled in university, compared to 22.5 per cent of all VET graduates proceeding to further study.[6] These patterns are accentuated for advanced diploma students compared to diploma students (NCVER, 2002, p. 13). Consequently, the majority of students who articulate to degree or higher-level studies in universities are most likely to come from relatively privileged backgrounds.

Short-cycle HE expressed as diplomas and advanced diplomas has not solved the access problem for students from disadvantaged backgrounds to HE. There is no reason to think that the introduction of associate degrees will do any better, particularly as these courses are likely to be full-fee paying.

Access to and mobility between sectors/institutions

As with other OECD countries, the Australian HE sector has grown from an elite to a mass and near universal system. However, the expansion in Australia has not been sufficient to keep pace with demand, with most Australians aspiring to a university education.

Karmel and Nguyen (2003, p. 8) explain that while the HE system has expanded overall, access to HE has declined from a high point in 1996, where it was expected that 44 per cent of individuals would enter HE at some point in their lives, to 40 per cent in 2000. They have estimated (based on 2001 data) the lifetime probability of individuals receiving a qualification in Table 3.

Table 3. Lifetime probability of getting a qualification.

Qualification	(%)
Degree	28
Diploma	14
VET (excluding diplomas)	42
Diploma or VET	55

Source: Karmel and Nguyen, 2003, p. 10

The AVCC estimated that 27.5 per cent (or approximately 63,000) of eligible applicants missed out on a HE place in a university in 2003, an increase of 17 per cent from the previous year. Mature-age applicants fared worst, constituting approximately ten per cent of all applicants, yet accounting for 32 per cent of those who missed out on a place (AVCC, 2003, p. 1). Students from low socio-economic status backgrounds and other disadvantaged groups are most likely to have lower tertiary entrance ranks (Teese, 2000), and so it can be extrapolated that they would be disproportionately represented among those who miss out on a place.

The issue of pathways to HE is thus becoming *more* important for policy, particularly policy concerned with equity, social justice, and building social capital. VET students are more likely to be part time, older, and from disadvantaged backgrounds in proportion to their numbers in the general community. Students from low socio-economic status backgrounds are under-represented in HE: 15.3 per cent of students from a low socio-economic background participate in HE, while they are 25 per cent of the population (Karmel and Nguyen, 2003, p. 6), and this under-representation is accentuated in the elite universities (James, 2002, p. 8).

Access to elite universities

While increasing numbers of students are moving from VET to HE and obtaining qualifications in both, as with other nations (Osborne *et al.*, 2000; Osborne *et al.*, 2002; Gallacher, 2003), transferring students are much less likely to gain access to elite universities (Moodie, 2003a). Paradoxically, it seems that university sectors that are 'unified' (as in Scotland and Australia) are less likely to facilitate access to elite universities for transfer students (from FE in Scotland and VET in Australia) than are systems that are formally differentiated into elite universities and the rest, as in many US jurisdictions. Unified systems are informally, but powerfully, differentiated by status (Marginson, 1997), and this appears to be a bigger obstacle in accessing elite universities than those systems which have mandated access and credit transfer policies, as in the US. Moodie (2003a, p. 5) demonstrates (in Table 4) the ratio of access by transferring students from FE in Scotland, VET in Australia, and community colleges in the US states to elite and moderately selective institutions. Whereas elite universities in the US admit one student for every two, the moderately selective universities admit, in Scotland this ratio is 1:5, and in Australia it is 1:4.

Moodie (2003a, p. 5) draws two conclusions from his analysis:

> *First, the formal segmentation of institutions into sectors does not always structure opportunities for students as much as the informal differences between institutions. Secondly ... many U.S. states have much higher transfer rates than Australia and Scotland because of their strong transfer practices and policies required by legislation.*

Table 4. Ratio of students transferring from VET/FE/CC to university in Scotland, Australia, California, Colorado and Texas

Jurisdiction	Highly selective institutions	Moderately selective institutions	Ratio of highly selective to moderately selective
Scotland	5%	24%	1 : 5
Australia	2%	8%	1 : 4
California	6.5%	13%	1 : 2
Colorado	3%	6%	1 : 2
Texas	15%	26%	1 : 1.7

Source: Moodie, 2003a, p. 5

He concludes that 'Informal distinctions are just as important as formal segmentation' and that universities have to be either 'bribed or coerced' to accept transferring students (Moodie, 2003a, p. 5). The evidence seems to support this argument.

Student movement between the sectors

While the VET sector has many more students than HE (approximately 1.7 million and 726,000 in each respectively)[7], it takes approximately 4.5 students to make an effective full-time student unit in VET and 1.25 students in HE (Karmel and Nguyen, 2003, p. 2).[8] Approximately 7 per cent of commencing students were admitted to HE in 2001 on the basis of VET study, and of 'commencing undergraduate students, 11.5% had a TAFE award and 8.8% had other awards' (Karmel and Nguyen, 2003, p. 10). This is likely to be an underestimate, and internal research in at least two universities shows that approximately 20 per cent of commencing students had prior TAFE study (Ramsay *et al.*, 1998; Wheelahan, 2001). The official data does not, among other things, take account of 'swirling' – 'students' multiple enrolments in and transfers between institutions' (de los Santos and Wright, 1990). There are also many students transferring from HE to VET: approximately 88,500 VET students had a degree or higher degree in 2002 (Karmel and Nguyen, 2003, p. 10). This is approximately 5.23 per cent of VET student enrolments (derived from NCVER, 2003). However, we can indirectly get an idea of the extent of 'swirling' by looking at the number of qualifications per person: Karmel and Nguyen outline the average number of qualifications per person and

Table 5. Growth in qualifications, 1993 and 2001.

| | Qualified persons ('000) | | Qualifications per person | |
	1993	2001	1993	2001
Higher Education	993.9	2169.3	1.59	1.74
VET	2903.6	4712.5	1.29	1.45

Source: Karmel and Nguyen, 2003, p. 4

the growth that has occurred from 1993 to 2001 in Table 5.

Moreover, Karmel and Nguyen provide evidence that many people have qualifications from *both* sectors. They separate diplomas and advanced diplomas from VET qualifications, and look at the percentage of all those with a VET qualification who also have a diploma or a degree, and the percentage of all those who are degree qualified who also have a diploma or a VET qualification. This is shown in Table 6. However, they also note that the diploma is declining in importance in HE for some age groups, which is a worrying trend given the importance of diplomas as an access mechanism to HE (Karmel and Nguyen, 2003, p. 11). In looking at their table, it appears also that the diploma is declining in importance as a stepping-stone for those with VET qualifications. If these trends continue, it is likely to result in declining access for VET qualified students to HE. It will also result in less credit transfer for students once they are in HE, as credit transfer – where it is available at all – is most likely to be granted for diplomas and not for VET-only qualifications.

Table 6. Persons with cross-sectoral qualifications, 1993 and 2001 (%).

| | VET qualified | | | | Degree qualified | | | |
| Age group | With a diploma | | With a degree | | With a diploma | | With a VET qualification | |
	1993	2001	1993	2001	1993	2001	1993	2001
15–24	5.5	4.9	1.0	2.6	4.6	5.7	3.0	6.7
25–34	10.4	8.3	2.4	5.3	17.0	11.1	5.1	7.1
35–44	9.7	8.8	2.7	7.0	24.5	16.8	4.7	11.4
45–54	12.6	10.4	4.6	7.3	20.0	23.1	10.8	11.1
55–64	12.5	7.8	3.1	5.8	20.2	23.8	9.9	13.2

Source: Karmel and Nguyen, 2003, pp. 10–11

The extent of credit transfer

There are two ways of trying to determine the extent of credit students are granted in HE on the basis of their prior VET (or at least TAFE) studies: the first is to examine the level of credit articulating students receive, based on student self-report; the second is to examine the total amount of credit granted based on prior TAFE study reported by universities as part of their annual reporting.

First, of those TAFE graduates who enrolled in a degree or higher level course in 2001, almost 53 per cent applied for and received some credit in their degree course,[9] just over 30 per cent said they had no intention of applying, approximately 9 per cent applied for credit but did not receive it, with the remainder indicating that they would apply in the future, or didn't know if they would (NCVER, 2002, pp. 13–14). However, the extent of credit students receive is small: over three-quarters of students who said they received credit received it for a third of their course or less (DEST, 2002, p. 11).

Second, government figures (based on enrolment data) show that the number of commencing degree students receiving credit for prior TAFE studies grew by 98 per cent from 1993 to 2001, growth which exceeded growth in commencing load overall for the same time (38 per cent) (DEST, 2002, p. 11). However, if the *percentage* of students receiving credit for prior TAFE study as a total percentage of commencing students is calculated, using the same numbers the government has provided, it can

Table 7. Students commencing bachelor degrees (or below) by exemption status and means of exemption, 1993 to 2001.

	1993	1994	1995	1996	1997	1998	1999	2000	2001
Students receiving exemptions for TAFE studies	1.65	2.32	2.59	2.50	2.66	2.55	2.80	2.83	2.36
Students receiving exemptions by means other than TAFE studies	10.37	10.21	11.96	11.42	13.99	13.81	13.86	15.16	13.77
Students receiving no exemptions	87.98	87.47	85.45	86.08	83.35	83.64	83.35	82.01	83.88
Total commencing students	100	100	100	100	100	100	100	100	100

Source: Derived from DEST, 2002: Table 6

be seen that the growth has been trivial, as demonstrated in Table 7. It demonstrates that credit transfer has *declined* for previous TAFE studies from the mid- to late 1990s, which approximately coincides with the introduction of training packages.[10] The literature is replete with findings that the introduction of training packages adversely affected the articulation and credit transfer arrangements between TAFE and HE.

Alternative access programmes

Australia has not had a strong and systematic national programme to increase access to HE by students from disadvantaged backgrounds comparable to the Scottish Wider Access Programme established in 1987 (Gallacher, 2003). The only national programme is the Commonwealth's higher education equity programme grant, which is 0.1 per cent of institutions' general operating grant. One third of this grant is allocated by performance and 40 per cent of the performance formula is for the number of enrolled students from socio-economically disadvantaged backgrounds and their academic success and retention (DEST, 2003, p. 74). As a result, access by students from disadvantaged backgrounds rests on individual institutions' initiative and universities' localised enabling programmes, which were only 1.3 per cent of all domestic commencing load in 2001 (DETYA, 2001, derived from Table 1).

Individual universities have developed access programmes, and these take the form of targeted courses for specific groups of students from disadvantaged backgrounds, the successful completion of which guarantees the student access to a degree programme. In addition, there are two types of alternative access mechanisms leading directly to degree courses: the first is to develop large-scale programmes that encompass all students without selecting students on the basis of specific equity related criteria, but which are premised on criteria that include disadvantaged students. Not many universities offer these programmes, and those that do are more likely to be universities that need to 'recruit' students as opposed to those that 'select' students (Maclennan, Musslebrook and Dundas, 2000, p. 12). The second approach is to develop programmes that include students on the basis of their membership of a target equity group. This is the basis of most access programmes, and they tend to be smaller in scope (Ramsay *et al.*, 1998, p. 64).

It is likely that specific access programmes – whether enabling or bridging courses, or alternative access mechanisms to degree level courses

– will remain small scale, and localised. Consequently, pathways from VET to HE assume more importance.

Improving student access and mobility: Credit transfer, institutional arrangements, course links and pathways

Australia has been experimenting with different ways of constructing pathways, through credit transfer, course links, and institutional links. A plethora of pathways and credit transfer arrangements have developed in Australia over the last ten years. A common language is gradually emerging to describe these arrangements, as a consequence of their increasingly diverse and widespread character, but also because there are now AQF credit transfer guidelines which have been endorsed by the peak bodies in both sectors (AQFAB, 2002; Carnegie, 2000).

National and state-based initiatives to increase credit transfer

Notwithstanding the AQF credit transfer guidelines, there is currently no systemic arrangement to support student transfer between the sectors – from VET to HE or HE to VET. There is no regulatory arrangement for credit transfer, advanced standing or access from one sector to another. Such arrangements that do exist are local, but they are unfunded, unco-ordinated, unregulated, not monitored, and are excluded from performance indicators in both sectors.

The Ministerial Council on Education, Employment, Training and Youth Affairs (MCEETYA) at its July 2003 meeting resolved that the states and territories 'agree to work with the Commonwealth to develop national arrangements for articulation and credit transfer between the higher education sector and the vocational and training sectors.' However, apart from making proclamations, there has been little political will shown at the national level to implement any real arrangements. The Commonwealth government conducted a review of HE in 2002, and promised to address the issue of sectoral relations through a discussion paper (one of six published as part of the review process) devoted to the VET/HE interface. However, the resulting policy mentions VET twice, and then only in passing. Much was promised through the review of HE, but nothing was delivered, and so the Commonwealth has lost its opportunity for the foreseeable future to plan and support relations between the sectors at the national level.

However, progress is occurring at the individual state level. The Victorian State Government is planning to introduce a 'credit-matrix' to facilitate credit transfer, articulation and student pathways. This is the first serious attempt in many years by a government or statutory body in Australia to establish a policy that facilitates credit transfer and articulation between the sectors. The Victorian credit matrix proposal was influenced the Scottish Credit and Qualifications Framework, but also by Ireland, New Zealand and South African qualifications frameworks. The Victorian credit matrix will look quite different to all of these however; it is state-based and not national, it must reflect local circumstances *and* it must in some way relate to the AQF. The credit matrix is a mechanism for evaluating the level of complexity and volume of learning, and then comparing this to the volume and complexity of learning in other qualifications. The Victorian Qualifications Authority has consulted widely, and anticipates that many of the eight Victorian universities will participate. Other states will watch the outcomes with interest.

In addition, other state governments have tried to establish arrangements to facilitate state-wide agreements between TAFE institutions and HE institutions – either individually or collectively, largely through memoranda of understanding (NCVER, 2002). It is possible that these initiatives combined will result in national policy to support credit transfer and student pathways.

Credit transfer arrangements

Despite the lack of national frameworks, two approaches have emerged, 'from the ground up' to negotiate credit transfer in Australian tertiary education. The first is based on block credit, where a completed TAFE qualification is deemed to be equivalent to a block of study in the degree. Usually a TAFE diploma[11] equals one year or one third of an ordinary three-year HE degree, often the first year.[12] Credit is based on the presumed commonalities derived from shared disciplines, rather than a detailed mapping of the content of both courses.

The second model is based on curriculum mapping, which focuses on mapping the content, learning outcomes, standards required in assessment, and sometimes approach to teaching and learning, with varying degrees of rigour. This is more likely to occur in dual-sector institutions (which are described in the next section) and other institutional arrangements that generate close relationships between the parties, for example, in the co-located institutions (Schoemaker *et al.*, 2000; Wheelahan, 2000). This approach can also occur between stand-alone institutions, but is less likely to occur at an institutional level. In this instance it is most likely at a course level where pockets at one institution develop relationships with pockets at another. The advantage of the curriculum mapping approach is that it can result in more credit being granted to articulating students. These arrangements are, however, expensive to maintain, as every time courses change in one or the other sector the pathway has to be renegotiated.

As self-accrediting bodies, universities are under no compulsion to develop pathways or grant credit. The extent to which universities do develop pathways and grant credit varies, with the newer, less prestigious 'recruiting' universities more likely to make such arrangements.

The CBT model in VET and the curriculum-input model in HE are not easily reconcilable. The move to CBT-based training packages in VET is widely regarded as an obstacle to articulation, credit transfer and other forms of course links between TAFE and HE (AVCC, 2001; Carnegie, 2000; NCVER, 2002; Senate, 2003; Wheelahan, 2000). This is for two reasons: first, HE is unable to understand the extent to which TAFE students with credit share the same underpinning knowledge as do other students. Second, assessment outcomes are usually ungraded,[13] and this disadvantages VET students in seeking entry to HE through competitive entry processes (Wheelahan and Carter, 2001).

Institutional dual-sector arrangements: Dual-sectors and co-locations

There are three types or models of institutional arrangements in Australian tertiary education: single-sector, stand-alone HE and VET institutions with various links and relations between the sectors; dual-sector universities (containing a HE and TAFE division); and co-located campuses. Each model has policies that govern credit transfer and other arrangements that support the movement of students across the sectors.

Single-sector institutions are the most numerous, but institutions vary considerably in the importance they give to inter-sectoral collaboration.

There are five universities regarded as dual-sector universities in Australia, four of which are in Victoria, with the fifth in the Northern Territory. The TAFE and HE sectors within the dual-sector universities are integrated to varying degrees, with teaching and courses remaining sectorally based in all institutions,[14] whereas most corporate and administrative services, and services for students are fully integrated.

Outside Victoria, co-located campuses, mostly comprising senior secondary school, a TAFE and a HE campus, are emerging as an important model for providing access to comprehensive post-compulsory education in regions beyond commuting distance from the major cities that can support separate institutions. They are integrated to varying degrees, but the partners are mostly administratively and financially independent, with many administrative, corporate and student services remaining distinct to a greater or lesser extent.

Relationship between institutional type and credit transfer

Broadly speaking, different institutional types approach credit-transfer differently. However, regardless of approach, the outcomes are most successful when staff from the different sectors have established good, collaborative, and trusting relationships (Schoemaker, *et al.*, 2000; Sommerlad *et al.*, 1998; Wheelahan, 2000; Wheelahan, 2001). This is most likely to happen when designated staff are employed to develop links between the sectors, a role described by Sommerlad *et al.* (1998) as that of 'boundary spanner'.

The dual-sector universities have an advantage to the extent that they are part of one institution, and are more likely to collaborate over the content of courses in each sector, rather than only developing pathways on the basis of completed qualifications. This has led to a range of models, some of which include components drawn from both sectors. The dual sectors also attempt to provide administrative support to their students in navigating the requirements of moving sectors, with varying levels of success. The dual-sectors are large institutions, and as such are sites of contested organisational and political culture, with relationships ranging from close and collaborative, to hostile. This can result in 'transfer-inhibiting practices' as Prager (1993, p. 551) observed for similar institutions in the US. However, this isn't necessarily always negative; it is sometimes a sign of *engagement* of staff in the dual-sector character of the university.

Co-located institutions must cope with the problems the dual sectors experience, but must also contend with complexities deriving from the fact that the partners are usually satellite campuses of a parent body, and most often do not have a common pool of funding for joint curriculum initiatives. Their administrative separation means that it is difficult to develop seamless arrangements for students.

Single-sector institutions vary in the extent to which they see collaboration as important. Those committed to collaboration (Sommerlad *et al.*, 1998) have created many pathways between courses in each sector, but these are mostly on the basis of completed qualifications, rather than detailed curriculum mapping which identifies equivalencies or at least inter-course relationships at levels lower than completed qualifications.

Course links: Pathways

Pathways (or articulation arrangements) link VET and HE courses and establish credit transfer arrangements. A pathway sometimes consists only of a link between two courses, so that successful completion of one may be used as the basis for an application to enter another, with no credit transfer granted. Alternatively, a pathway may link a VET and HE course, and it may also provide credit transfer.

Pathways can be *standardised* or *customised*. Standardised pathways are formally approved by the institutions involved, and ensure that all students meeting the specified conditions are granted the same benefit, usually credit transfer. Customised pathways are developed where no standardised pathway exists, or to meet the specific needs of individual students or groups of students.

Increasingly, *enhanced* pathways are being developed in Australia. Enhanced pathways offer articulating students more credit or advanced standing in the destination course than would otherwise be the case. An enhanced pathway is developed by both parties (TAFE and HE), but most often delivered in the TAFE institute. At dual-sector universities enhanced pathways are increasingly offered, which in some instances combine modules and subjects from both sectors, but which have been packaged into the TAFE course. This occurs through cross-crediting the TAFE modules and HE subjects against each other.

Guaranteed pathways are also becoming more prominent. Most often, TAFE students must win access to the destination HE course through competitive entry processes before they are able to attain the credit transfer specified in the agreement. In contrast, guaranteed pathways reserve a place for the articulating student, provided they meet the standards of performance specified in the pathway agreement.

Course links: Dual-sector awards and nested awards

There are two main types of dual-sector programme: dual-sector awards and nested awards. While they are not numerous, they are increasing (DEST, 2001), mainly in dual sectors and co-locations, to obtain market positioning.

Dual-sector programmes combine two awards, one from each sector, so that students complete both in less time through cross-crediting subjects in each. They have been developed by analogy from joint HE courses such as the joint arts/law degree and the joint accounting/information systems degree that have proliferated in Australian HE in the last decade. Dual-sector awards may draw on complementary fields of study, for example information technology or accounting. Alternatively, they may draw on the same discipline, but in a way that embeds TAFE qualifications in degree programmes (for example, a certificate as a lab technician within a science degree), allowing students to obtain an early credential to use for part-time or casual work. Dual-sector programmes of this nature do not really offer great potential for increasing access to students from disadvantaged backgrounds because to gain entry to such a programme students must first meet the entry requirements of the HE component of the award (Schoemaker *et al.*, 2000; Wheelahan, 2000).

Nested awards, on the other hand, do have potential to increase participation. Nested awards commence in TAFE and conclude in HE with various exits along the way. Students are able to work in areas related to their study, or they can leave and re-enter study at a later time. Nested awards particularly lend themselves to supporting students to move from para-professional to professional areas (like nursing), again providing students with an early credential. They may also appear more accessible to students from non-traditional backgrounds, both in gaining admission, and in developing aspirations for HE. This is because they offer school-leavers and mature-aged students 'progression by internal promotion (not selection by score)' which 'would provide the security that is currently the preserve of a minority of students at the top of the curriculum' (Teese, 2000, p. 229).[15]

Nested awards are institutionalised *within* sectors, for example, from certificate to diploma level in TAFE/VET, or the (now very common) graduate certificate to graduate diploma to coursework or taught Masters programme route in HE. Cross-sectoral nested awards remain underdeveloped, but are increasing in their importance.

Relations between the sectors and future developments

Credit transfer, dual-sector awards and the extent of student movement between the sectors remains underdeveloped, even at dual-sector universities and co-located institutions. This is in part because of the different reporting, funding and accountability requirements to different levels of government in each sector. The dead weight of administrative requirements is an almost irresistible counterforce to policy that seeks to deepen and extend collaboration. Industrial issues are often masked as disputes over philosophy, teaching style and standards, but upon closer examination are just as often as much about preserving jobs and status in each sector. The different accreditation and curriculum models in each sector also militate against collaboration. These are pressures towards divergence, and contribute to maintaining the unusually strong distinctions between the sectors compared to other Anglophone liberal market economies.

These tensions are compounded by historical factors: VET policy in Australia has been in part shaped by the need for the sector to define itself in distinction to the HE sector, and more recently in distinction to the senior school sector as well, as schools increasingly offer VET qualifications as part of their senior secondary school programme. VET (or TAFE as it was then) was established by the Kangan Committee in 1974 as a national system of teaching and learning that *didn't* happen in universities or colleges of advanced education; that is, TAFE was defined residually (Kangan, 1974). The creation of a national VET market in 1992 helped to define and distinguish VET from the other sectors. Qualifications were restructured on competencies and re-oriented towards specific occupations. A purchaser–provider model was established in which public TAFE institutions were only one type of provider, albeit the overwhelmingly dominant type.

However, this distinction was never complete. HE claims to prepare graduates for work, so the distinctions based on vocational orientation have begun to break down, as has the notion that vocational preparation is limited to narrow skill development. There are also pressures towards convergence, similar to those experienced in the other Anglophone liberal market economies. The distinctions between the sectors continue to blur as a consequence of the fuzziness of the distinctions between vocational and general (or academic) education (Gallagher, 2001; Karmel, 1998; Raffe and Howieson, 1998).

The sectors are distinguished by their different levels of awards, accreditation frameworks, curriculum (competency-based training in VET and a curriculum input model in HE), and reporting requirements, rather than intrinsic differences in mission. These differences between the sectors disguise the considerable, although as yet largely unacknowledged, common aims of their students; commonality of *content* in courses offered in both sectors, with both offering vocational and general courses; commonality of learning–teaching *process*, with both sectors promoting the virtues of flexible and workplace-based learning; and both sectors even adopting common *aims*, the promotion of economic benefit through the development of human capital, and increasingly (through government policy statements), building resilient and sustainable communities and regions through developing social capital.

The sectors are also being driven closer by pressure from the market: 22 (of 37) public universities[16] are registered to provide VET-level courses, mostly on a fee-for-service basis, while TAFE and other VET providers have been approved to provide some degrees and graduate certificates and diplomas. The Victorian State Government has recently passed legislation allowing TAFE to offer degrees in specific niche areas. This leads Karmel and Nguyen (2003, p. 1) to argue that '... there is no clear distinction between the sectors in terms of providers ... the level of the award defines the sectors rather than the provider.'

Now that associate degrees have been approved as HE awards, it is most likely that TAFE and other VET providers will seek to become large-scale providers of these awards. Apart from anything else, TAFE directors and private VET providers will use associate degrees to break free of the perceived restrictive nature of training packages (all publicly funded delivery in VET must be based on training packages). National seminars are being organised to advise TAFE on how to get such awards approved. TAFE will enter the HE market as private providers, in the same way HE has entered the VET market as private providers, and both can do so provided they meet the accreditation requirements of each sector. This will bring VET (particularly TAFE) into alignment with the analogous FE colleges in the UK and two-year or community colleges in the US, except that VET is not likely to receive public funding to do so – at least initially. However, like the early development of HE in FE in the UK (Parry and Thompson, 2002), this will take place in an unplanned and ad hoc manner.

This expansion of short-cycle HE in VET will also be driven by recent reforms passed by the Commonwealth Parliament, in which students who occupy full-paying HE places will be able to get income contingent loans up to $50,000 to pay fees.[17] Currently, while VET students pay fees that are considerably lower than the contribution paid by HE students, they must pay these fees up front, while HE students have the option of deferring payment of fees. Moreover, the VET sector runs many full-fee-paying courses, particularly in new economy areas, and students are not able receive government subsidies or loans for these fees. So while VET was ignored in the HE reforms passed by Commonwealth Parliament, they will nonetheless profoundly alter the relationship between the sectors, by increasing the competition between them for the same qualifications market, and providing the impetus for VET to become a large provider of short-cycle HE.

Conclusion

Australia's separation of vocational and higher education within a liberal market economy has not resulted in coherent frameworks to support student transition from one sector to another. The sectors are under pressure as a consequence of the blurring of their roles in light of the demands of the 'new economy', and from pressure on institutions and sectors to increase market share. Rhetoric of seamlessness is strong, but so is defence of the sectoral distinctions. It is anticipated that *students* will move taking from each sector what they need to craft their own individualised portfolios. This suggests that students have the 'market knowledge' needed to do so, and all research says this is not the case (James *et al.*, 1999).

While the Commonwealth government talks about seamlessness, it does little to facilitate it. State governments, on the other hand, are experimenting with a range of mechanisms to promote student articulation, particularly to support social justice and equity objectives as well as supporting economic and skills development within the state. Hopefully these efforts will eventually result in a more coherent national approach.

The Commonwealth government's HE reforms have the potential to reshape the relations between the sectors, through opening access to students enrolling in fee-paying HE courses to income-contingent loans. VET providers will flock to associate degrees to escape the constrictions of training packages, to enable their students to access income-contingent loans, to increase the extent of credit transfer awarded to articulating students, and to increase their share of the tertiary education market. It seems that the tensions caused by establishing very separate post-compulsory education sectors within a liberal market economy will be resolved in favour of the market. Over time the Australian sectors are likely to increasingly merge and overlap like their counterparts in other Anglophone countries. However, like the early development of HE delivery by FE in England, this will occur in an unplanned and ad hoc manner (Parry and Thompson, 2002). This is not the basis for a lifelong learning policy for Australia, and nor is it the basis for increasing access to HE for students from disadvantaged backgrounds.

Notes

[1] This refers to the Higher Education Contribution Scheme (HECS). Students on publicly funded HE courses are charged fees which are a 'contribution' of about a third of the cost of their tuition, with the Commonwealth government paying the rest. Students can defer the payment of HECS until their income reaches a threshold ($35,000 per annum in 2005, which is approximately 70 per cent of average weekly earnings), and they repay their debt through the taxation system on a sliding scale aligned with their income. HECS debts are increased by the consumer price index to maintain their real value but no real rate of interest is charged.

[2] See Richardson (2000) for an account of the 'approaches to learning' literature.

[3] Even the Commonwealth Department of Education, Science and Training is internally divided with separate departments for VET and HE. The AQF Advisory Board is therefore a crucial source of advice to government, spanning all of post-compulsory education and training.

[4] In some states ACE accredits its own programmes, where there is an independent statutory board – however, this does not happen in all states. ACE qualifications are subsumed under VET qualifications, are counted as VET qualifications, and are not a separate component of the AQF.

[5] The Commonwealth, State and Territory education and training ministerial council agreed to designate associate degrees as HE awards, despite the opposition of ANTA and the deep unhappiness of many of the state VET jurisdictions. As a

consequence, the ministers endorsed associate degrees as HE awards subject to an inquiry on the impact of this on diplomas and advanced diplomas and the VET sector more generally. This could be interpreted as a way of placating the VET sector. One should never underestimate the power of vice-chancellors combined!

[6] With the exception of students with a disability and students who come from a non-English-speaking background.

[7] This is based on student enrolment data in the two sectors.

[8] This is based on what Karmel and Nguyen (2003) call a 'courageous' estimate – Australia does not have consistent data collections in the two sectors, and this makes it very difficult understand the extent of traffic between the two sectors, and also to gauge accurately the size of the sectors, as census data, Australian Bureau of Statistics surveys (based on population samples), other surveys based on population samples, and statistical collections based on enrolment data in both sectors yields quite different results. This is compounded by the problem that the sectors have different and largely incommensurable measures for student load, and the sectors report to different levels of government.

[9] But we cannot say with certainty whether this was on the basis of their prior TAFE study – we can presume most of it is.

[10] Although caution must be used here, as other factors could also contribute to this decline, including the level of unmet demand for HE places – the higher the level of unmet demand, the more likely are students to use VET studies as a pathway to HE.

[11] Which is often two years study, but this has become variable since the introduction of training packages, and is often less.

[12] But sometimes credit is spread across different years of a degree, creating sequencing problems for students.

[13] However, TAFE institutions (both stand-alone and dual sector) are increasingly providing graded assessment to help students access HE, but also, in response to demands by employers and students for results that discriminate between VET graduates.

[14] This is a little different at the Charles Darwin University in the Northern Territory: courses are institutionally based, but an enterprise agreement involving unions from all sectors has resulted in an agreement that permits cross-sectoral teaching.

[15] Teese is here referring to integrated programmes spanning senior secondary school and TAFE, but this is within the context of a discussion that includes HE, particularly HE institutions serving the most vulnerable sectors of the population.

[16] Australia has two small private universities, with the remainder all public.

[17] Fee-HELP (Higher Education Loan Programme) will differ from HECS, because students would have to repay full tuition fees, while HECS-funded places are subsidised by the Commonwealth government.

References

Australian National Training Authority (ANTA) (2002) *Response to the Commonwealth Department of Education, Science and Training Discussion Paper Varieties of Learning: The Interface Between Higher Education And Vocational Education And Training*. Canberra: DEST. Online at:
http://www.dest.gov.au/crossroads/issues_sub/pdf/i274.pdf

Australian Qualifications Framework Advisory Board (AQFAB) (2002) *Australian Qualifications Framework Implementation Handbook*. Melbourne: AQFAB.

Australian Vice-Chancellors Committee (AVCC) (2001) *Cross-Sector Qualification Linkages Between Higher Education and VET*. Canberra: AVCC. Online at: http://www.avcc.edu.au/students/credit_transfer/index.htm [27 January 2002].

Australian Vice-Chancellors Committee (AVCC) (2002) *Forward from the Crossroads: Pathways to Effective and Diverse Australian Universities*. Canberra: DEST. Online at: http://www.dest.gov.au/crossroads/issues_sub/pdf/i354.pdf

Australian Vice-Chancellors Committee (AVCC) (2003) *Survey of Applicants for Undergraduate Higher Education courses 2003*. Canberra: AVCC. Online at: http://www.avcc.edu.au/policies_activities/resource_analysis/key_stats/Survey_Apps_HigherEd_2003.pdf

Carnegie, J. (2000) *Pathways to Partnerships: Qualification Linkages Between Vocational Education and Training and Higher Education*. Report and draft policy guidelines of the ANTA/AVCC joint study on credit transfer and articulation between the Vocational Education and Training (VET) and Higher Education (HE) sectors. Canberra: Australian National Training Authority/Australian Vice-Chancellors' Committee. See www.avcc.edu.au

Clark, B.C. (1983) *The Higher Education System: Academic Organization in Cross-National Perspective*. Berkeley, CA: University of California Press.

De los Santos, A.G. Jr and Wright, I. (1990) 'Maricopa's swirling students: earning one third of Arizona State's bachelor's degrees', *AACJC Journal*, Jun/Jul, pp. 32-4.

Department of Education, Science and Training (DEST) (2002) *Varieties of Learning: The Interface Between Higher Education and Vocational Education and Training*. Canberra: DEST.

Department of Education, Science and Training (DEST) (2003) *Higher Education Report for the 2003 to 2005 Triennium*. Online at:
http://www.dest.gov.au/highered/he_report/2003_2005/default.htm

Department of Education Training and Youth Affairs (DETYA) (1998) *The Characteristics and Performance of Higher Education Institutions*, Occasional Paper Series, Report No. 1A-98, November. Higher Education Division, Department of Education, Training and Youth Affairs.

Department of Education Training and Youth Affairs (DETYA) (2001) *Students 2000: Selected Higher Education Statistics*. Canberra: DETYA.

Dobson, I., Sharma, R. and Haydon, A. (1998) *Undergraduates in Australian Universities: Enrolment Trends and Performance of Commencing Students 1993–1996*. Canberra: AVCC.

Fuller, R. and Chalmers, D. (1999) 'Approaches to learning of TAFE and university students', *Australian and New Zealand Journal of Vocational Education Research* 7(1), pp. 127–44.

Furth, D. (1973) 'Short-cycle higher education: some basic considerations', in: D. Furth (ed.) *Short-Cycle Higher Education: A Search for Identity*. Paris: OECD, pp. 13–42.

Gallacher, J. (2003) *Higher Education in Further Education Colleges: The Scottish Experience*, Report for the Council for Industry and Higher Education (CIHE), March. Glasgow: Centre for Research in Lifelong Learning, Glasgow Caledonian University.

Gallagher, M. (2001) *Lifelong Learning: Demand and Supply Issues, Some Questions for Research*. Sydney: The Business/Higher Education Roundtable Conference on The Critical Importance of Lifelong Learning.

Golding, B., Davies, M. and Volkoff, V. (2001) *Review of Research: A Consolidation of ACE Research 1990–2000*. Adelaide: National Centre for Vocational Education Research.

Hall, P.A. and Soskice, D. (2001) 'An introduction to Varieties of Capitalism', in P.A Hall and D. Soskice (eds) *Varieties of Capitalism: The Institutional Foundations of Comparative Advantage*. Oxford: Oxford University Press, pp. 1–68.

James, R. (2002) *Socioeconomic Background and Higher Education Participation: An Analysis of School Students' Aspirations and Expectations*. Evaluations and Investigations Programme. Canberra: Department of Education, Science and Training. Online at: http://www.dest.gov.au/highered/eippubs/eip02_5/eip02_5.pdf

James, R., McInnes, C. and Baldwin, G. (1999) *Which University? The Factors Influencing the Choices of Prospective Undergraduates*, Evaluations and Investigations Programme, 99/3. Canberra: Higher Education Division.

Kangan, M. (chair) (1974) *TAFE in Australia: Report on Needs in Technical and Further Education*. Canberra: Australian Committee on Technical and Further Education.

Karmel, T. (1998) *Universal Participation: Implications for Policy Makers, Institutions and Students*. OECD Thematic Review of the First Years of Tertiary Education Australia Seminar. Sydney: DETYA.

Karmel, T. and Nguyen, N. (2003) *Australia's Tertiary Education Sector*. Centre for the Economics of Education and Training 7th National Conference, Monash University, Melbourne.

Keating, J. (2000) *Qualifications Frameworks in Britain and Australia: A Comparative Note*. Melbourne: RMIT University.

Keating, J. (2003) 'Qualifications frameworks in Australia', *British Journal of Education & Work* 16(3), pp. 271–88.

Maclennan, A., Musslebrook, K. and Dundas, M. (2000) *Credit Transfer at the FE/HE Interface*. Scottish Higher Education Funding Council/Scottish Further Education Funding Council. Online at: http://www.sfefc.ac.uk/publications/other/wideopps.pdf

Marginson, S. (1997) *Markets in Education*. St Leonards: Allen & Unwin.

Ministerial Council for Employment Education Training and Youth Affairs (MCEETYA) (2002) *Ministerial Declaration on Adult Community Education*. Melbourne: Victorian Government Department of Education and Training, on behalf of MCEETYA

Moodie, G. (2003a) *Comparative National and International Transfer Rates from TAFE/Further Education/Community College to University*. Enhancing university-TAFE partnerships, University of New England.

Moodie, G. (2003b) 'The missing link in Australian tertiary education: short-cycle higher education', *International Journal of Training Research* 1(1), pp. 44–63.

National Centre for Vocational Education Research (NCVER) (2002) *Submission to the Review of Higher Education*, 5 July. Adelaide: NCVER.

National Centre for Vocational Education Research (NCVER) (2003) *Australian Vocational Education and Training Statistics: Students and Courses 2002 – At a Glance*, Adelaide: NCVER.

Osborne, M., Cloonan, M., Morgan-Klein, B. and Loots, C. (2000) 'Mix and match? Further and higher education links in post-devolution Scotland', *International Journal of Lifelong Education* 19(3), pp. 236–53.

Osborne, M., Gallacher, J. and Murphy, M. (2002) *A Research Review of FE/HE Links: A Report to the Scottish Executive Enterprise and Lifelong Learning Department*. Stirling: Centre for Research in Lifelong Learning, University of Stirling and Glasgow Caledonian University.

Parry, G. and Thompson, A. (2002) *Closer by Degrees: The Past, Present and Future of Higher Education in Further Education Colleges*. London: Learning and Skills Development Agency. Online at: http://www.lsda.org.uk

Prager, C. (1993) 'Transfer and articulation within colleges and universities', *The Journal of Higher Education* 64(5), pp. 539–54.

Raffe, D. and Howieson, C. (1998) 'The unification of post-compulsory education: Towards a conceptual framework', *British Journal of Educational Studies* 46(2), pp. 169–87.

Ramsay, E., Tranter, D., Charlton, S. and Sumner, R. (1998) *Higher Education Access and Equity for Low SES School Leavers: A Case Study*. Evaluations and Investigations Programme, October 1998, 98/18. Canberra: Higher Education Division, DEYTA.

Richardson J.T.E. (2000) *Researching Student Learning: Approaches to Studying in Campus-Based and Distance Education*. Buckingham: SRHE/Open University.

Schoemaker, A. *et al.* (2000) *Multi-Partner Campuses: The Future of Australian Higher Education?* Canberra: DETYA.

Senate Employment Workplace Relations Small Business and Education Committee (2003) *Bridging the Skills Divide*. Canberra: The Parliament of the Commonwealth of Australia.

Senate Standing Committee on Employment, Education and Training (1991) *Come In Cinderella: The Emergence of Adult and Community Education*. Canberra: The Parliament of the Commonwealth of Australia.

Smith, P. (2001) 'Learning preferences of TAFE and university students', *Australian & New Zealand Journal of Vocational Education Research* 9(2), pp. 87–109.

Sommerlad, E., Duke, C. and McDonald, R. (1998) *Universities and TAFE: Collaboration in the Emerging World of Universal Higher Education*. Canberra: Higher Education Council. Online at: http://www.deetya.gov.au/nbeet/publications/hec/overview.html

Teese, R. (2000) *Academic Success and Social Power: Examinations and Inequality*. Carlton South: Melbourne University Press.

Wheelahan, L. (2000) *Bridging the Divide: Developing the Institutional Structures that Most Effectively Deliver Cross-Sectoral Education and Training*. Adelaide, South Australia: NCVER.

Wheelahan, L. (2001) *The 'Best Fit' or 'Screening Out': An Evaluation of Learning Pathways at Victoria University*. Melbourne: Victoria University of Technology.

Wheelahan, L. (2003a) 'Global trends and local bends: Australian VET developments,' *Journal of Continuing and Adult Education* 9(1), pp. 32–50.

Wheelahan, L. (2003b) *Pressure on the Australian Qualifications Framework:*

Implications for Cross-Sectoral Collaboration. Enriching Learning Cultures, 11th Annual International Conference on Post-Compulsory Education and Training, Parkroyal Surfers Paradise, Gold Coast, Queensland, Australia.

Wheelahan, L. and Carter, R. (2001) 'National Training Packages: A new curriculum framework for vocational education and training in Australia', *Education and Training* 43(6), pp. 303–16.

Review of further education/higher education links in Canada

Brian Burtch

Introduction

Canadian post-secondary education is administered by the ten provinces and three territories. Community colleges have been an integral part of higher education (HE) since the 1960s, complementing the post-secondary role of Canadian universities. Some brief background points should be mentioned for those unfamiliar with Canada. The Canadian population is approximately 30 million (28,846,761 according to our 1996 census), with about 80 per cent of residents living in urban areas (Micromedia, 2002, pp. 1–50). Constitutionally, responsibility for the administration of education is vested with the provinces and territories of Canada, not with the federal government. This decentralised approach can be seen as a mixed blessing, avoiding a centralised, standardised approach to further and higher education, but also encouraging a parochial (provincial) focus on educational offerings. Canada has one of the highest post-secondary participation rates for 18–21 year olds and has 92 universities and 175 community colleges affiliated with the Association of Universities and Colleges of Canada (AUCC, 2001; Council of Education Ministers, Canada and Statistics Canada, 2003).

With the second largest landmass of any nation, provincial and territorial control of education, and considerable linguistic and cultural diversity, it is not surprising that post-secondary education in Canada is both diversified and complex. Links between community colleges, universities, and institutes might fairly be termed strong, tenuous, and sometimes non-existent. Research on post-secondary institutions and experiences has tended to focus on universities, with rather limited studies of Canadian community colleges in the past five years. In fairness, there are signs of increased interest in community college programmes. These include studies of students' articulation and transfer experiences in British Columbia (Karlinski, 2003) and significantly, the inclusion of profiles of 128 Canadian community colleges in the recent Maclean's survey of HE (Johnston, 2001). Initially, the Maclean's researchers surveyed only universities.

This report will highlight some arrangements between the colleges and other post-secondary institutions, available research findings on transfer credit for example, and recurrent themes and issues associated with further and higher education in Canada.

Community colleges in Canada

The term 'community college' is not used in all Canadian jurisdictions. For example, the term 'regional college' is used in Saskatchewan, 'public college' in Alberta, and Collège d'enseignement général et professional (CEGEP) – College of General and Vocational Education or simply 'junior college' – in Québec (AUCC, 2001, p. xxiv; Johnson, 1990, p. 125). For the sake of simplicity, the generic term 'community college' will be used to indicate a post-secondary, publicly-funded institution other than universities. In British Columbia (BC), community colleges' offerings are divided into four broad categories: academic (with transfer credit to university), career and technical (with specific programmes targeted for work), vocational ('short applied programmes'), and adult basic education (for people who have completed high school graduation requirements) (Francis, 2000).

George Butlin (2000) noted that unlike many American colleges, Canadian community colleges act as 'commuter institutions', not offering degrees, and facilitating eventual entrance to university studies. As will be noted below, there are various degrees of articulation between colleges and universities, with some provinces – BC, Alberta, and Québec – establishing considerable transfer of credits from college studies to university programmes. There are also innovations such as university colleges in BC – which grant undergraduate degrees and are now able to propose graduate programmes. The BC university college initiative is essentially the 'exception to the rule' in Canada, where many colleges are mostly focused on vocational/technical programmes. Again, there is considerable variation in the colleges' provision of courses that transfer smoothly should a college student enter university.

As of 1994, there were approximately 150 community colleges with over 700 'satellite campuses' across Canada. It was estimated that 1.5 million students were taking non-credit courses and 500,000 were registered on credit courses (Dennison, 1995a, p. 3). In the 1998–99 academic year, full-time enrolment (FTE) in Canadian community colleges was approximately 403,500. The numbers increased by 1.2 per cent over the 1997–98 academic year. Statistics Canada reported that these enrolments had increased by 9.3 per cent over enrolments five years previously (Canadian Press, 2000a).

Table 1 gives an overview of community colleges in the ten provinces and three territories (North West Territories, Yukon, and Nunavut).

Table 1. Community colleges in the territories and provinces of Canada.

Province/territory	College designation	# of colleges
British Columbia	Community college University college	15 (including 5 university colleges)
Alberta	Public college	10
Manitoba	Community college	4
New Brunswick	Community college	9
Newfoundland	Provincial college	1
North West Territories	Community college	1
Nova Scotia	Community college	1
Nunavut	Community college	1
Ontario	College of applied arts and technology	25
Prince Edward Island	Community college	1
Québec	Collège d'enseignement général et professional (CEGEP), or 'junior college'	48
Saskatchewan	Regional college	8
Yukon	Community college	1
Total		125

Source: Adapted from Micromedia (2002), section 9; Heritage College (2002)

Some jurisdictions report a growing demand for community college programmes. In Manitoba, the number of full-time students in community colleges increased by over 40 per cent between 1993 and 2000. As a case in point, Red River College (Winnipeg, Manitoba) experienced 'a record-setting increase of over 500 full-time students' in one year. Enrolment increased by 12 per cent, leading to problems of overcrowding, lack of established classroom space, and demands for additional government spending (Canadian-Press-Newswire, 2000). In contrast, several college campuses were closed in Nova Scotia in the mid-1990s (*Teacher*, 1996). There appears to be a clash between restraint in post-secondary education costs on the one hand, and demands for career-directed offerings by the colleges. However there does not appear to be any systematic study of factors that might explain why some provinces expand their college offerings, while others are at a standstill or are reducing access.

Butlin (2000) traced wide variations in community college employment patterns in the various provinces and territories. Only 35 per cent of college staff in Saskatchewan and the Yukon were employed full time, compared with 95 per cent of college employees in New Brunswick, and 90 per cent of their counterparts in Manitoba. Regional differences were also noted with respect to 'dropouts' from colleges and universities in Canada. Thus, both university and college students in British Columbia, the Prairies, and the Atlantic provinces were more likely to leave post-secondary studies than students in either Ontario or Québec (Butlin, 2000).

Transfer credit between the colleges and universities

Community colleges do not have a uniform linkage with Canadian universities. As mentioned above, only a minority of provinces – Québec, Alberta, and BC – have 'articulated models' to ease transfer from colleges to universities. Formal arrangements allow college students with designated prerequisites to gain credit in university programmes, ideally providing greater access to further educational opportunities. While problems in transfer credit have been identified, the point remains that for most provinces, links between the colleges and universities are not particularly well developed (Andres, 2001).

For example, in BC, articulation of credit between colleges and universities was part of the mandate for community colleges (Andres, 2001). Some 'comprehensive' community colleges may offer the equivalent of the first two years of university education, mounting first and second year courses that are given transfer credit at some universities. This arrangement is a boon to students, since more students commence degree studies through community colleges, university colleges, or institutes than through direct entry to BC's universities (BCCAT, 2001, p. 5). Credit may be assigned directly where college and university courses are deemed to be essentially similar, i.e. there is a 'match' between the courses. In some cases, block transfer can be given between a sending institution (college) and a receiving institution (university). This allows students to proceed into upper-level coursework without undertaking costly, time-consuming, lower-division prerequisites. Even where direct credit is not granted, a student may receive unassigned credit for certain courses. This is where a course is equivalent in credit terms, but there is no equivalent at the university. Unassigned credit may help a student to complete breadth requirements of a degree, if not the more specific requirements of a major or minor concentration. In some cases, no credit may be given.

In BC, transfer credit is an important link, allowing students to obtain equivalent first or second year education at lower tuition costs than universities, often in a more convenient, accessible, and affordable location than those of the four major provincial universities. Students may thus transfer in to universities with equivalent standing to students who entered university directly in the first year. Karlinski (2003) reported that two-thirds of BC college students transferred to BC universities, with only 10 per cent continuing in community college programmes and 6 per cent in university college programmes. Transfer mechanisms are guided by 'general principles for flexible and innovative transfer.' These principles are:

- Students should be able to complete all lower division (1st and 2nd year courses) degree requirements at a college, provided that the college offers a reasonable variety of courses in their chosen discipline.
- Neither transfer nor direct entry students should be advantaged or disadvantaged as a result of the transfer process. (BCCAT, 2001, p. 7)

BCCAT is responsible for facilitating and co-ordinating credit among post-secondary institutions, and providing an annual report – in print and online formats – that denotes specific credit arrangements. BCCAT undertakes in-house research, funds provincial articulation meetings, and produces the *BC Transfer TIPS Handbook* (the acronym TIPS stands for Transfer Information for Post-secondary Success). Updated information is available on the Council's Website (www.bccat.ca).

In Québec, the situation is quite different. Their CEGEP system requires that all Québec students undertake 'pre-university programs' and obtain a diploma before applying to a Québec university (Butlin, 2000; Dennison, 1995a, p. 6). Students enter a CEGEP after their eleventh year of education. This contrasts with other provinces where students complete grade 12 (or 13, for the moment, in Ontario) and then proceed directly into college or university programmes. As noted in Table 1, there are 48 CEGEPs in Québec, allowing students ready access to such preparatory institutions. In Canada's largest province, Ontario, a 'parallel' system is in place, with universities seen as quite distinct from many community colleges. This arrangement does not allow for the ready integration of credit transfer between the two, unlike the BC system (Dennison, 1995b).

The Centre for Education Information (2001) explored experiences of over 6,000 BC students who, after enrolling in institutes, university colleges, or community colleges, continued on to further education (FE). Most (65 per cent) continued on university studies, primarily the University of British Columbia, Simon Fraser University, and the University of Victoria. The great majority (86 per cent) of respondents were either 'very satisfied' or 'satisfied' with transfer of credits between institutions. On the downside, students who had completed work in fairly specialised programmes such as 'Visual, Performing and Fine Arts' were more likely to be disappointed in transfer credit decisions (Centre for Education Information, 2001). A subsequent study found that 88 per cent of college students were either 'very satisfied' (48 per cent) or 'satisfied' (40 per cent) with their experience with transfer credit (Karlinski, 2003).

Even where clear transfer links are articulated, concerns have been voiced over what appears to be the relatively weak performance of students transferring from college to university programs. Lesley Andres (2001) reported that students who begin university studies directly from high school, i.e. enter first-year university classes, are more likely to receive degrees than their transfer-in counterparts from colleges. Some of these findings date back to the 1980s, and we should be cautious about treating such differences as axiomatic. Indeed, of all the students who receive degrees in BC, more begin their post-secondary studies in colleges, university colleges, or institutes than through direct entry to university. Andres (2001) used interviews with 47 lower mainland (Greater Vancouver) students who transferred from a local community college to a university in Greater Vancouver. She found that most respondents planned to transfer from college to university studies (indeed, 37 per cent of students at this college were enrolled in university transfer studies, as opposed to applied programmes (31 per cent) and general studies (32 per cent). Reasons cited for attending college included proximity to home, lower tuition fees, reduced requirements for admission, and using college as a 'stepping stone' to ease into university studies. Andres (2001) found that while most respondents were generally complimentary about transfer credit arrangements, concerns were expressed over declines in GPA (grade point average), misleading or unhelpful advising (primarily in the college, not university context), loss of credit, difficulties interpreting the BCCAT Transfer Guide, and difficulties adjusting to the more impersonal environment of university. Loss of credit and poor academic performance can lead to delays in degree completion, higher costs of education and, in some cases, being placed on academic probation and/or being required to withdraw from university. Andres (2001) recommends that students considering transfer to universities should have access to pertinent information, that applicable 'policies, practices, and procedures' should be more understandable, and that colleges and universities should work together to provide better matches between curriculum and pedagogy. Other concerns include 'transfer shock' manifested in lowered grades, usually in the first semester of university attendance. The British Columbia Council on Admissions and Transfer reported that international students and students arriving from distant sites such as northern communities generally experienced the most transfer shock (BCCAT, 2001, p. 3).

However, we do not have a tradition of systematic research on college and post-college experiences, and certainly not a tradition of inter-provincial/territorial comparisons of linkages between colleges and other post-secondary institutions. Butlin (2000) is an exception to this pattern, as his research incorporates a national focus.

Other transfer links

The previous section focused on transfer of academic credits among community colleges, university colleges and universities. Wider initiatives have also been undertaken to strengthen recognition of work done at other institutions or in the workplace. Mobility and transferability are listed as fundamental advocacy issues by members of the Association of Canadian Community Colleges. For example, as of 1999 there were 102 college signatories to the pan-Canadian protocol. This protocol involves acknowledgement and transfer of 'learning acquired through formal education, workplace training and work and life experience' (Association of Canadian Community Colleges, 2002). The rationale for this protocol is set out in Figure 1.

Despite such initiatives to increase recognition and transfer of credit, most studies of community colleges have focused on more specific issues, such as dropout (or 'post-secondary leaving') rates (Grayson, 1997; Koodoo and Pachet, 1998). However, as has been noted above, Butlin (2000) argues that, unlike many American colleges, Canadian community colleges act as 'commuter institutions', not offering degrees, but facilitating eventual entrance to university studies for those who are not taking strictly vocational/technical programmes. Community college students may, for example, obtain a two-year diploma from their institution, then transfer in to a university to obtain a baccalaureate degree. In our terminology, the diploma may 'ladder' into degree-based studies.

There were also regional variations in dropout rates. For example, more than one-third of high school graduates in BC left university, while only 13 per cent of their Ontario counterparts left university. Intermediate rates of university leaving (approximately 25 per cent) were identified for students in the Atlantic region (Newfoundland and Labrador, Nova Scotia, Prince Edward Island, and New Brunswick) and the Prairie region (Manitoba, Saskatchewan, and Alberta). With respect to community colleges, Butlin (2000) reported that '[High school or equivalent] Graduates from the Atlantic region and Prairie provinces had odds nearly 2 times higher for community college leaving compared to Ontario students ... The odds of community college leaving were 3.3 times higher for British Columbia students compared to Ontario students'. I find these two paragraphs a bit confusing. I think they are comparing the experience of high school graduates with former community college students in universities in different provinces, but I'm not really sure, and wonder if it could be more clearly expressed?

Factors positively correlated with post-secondary leaving included parents without post-secondary education (20 per cent of school leavers, compared with 15 per cent of students whose parents had no post-secondary education). Nevertheless, 'Parents' level of educational attainment did not affect the odds of university leaving, after controlling for the effects of other predictors such as high school marks, high school leaving and failing a grade in elementary school.' Butlin (2000) points out that the:

Figure 1. Rationale for pan-Canadian protocol among 102 community colleges.

There is a growing recognition in all sectors related to post-secondary education (school, student, government and industry), that to compete in the new knowledge-based economy, Canada needs to build a capacity for learning and training that widens access to learning opportunities for individuals and for enterprises, and increases labour force productivity.

To meet the requirements of rapid change in post-secondary education and in the labour force, colleges are increasingly entering into agreements with industry for employee training, and with each other for program sharing and the transferability of learning.

At the same time, colleges, along with governments at the provincial and federal levels, are developing policies to address the need for increased student mobility and accessibility to post-secondary education and skills training. What is needed now is a Pan-Canadian protocol on the transferability of learning that can be ratified by colleges across the country. It is becoming increasing apparent that the ability to move easily between work and school, and between post-secondary institutions, increases the efficiency of learning and saves valuable time and cost to the individual, to industry and to society.

If Canada is going to compete successfully in the global market and continue to be productive domestically, the labour market requires more advanced skills and education and a frequent renewal of skills. Skilled human capital is rapidly becoming a major source of competitive advantage, wealth and prosperity. The easier it is to access education for individuals, and the more mobility they are afforded by post-secondary institutions, the more likely individuals are to upgrade their skills on a continuous basis. Credit transfers and prior learning assessment are an effective and efficient way of providing opportunity for these workers to upgrade their skills and knowledge base.

A protocol would furthermore allow colleges to identify common standards; encourage dialogue between institutions and college systems; set or target provincial and national standards; maximize the use of resources; and, increase awareness of articulation goals and principles.

A Pan-Canadian protocol for the transferability of learning among colleges benefits everyone. The clear advantages to the student are greater mobility and accessibility, both in studying and in the workplace. The ability to transfer credits easily between institutions, and the ability to move easily from work to school and back, encourages increased college participation, and a more active, knowledgeable and skilled workforce.

(Taken verbatim from Association of Canadian Community Colleges (2002), www.accc.ca)

higher odds of university and community college leaving in British Columbia may have something to do with the university transfer system in this province. British Columbia has a highly developed university transfer system in which students can transfer to a university without earning a community college/CEGEP diploma ... in addition, British Columbia has a relatively high number of part-time students at both the community college and university levels. Part-time students are more likely to leave without completing their programs than full-time students ... (Butlin, 2000)

The progression of high school to community college and then possibly to university is not always straightforward. Some university graduates undertake community college or other, non-university studies to complement their degrees. For example, the Information Technology Institute (ITI) is a private instructional technology institution, which requires applicants to complete a university degree prior to admission (Sibley, 2000).

Privatisation and government cutbacks

Government policies and private sector influences on education have generated an ongoing debate about post-secondary education. A noticeable trend has been an entrepreneurial focus, tied in with the federal government's support for vocational training. Another trend has been a policy of cutting back federal contributions to public education and other social welfare activities (Dennison, 1995a, p. 13). Such a 'restructuring' of government expenditures and emphasis on privatisation and the private sector is often presented as the major influence on the direction of community college offerings (Witchell, 1990). One instance of this is the announcement of a new post-secondary institution in Ontario, based on a partnership between Durham College (Oshawa) and the newly formed Ontario Institute of Technology. The new institution will focus on 'high-waged employment' and will grant both diplomas and degrees (Daily Commercial News, 2001). Advocates of stronger linkages between the private sector and the colleges cite many benefits to such collaboration, including lessened demands on government budgets, and work-oriented curricula that can ease the transition from formal studies to employment. Links between business, industry, and community colleges are often celebrated as a means of increasing revenues and tailoring programmes to ever-changing work contexts (Wells, 1998).

Private-sector influences and government cutbacks have also attracted criticism. Concerns over corporate influence in the colleges have been voiced by John Ralston Saul and others. These concerns include undue control over curriculum, amount of time required for fundraising, and pressures to value 'training' over more academic education. Ralston Saul urged college administrators to resist what he termed a 'corporate, managerial approach' and to preserve core educational approaches and programmes (Canadian Press, 2000b).

Levin (2000) contends that there is clearly a trend toward a corporate-style, managerial approach in community college governance, but there are countervailing pressures to heighten staff and student input for decision-making. In several American and Canadian jurisdictions studied, it appears that only BC and California 'requires or encourages shared or participatory governance' through such measures as faculty involvement on governing boards and the presence of educational councils. Other commentators highlight the impact of declining government expenditures on post-secondary education, and gender-based issues such as the appreciably higher number of women instructors with part-time and limited-term appointments, compared with male instructors (Barnetson, 2001).

Attracting non-traditional populations

In a general sense, community colleges have long served the needs and interests of non-traditional populations, for example through an emphasis on work training, unlike the more 'academic' focus of the universities (*Nova Scotia Business Journal*, 1998). Nevertheless, there is a strong scholarly tradition in Canada that explores the difficulties some populations experience in gaining occupational and educational opportunities within Canada's 'vertical mosaic' (Helmes-Hayes and Curtis, 1998; Porter, 1965). The recent literature identifies more specific populations that have not traditionally enjoyed access to post-secondary education.

Women's participation in post-secondary studies has increased dramatically in the past 30 years, with female undergraduate students outnumbering male students in virtually all Canadian universities and community colleges. Nevertheless, concerns have been raised about under-representation in some programmes. At Toronto's Instructional Technology Institute (ITI), women accounted for just over a quarter (28 per cent) of the incoming students in May 2000 (Sibley, 2000). Sibley adds: 'The figures are equally dismal for women enrolled in computer science courses in Canadian universities ... while there were 15,270 male students in computer science programs in 1998, there were only 4,130 women' (2000).

In recent years, considerable attention has been given to ways of attracting and retaining Aboriginal students. This category is quite broad, including status and non-status Indians, Metis, and Inuit. At approximately 700,000 people, the Aboriginal population is estimated at 2 per cent of the Canadian population (Baker, 1995, p. 209), although some place this as high as 4 per cent of the total population. Studies have confirmed that First Nations people have a much lower participation rate in post-secondary education. Specifically, they are one-seventh as likely as the general population to graduate from university, and only half as likely to graduate from high school (Wright, 1998). The 1991 Canadian census found disparities in educational attainment between Indian and non-Indian populations, with only 3 per cent of the former completing degrees compared with 15 per cent of the general population (Baker, 1995, p. 209).

To remedy this, some colleges have established tribal councils, steering committees, and have modified their offerings to reflect Aboriginal concerns and values. Indeed, there has been a renaissance of educational initiatives within Aboriginal communities, oftentimes in partnership with non-Aboriginal stakeholders (see Castellano, Davis and Lahache, 2000). In some cases this involves bilateral negotiations between college administrators and First Nations representatives. It may also involve on-reserve resources such as learning centers, which provide assessment and preparation for post-secondary studies or completion of high school equivalency. In this case, the First Nations band has formed a formal partnership with Capilano College in North Vancouver, BC (Wright, 1998, p. 85). There are many other examples, such as the partnership between Heritage College and the James Bay Cree School Board, which provides college preparation for Cree students in northern Québec (Heritage College, 2002). Also of interest to the postsecondary sector is an historic signing between the First Nations Steering Committee, Indian Affairs and Northern Development, and the BC government in July 2003. This formal understanding 'lays the groundwork for greater First Nations control and authority over K-12 [kindergarten to grade 12] education on-reserve as well as increased influence in the public school system' (Indian and Northern Affairs Canada, 2003).

There has been a positive trend toward greater educational

participation of Aboriginal students, with a 30 per cent increase in Aboriginal adult students in colleges and universities between 1986 and 1992 (Baker, 1995, p. 209). Baker isolates several factors associated with success of Aboriginal students. These include location, preparation, community linkages, peer support, cultural support, family and childcare services (the majority of Aboriginal students in the mid 1990s were mature women with children), and a 'culturally hospitable environment' (1995, pp. 211–12). The province of Saskatchewan has had a strong legacy of encouraging college and university attendance by Aboriginal people. The Saskatchewan Indian Federated College (SIFC) and Saskatchewan Indian Institute of Technologies (SIIT) were established in 1976. SIFC began with less than ten students, and now has over 1,300 students, while SIIT has over 2,000 students in the 1999/2000 academic year (Windspeaker, 2001). It is fair to stay that the community college sector has a vital role to play in providing opportunities for Aboriginal people.

Summary

While the colleges play a major role in the sociocultural and economic life of this country, very little systematic effort has been made to document their contributions, to analyze the changes that are occurring within them, or to examine the issues which must be addressed if they are to continue to play a viable role. (Dennison 1995a, p. 9)

Community colleges are a relatively new addition to Canadian post-secondary education, tied to the expansion of educational opportunities in the 1960s and 1970s, but often out of the limelight-accorded Canadian universities. While some community colleges have become degree-granting, their primary roles seem to be diploma and certificate programmes, often of an applied nature, with some linkage to further studies at the 'upper levels' (third and fourth years) of university programmes. The growth of degree-granting university colleges in BC is a recent innovation that spans the traditional roles of colleges and universities.

Pan-Canadian accords (protocols) have also been forged to increase recognition of work undertaken within and outside community colleges (www.accc.ca). Students interested in post-secondary studies can also avail themselves of a number of print and electronic resources devoted to college and university programmes (www.canlearn.ca). These initiatives and resources should be considered in light of the lack of a national educational policy in Canada and a tradition of local and provincial autonomy in the administration of educational initiatives. There is also an overarching pressure to 'restructure' expenditures and programmes to conform to market-oriented, cost-recovery principles. This highlights privatisation and greater involvement of the private sector generally in educational matters.

Even where formal inter-institutional links are established, there are persistent problems of poor access to useful information, lack of preparation for FE at university, and shortfalls in credit recognition for some community college courses and programmes. The recent literature highlights not only successful and unsuccessful example of linkage (credit recognition and transfer credit, for example), but also wider concerns over programme content, reduced government funding despite increased demand for places, and a 'restructuring' tendency that adversely affects students, instructors, and other staff (Meaghan, 1997).

Rising tuition costs and general financial pressures on students have been identified as factors of social exclusion. This is often presented in a general context of privatisation, where post-secondary costs are passed on to students or non-government sectors, as federal and/or provincial governments retrench their expenditures on post-secondary education (Dennison, 1995a, p. 8). Specific populations such as women and Aboriginal peoples have been identified within this exclusionary framework. In addition, many cite instances of resisting and reducing exclusionary practices for such non-traditional populations.

The diverse and divided nature of the Canadian educational landscape has not been captured in a comprehensive review of the community college sector, let alone its links with other educational institutions, particularly universities. This overview highlights key themes within the provincial and territorial post-secondary systems, but it cannot provide more than a starting point for future, comparative (cross-national) studies of FE and HE.

References

Andres, L. (2001) 'Transfer from community college to university: perspectives and experiences of British Columbia students', *Canadian Journal of Higher Education* 31(1), pp. 35–74.

Association of Canadian Community Colleges (2002) *Pan-Canadian Protocol*. Online at: www.accc.ca

Association of Universities and Colleges of Canada (AUCC) (2001) *The Directory of Canadian Universities 2001*. Ottawa: AUCC. See: www.aucc.ca

Baker, D. (1995) 'Aboriginal education in community colleges', in: J. Dennison (ed.) *Challenge and Opportunity: Canada's Community Colleges at the Crossroads.* Vancouver: University of British Columbia Press, pp. 208–19.

Barnetson, B. (2001) 'Part-time and limited-term faculty in Alberta's colleges', *Canadian Journal of Higher Education* 21(2), pp. 79–102.

British Columbia Council on Admissions and Transfer (BCCAT) (2001) *British Columbia Transfer Guide 2001-2002*. Vancouver: BCCAT. See: www.bccat.bc.ca

Butlin, G. (2000) 'Determinants of university and community college leaving', *Education Quarterly Review* 6(4), pp. 8–23.

Canadian Press (2000a) 'Enrolment at community colleges increases in 1998–1999 school year', *Canadian Press Newswire* [October 3].

Canadian Press (2000b) 'Community colleges urged to turn down corporate sponsorship', *Daily Commercial News* 73(120), 21 June, p. B14.

Canadian-Press-Newswire (2000) 'Winnipeg's crowded Red River College forced to hold classes in washrooms', *Canadian Press Newswire*, 5 September.

Castellano, M.B., Davis, L. and Lahache, L. (eds) (2000) *Aboriginal Education: Fulfilling the Promise*. Vancouver: University of British Columbia Press.

Centre for Education Information (2001) *Admissions and Transfer Experiences of Students Continuing their Studies in British Columbia*, Research Report, British Columbia Council on Admissions and Transfer (February), 4 pp. Online at: www.bccat.bc.ca/pubs/rr_feb01.pdf

Châteauneuf, L. (1996) 'Sursis ... l'éxecution au Manitoba [Collège universitaire de Saint-Boniface]', *University Affairs* 37(7), pp. 10–11.

Council of Education Ministers, Canada and Statistics Canada (2003) *Education Indicators in Canada: Report of the Pan-Canadian Education Indicators Program 2003*. Toronto: Canadian Education Statistics Council.

Daily Commercial News (2001) 'First new university in 40 years planned for Durham site', *Daily Commerical News* 74(194), p. A5.

Dennison, J.D. (1995a) 'Introduction', in: J. Dennison (ed.) *Challenge and Opportunity: Canada's Community Colleges at the Crossroads.* Vancouver: University of British Columbia Press, pp. 3–12.

Dennison, J.D (1995b) 'Community college development in Canada since 1985', in: J. Dennison (ed.) *Challenge and Opportunity: Canada's Community Colleges at the Crossroads.* Vancouver: University of British Columbia Press, pp. 13–104.

Francis, D. (2000) 'Community colleges', in: D. Francis (ed.) *Encyclopedia of British Columbia*. Vancouver: Harbour Publishing.

Grayson, J. (1997) 'Institutional failure or student choice? The retention of adult students in Atkinson College', *Canadian Journal for the Study of Adult Education* 11(2), pp. 7–30.

Helmes-Hayes, R. and Curtis, J. (eds) (1998) *The Vertical Mosaic Revisited*. Toronto: University of Toronto Press.

Heritage College (2002) Home page: www.cegep-heritage.qc.ca

Indian and Northern Affairs Canada (2003) 'Education for sustainable communities' [special promotional feature], *The Province* October 18, p. A23.

Johnson, W. (1990) 'The radical pedagogy of a CEGEP instructor', in: J. Muller (ed.) *Education for Work, Education as Work: Canada's Changing Community Colleges.*

Toronto: Garamond Press, pp. 125–41.

Johnston, A.D. (2001) *The MacLean's Guide to Canadian Universities and Colleges*. Rogers Media.

Karlinski, J. (2003) *2002 Admissions and Transfer Experiences of Students Continuing their Studies: Findings from a College Outcomes Survey*. 2nd Biennial Conference on Articulation and Transfer, 'Policies and Practices in Transfer: Putting the Pieces Together', University of South Florida and Hillsborough Community College, Tampa, Florida, 28–29 July.

Koodoo, A. and Pachet, N. (1998) 'A comparison of the graduation rates of pre-employment plumbing students who entered the program at Red River Community College with 20G courses and those with 20S courses', *Manitoba Journal of Counselling* 35(1), pp. 17–20.

Levin, J.S. (2000) 'What's the impediment? Structural and legal constraints to shared governance in the community college', *Canadian Journal of Higher Education* 30(2), pp. 87–122.

Meaghan, D. (1997) 'Restructuring and ravaging Ontario's community colleges', *Education Monitor Reporting on Education and Public Policy Issues* 1(4), pp. 16–19.

Micromedia (2002) *Canadian Almanac and Directory 2002*. Toronto: Micromedia (a division of HIS Canada).

Nova Scotia Business Journal (1998) 'Nova Scotia [Community College] offers variety of quality training options', *Nova Scotia Business Journal* 13(6), p. B2.

Porter, J. (1965) *The Vertical Mosaic*. Toronto: University of Toronto Press.

Sibley, K. (2000) 'Women's work: Females are still under-represented in the intake numbers of technology training courses', *Computing Canada* 26(18), pp. 17–18.

Teacher (1996) 'Closing Shop [five Nova Scotian Community College campuses]', *Teacher* 35(1), p. 8.

Wells, L. (1998) 'Community college curriculum a carrot to attract call centres to Nova Scotia', *Nova Scotia Business Journal* 13(3), p. A10.

Windspeaker (2001) 'Celebrating 25 years of post-secondary education', *Windspeaker* 19(3), p. 31.

Witchell, C. (1990) 'Teacher unionism and college education in post-referendum Québec', in: J. Muller (ed.) *Education for Work, Education as Work: Canada's Changing Community Colleges*. Toronto: Garamond Press, pp. 49–68.

Wright, D.A. (1998) 'Preparing First Nations students for college: The experience of the Squamish Nation of British Columbia', *Canadian Journal of Native Education* 22(1), pp. 85–92.

Higher education in the learning and skills sector: England

Gareth Parry

Introduction

In the dual system of post-secondary education in England, higher education (HE) is the central responsibility of one sector and a secondary or minor concern of another. In the HE sector, universities and other establishments of HE are funded by the state to pursue teaching at the undergraduate and postgraduate levels, alongside research and the transfer of knowledge. In the learning and skills sector, a wide range of organisations, including colleges of further education (FE), are publicly funded to deliver education and training at the upper secondary and tertiary levels. This structural and organisational separation has been maintained at the same time as relationships between institutions in each sector have multiplied. More significantly, these divided structures have survived into an era during which FE colleges are expected to play a major role in the future expansion of HE.

Since the end of the 1990s, FE colleges have been implicated in a major policy experiment intended to change the traditional pattern of demand for English HE, away from the first degree studied at HE establishments and toward sub-degree qualifications delivered by FE institutions. The difficulties encountered by this latest attempt to bring parity of esteem to vocational and academic education in the English system reflect a deep ambivalence and unease about according colleges a larger role in the conduct of HE. Neither within the HE sector nor inside the learning and skills sector is there a shared conviction that FE colleges, collectively or severally, should incorporate HE into their core mission. Nevertheless, these institutions continue to account for around one in nine of all students undertaking courses of HE in England and, for the Westminster government, they occupy a central place in the drive to wider participation and near universal access by the end of the decade.

In what follows, an account is given of the past and present contribution of colleges to English HE, especially in the transition to mass levels of participation. The nature of this contribution has received relatively little attention, whether from academic researchers, policy officials or professional politicians (Parry and Thompson, 2002). Unlike in Scotland, the short-cycle sub-degree courses offered by the English colleges represented neither a significant share nor a discrete segment of the HE system. Furthermore, the rapid expansion that produced the decisive shift to mass HE in England was taken largely by establishments of HE, not by institutions of FE. The evolution of this pattern, including the reform measures that shaped its contemporary character and development, are examined in the next section.

Having moved to a mass system at a time when HE in FE was a matter of 'low' policy, the sudden elevation of this territory into 'high' policy was made in circumstances less than favourable to colleges leading the next phase of growth. The new policy expectations placed on colleges and the conditions for their realisation are reviewed in later parts of the paper. Necessarily, only an outline description and examination are presented here. For specific and separate accounts of the evolution of the FE and HE sectors in England, the reader is directed to the relevant standard works (see, for example, Cantor and Roberts, 1986; Cantor, Roberts and Pratley, 1995; Matterson, 1981; Pratt, 1997).

Long history and low policy

Historically, the formal separation of FE colleges from those institutions that have HE as their primary purpose is a recent phenomenon. Up to the 1980s, the colleges were part of a local authority system of advanced and non-advanced FE that included the polytechnics and, following the rationalisation of teacher education in the 1970s, the colleges of HE. These three types of institution each offered courses of 'advanced' FE (as local authority HE was then described) in the maintained or non-university sector of HE. Such courses were funded through local government and were approved, validated and inspected by external bodies. The university sector of HE, by contrast, comprised self-governing universities financed directly by central government (on the advice of an intermediary body) and legally empowered to award their own degrees.

In the FE system, local authority control of the polytechnics and colleges, together with a regional machinery for course approvals, meant that decisions about the distribution of advanced and non-advanced education were referenced to the needs of the locality and its region. In this 'national system, local administered', the administration and funding of FE, like that of schools, was conducted as a partnership between central government and the local education authorities, with the Whitehall department responsible for education as the major partner and central authority. The legal basis for this partnership was supplied by the 1944 Education Act where local authorities had a statutory duty to provide 'adequate facilities' for FE in their areas (Cantor and Roberts, 1972).

Colleges in the maintained system

Operating as a third 'tier' of HE providers in the maintained system, the FE colleges were among the most local, vocational and distributed parts of English HE. Unlike the 29 polytechnics and the 70 or more colleges and institutes of HE, the advanced courses offered at the colleges of FE were a minority of their provision; and some had no advanced work at all. Across the 300 or so FE colleges supporting advanced courses, most had small amounts of HE. Only in a handful of colleges was this a sizeable activity, contributing to their character as 'mixed economy' institutions. For the great majority of FE colleges, their main purpose was the education of young people and adults at the 'non-advanced' levels.

Apart from the size and proportion of advanced provision, the other main feature of HE in the colleges was the short-cycle vocational character of its courses. These were generally of two kinds. The first comprised two-year programmes leading to sub-degree qualifications awarded by the national councils for technician and business education: the full-time Higher National Diploma (HND) and the part-time Higher National Certificate (HNC). The second included an assortment of higher-level courses and examinations, some controlled by professional bodies and others recognised by employers, that met the education and training requirements of specific occupations.

Compared to the strong vocational orientation of advanced courses in the colleges, the curriculum of non-advanced FE provided a plural set of programmes and pathways, even where the technical tradition was strong. Most colleges offered a broad range of courses leading to academic and vocational qualifications (including entry to HE) as well as programmes catering for general, liberal, leisure and basic education. Except for a small number of specialist institutions in areas such as agriculture, art and design, and the performing arts, the span of subjects taught in general FE colleges was normally wide, although not without some hard boundaries around different types of college provision: between academic and vocational tracks; and between courses leading to qualifications and those, usually part time, pursued without the need for certification.

Over time, especially during the recession years of the 1970s and under the retrenchment policies of the first Thatcher government, colleges sought to diversify their non-advanced courses. As a consequence of the decline in the manufacturing industry and a corresponding reduction in apprenticeships, several colleges experienced a contraction of traditional 'day release' courses provided for trainee technicians and practitioners of trades. In their place, many embraced more general forms of vocational and work-related education. Included in these new activities were special training schemes for the unemployed and various programmes of vocational preparation aimed at recent school leavers.

Recession and unemployment also increased the demand for full-time courses. Many colleges developed their academic curriculum to rival that offered in secondary school sixth forms and sixth form colleges. Where previously it was the vocational route (not available in schools) that brought many young people into FE, this was now joined by increasing numbers of school-leavers choosing to take (or re-take) their upper secondary qualifications in the more 'adult' environment of the college. In another extension of their provision, opportunities for adults to return to study and to qualify for 'alternative' entry to HE were extended by the rapid growth of access and second chance programmes. Many access to HE courses involved the colleges in formal relationships with neighbouring HE establishments and a number of schemes gave students guaranteed progression to linked undergraduate courses.

These changes to the core territory of non-advanced FE coincided with pressure on some colleges to justify their continuing involvement in HE. Like their counterparts at the national diploma and certificate level, those HND and HNC programmes run in conjunction with local industry experienced an increasing unwillingness on the part of employers to release their workforce for blocks of study in the college. Such difficulties were not new. The period since the 1960s had been 'a generally hostile environment' for sub-degree and part-time courses (Scott, 1984). Not only had the mandatory grant system produced a bias in favour of full-time study, the 1966 binary policy looked to a concentration of full-time HE in the local authority system. The newly created polytechnics were expected to command the greater share of this higher-level work. The role of 'other' colleges in HE was to secure specialist provision or meet local needs. In these circumstances, the binary policy 'left the main body of further education colleges bereft of their star institutions and uncertain of their status and future' (Pratt, 2000).

Nevertheless, the polytechnics and the colleges remained under the control of local government and, through their involvement in the machinery for advanced course approvals, the local authorities were in a position to influence the regional and institutional pattern of HE, including the extent to which advanced provision was brought together in some institutions or dispersed among many. For their part, civil servants in central government were concerned from the beginning about the increasing costs of an expanding local authority system that entitled each authority to charge to a 'pool' its expenditure on advanced courses. Officials saw the answer to controlling expenditure in better national co-ordination and the rationalisation of provision. The concentration of scarce resources, they believed, demanded the selection and development of dedicated HE institutions (Sharp, 1987).

The local authorities interpreted these moves as attempts to loosen their control of the polytechnics, a process that would lead sooner or later, they feared, to the replacement of local authority HE by a new sector under central control. For the representatives of local government, one of the fundamental principles underpinning the FE system was the link between advanced and non-advanced provision: the 'seamless robe' that recognised common ground between HE and FE. Despite repeated efforts to concentrate advanced work in the larger and strongest institutions, the colleges of FE still accounted for around one in five of all HE students in the maintained sector by the beginning of the 1980s.

Colleges outside the two sectors of higher education

It was during this decade, however, that the structural separation of advanced and non-advanced was finally achieved. The Education Reform Act of 1988 removed the polytechnics and the major HE colleges from the local authorities and established them as incorporated institutions in their own HE sector. Like the university sector that was also reformed under this legislation, the two HE sectors each had their own funding council. National arrangements for the planning and funding of local authority HE had already been introduced after 1982. The local authorities were represented on the new planning body but, in advising the Secretary of State on the distribution and funding of places, the amount of money at its disposal was now fixed in advance by central government. In steering a difficult path between allocating a shrinking pool of resources and maximising access for students, one of the main ways that it looked to make savings was through further concentration of advanced work.

Although chided by ministers for not doing enough to rationalise the pattern of provision, the main policy justification for the abolition of the national advisory body was the need for the polytechnics to be freed from local constraints and encouraged to build on their individual strengths. In their recruitment and range of subjects, the polytechnics had become national institutions and, as 'mature' academic establishments, they sought more independence in their management and governance, as well as in the validation of courses.

In place of a system that gave undue weight to local interests, the Thatcher government looked to 'a more effective lead from the centre'; one that would allow polytechnics to meet the changing needs of industry and, following its 'revised' policy on access, provide in new ways for the wider range of students that would enter HE in the 1990s:

> The existing national planning arrangements are unsatisfactory. More progress needs to be made in rationalising scattered provision and concentrating effort on strong institutions and departments.

In addition:

> Many local authorities apply to their higher education institutions inappropriate detailed controls, some of which are designed for smaller institutions or other sources. (DES, 1987, p. 29)

Accordingly, the polytechnics and all other institutions 'of substantial size' (with 350 or more full-time equivalent HE students) and 'engaged predominantly' in HE (with more than 55 per cent of their activity in HE) were re-established as corporate bodies outside of local authority control.

There were political advantages too in taking HE out of the hands of local government. Most of the large metropolitan authorities were Labour-controlled, some of which had used their control of polytechnics and FE colleges to target resources at those who had benefited least from existing provision. Apart from the positive action and equal opportunity dimensions of such policies, it was under the aegis of local authorities that early articulation agreements and 'open college' arrangements were developed between higher, further and adult education (Parry, 1996).

When it came, the removal of the polytechnics and other HE institutions from the local authority system was also seen to bring benefits to the redefined FE sector. Not only was it relieved of responsibility for HE establishments, it was no longer burdened with the negative language of non-advanced FE. The small amounts of HE that remained with the colleges were officially regarded as 'residual'. In a reform that had created two sectors of HE, the idea of HE in FE was rendered untypical, if not anomalous. On the margins of the mainstream system, much of this remaining provision was placed outside the scope of a central planning authority.

This status was reinforced by a distinction between courses of 'prescribed' HE which were eligible for support from the Polytechnics and Colleges Funding Council (such as the first degree and HND) and courses of 'non-prescribed' HE (such as the HNC) that nominally remained with local government. Unlike the universities and polytechnics, each funded as institutions of HE, the colleges that provided prescribed and non-prescribed courses had to deal with two funding sources: one that had the polytechnics and HE colleges as their primary constituency; and another that was tied to the level of the rate support grant determined by central government. For their FE provision, on the other hand, the colleges continued to relate mainly to local government. Here as well, by delegating financial responsibility to governing bodies, the 1988 Act served to weaken the control exercised by local authorities over their colleges.

Although much reduced by the 1988 legislation, the overall size of the local authority part of HE was considerable. At least 92 colleges were funded for their prescribed HE and around another 300 had non-prescribed courses. Taken together, around 120,000 HE students were enrolled in FE colleges, most studying part-time and the great majority on sub-degree programmes. A report of Her Majesty's Inspectorate described this provision as 'substantial and diverse', including courses which met a specific need, those in unusual subjects, and some for which there was high demand. They increased the variety and geographical spread of HE in England and so played an important part in 'widening opportunities for students' (DES, 1989).

Colleges in their own sector

In another major policy turn, the existence of these courses, their vocational emphasis and their local accessibility were but a minor consideration in the reforms introduced by the Further and Higher Education Act of 1992. Like the polytechnics five years earlier, the colleges were established as independent corporations in their own sector and with their own funding body, the Further Education Funding Council (FEFC). At the same time, a single funding structure and a common quality assurance framework was created for a unitary sector of HE. Within the unified sector, the Higher Education Funding Council for England (HEFCE) was responsible for all institutions of HE, including the former polytechnics and the handful of HE colleges that were allowed to use the university title following the 1992 Act. In this dual structure for post-secondary education, FEFC inherited responsibility for the small quantities of non-prescribed HE at most of its FE colleges and, on assuming its responsibilities in 1993, HEFCE funded prescribed courses at more than 70 FE establishments.

In establishing some 500 colleges as free-standing FE institutions, including 100 or so sixth form colleges previously run under school regulations, the Major Government hoped that these establishments would emulate the success of the polytechnics in achieving the 'efficient expansion' of the late 1980s and early 1990s. The more market-led policies applied to HE under the third Thatcher Government and, continued by her successor, had seen a spectacular growth in the student population accompanied by a year-on-year decline in the average unit of resource. Overall numbers in the former polytechnics and colleges sector had grown by more than two-thirds and those in the former universities sector by more than a third.

This runaway expansion was brought to an abrupt end in 1994 when spiralling costs proved too much for the Treasury. In the new colleges sector, by contrast, ambitious annual growth targets were set for FEFC and its institutions. Not for the first time, government policies directed at the HE and FE sectors took divergent paths. However, the across-the-board expansion enjoined on FE also soon fell victim to increasing pressures on government finances and the demand-led funding incentive for colleges to expand was withdrawn in 1997.

From the beginning, FEFC showed no inclination to engage with the non-prescribed HE it was obliged to fund or with the prescribed provision in colleges supported by HEFCE. While not excluded from its remit, HE in FE became a zone of 'low' or 'no' policy for the new funding council. Only 5 per cent of the students in the FE sector were on HE courses and, given the priorities set for the sector by government, FEFC was anxious to guard against any dilution of its mission and that of constituent colleges. Nevertheless, this did not prevent its own inspectors describing HE as 'an integral part of the provision offered in many further education colleges' and displaying 'essential features of the drive to achieve national targets for lifelong learning' (FEFC, 1996).

High policy and the skills agenda

A deepening crisis of funding in both HE and FE was the context for the establishment of a national committee of inquiry into the future of HE (the Dearing Committee, 1996–97). Conspicuously, no such independent and wide-ranging exercise was felt necessary to investigate the condition of FE. Rather, an internal inquiry into widening participation in FE by FEFC (the Kennedy Committee, 1994–97) became the main vehicle by which the contemporary role of colleges was addressed alongside, but not in dialogue with, the Dearing process (FEFC, 1997; Parry, 2001). Equipped with bipartisan support, one of the central tasks of the Dearing inquiry was to recommend to a newly elected government in 1997 how 'affordable' future expansion might be secured while maintaining academic standards, retaining high completion rates, and widening participation in HE.

Although the funding model proposed by the inquiry was immediately rejected by the incoming New Labour Government, the political breakthrough made by the Dearing Committee was to recommend the introduction of tuition fees paid by home students for full-time undergraduate education. Much less noticed in the heated public debates that followed was the broad acceptance by the Blair Government of the Dearing assumptions and recommendations regarding resumed growth. In contrast to the pattern of previous expansion, the committee expected a major part of future growth to be expressed at the sub-degree levels. Equally controversial was the inquiry's proposal that priority in future growth at these levels should be accorded to FE colleges and that they should be funded directly for this provision.

Elaboration I: Direct funding and a special mission

After a period of unplanned and under-funded expansion that reproduced the English preference for full-time and first degree study in establishments of HE, the Dearing proposals marked the arrival of 'high' policy for HE in FE. The colleges were now at the front end of a major effort to change the dominant pattern of demand for undergraduate education in England. The 'special mission' that Dearing assigned to FE colleges was the first of three major policy interventions by the Blair Government, each intended to stimulate and steer future growth toward vocational sub-degree qualifications delivered mainly in FE settings.

Compared to the analysis and attention devoted to funding questions, the Dearing arguments for a return to growth by way of sub-degree HE were surprisingly under-developed and even more so in relation to the college contribution (Parry, 1999). Such provision, it was suggested, was better matched to the diverse aspirations, backgrounds, and credentials of many of those expected to enter this expanded system. It made for greater flexibility and more stopping-off points in support of lifelong learning. Importantly, it relieved pressure on the first degree and so helped to maintain 'one of the highest first degree graduation rates in the world'. Whatever the merits of these arguments, they confronted a history and growth trajectory in England based on the hegemony and popular appeal of the first degree. For the great majority of students, short-cycle qualifications and college-based programmes were not a first or preferred choice.

During the peak years of expansion that propelled the English system from an elite to a mass scale of HE, enrolments in sub-degree courses had been much slower than for first degree and postgraduate education (Table 1). With most of its provision at levels below the first degree, the expansion of college-based HE over this period was among the slowest recorded across all parts of English HE. Indeed, had it not been for the phenomenon of 'franchising', there would have been a reduction in the share of HE undertaken in the FE sector.

Franchising was the means by which an HE establishment funded one or more FE colleges to deliver some of its courses. These were nearly always at the undergraduate levels where the whole or part of such programmes might be taught in college environments. The number and type of franchise arrangements increased rapidly as the polytechnics in particular looked for ways to expand student numbers. Franchising was an attractive option when their campuses were unable to absorb further

Table 1. Higher education students enrolled at higher education institutions (including Open University) and further education colleges by level and type of qualification, England (thousands).

	1989/90	1994/95	(% change)
Postgraduate			
Higher education institutions	123.3	253.6	(+106%)
Further education colleges	1.9	2.2	(+16%)
Total	125.2	255.8	(+104%)
First degree			
Higher education institutions	499.1	822.0	(+65%)
Further education colleges	5.4	12.6	(+133%)
Total	504.5	834.6	(+65%)
Other undergraduate			
Higher education institutions	164.2	201.6	(+23%)
Further education colleges	103.9	116.8	(+12%)
Total	268.1	318.4	(+19%)
All levels			
Higher education institutions	786.6	1277.2	(+62%)
Further education colleges	111.2	131.6	(+18%)
Total	897.8	1408.8	(+57%)

Notes:

1. Figures for franchise students were not collected for these years and therefore not indicated.

Sources: Department for Education/Department for Education and Employment and Ofsted Departmental Reports

growth or where they sought to take courses into the community and region. Such relationships brought benefits for students and their colleges, as well as for HE institutions. They increased the local availability of HE, taking new courses and new subjects into colleges, enhancing progression within and between partner institutions, and bringing some colleges into HE for the first time (Abramson *et al.*, 1996; DES, 1991).

Franchising, especially in its 'multiple' and 'serial' forms, was the subject of some of the most prescriptive recommendations in the Dearing report. There was a worry that some colleges might be extending themselves too broadly and entering into too many relationships to be able to ensure quality and standards. For such arrangements to continue, the report stated, there needed to be rigorous criteria specifying the 'proper limits' of franchising and a regulatory framework to ensure 'compliance' with these requirements. In its response to these proposals, the government invited the newly formed Quality Assurance Agency for Higher Education (QAA) to be flexible in allowing franchisees to have more than the one higher partner originally recommended by the Dearing committee.

The disquiet evoked by franchising was one reason why the inquiry wanted to see HE in the colleges funded directly. It also wanted to prevent any upward drift in their 'distinctive' sub-degree mission and proposed that no growth be allowed in first degree and postgraduate qualifications in colleges:

> *We are keen to see directly-funded sub-degree higher education develop as a special mission for further education colleges. In general, over time, we see much more of this level of provision being offered in these colleges, although we recognise that particular circumstances might apply in some cases. We also see no case for expanding degree or postgraduate work in further education colleges. In our view, this extra discipline to the level of higher education qualifications offered by further and higher education institutions will offer each sector distinctive opportunities and best meet growing individual, local and national needs, although we recognise there may be different circumstances in the different countries of the UK. (NCIHE, 1997a, p. 260)*

The example of Scotland was a major influence on this set of proposals. With little investigation undertaken into the history and nature of HE in the English colleges, the inquiry was made keenly aware of the situation north of the border by the work of its own Scottish committee (NCIHE, 1997b).

The higher participation rate in Scotland (44 per cent) compared to England (33 per cent) was attributed, in part, to a recently introduced structure of qualifications which supported progression from school, through FE and into HE, and to 'the wide scope there to study sub-degree HE in FE colleges'. In Scotland, it was reported, some 40 per cent of HE was at sub-degree levels and over a quarter (27 per cent) of the total provision was delivered by the colleges. In England, a smaller proportion of HE was offered at the sub-degree levels (around 28 per cent) and, counting both franchised courses and those owned by the colleges themselves, the colleges still only accounted for an estimated one in nine of the student population in HE.

Elaboration II: Plural funding and a new qualification

The early years of this policy encountered a combination of damp demand for sub-degree courses, a concern about low subject review ratings in some colleges, and a response from within the HE sector that reflected a mixture of ambivalence, unease and hostility. Nor did the colleges themselves engage collectively or actively with the Dearing proposals. In its own response to the Dearing report, HEFCE was unconvinced by the evidence of demand for sub-degree entry or by the case for any immediate concentration on this level of provision. It was equally sceptical about limiting the expansion of sub-degree courses to the colleges, especially if this was assumed to be a cheaper option.

The funding council had earlier conducted its own review of the extent and nature of the 'interface' between HE and FE (HEFCE, 1995). In a subsequent consultation report, it recommended that future funding of HE in colleges should be based on collaborative arrangements with institutions of HE (HEFCE, 1996). This work was overtaken by the establishment of the Dearing committee but was used again by the HEFCE to suggest that the funding of HE in FE was 'more complex' than the inquiry report indicated.

Contrary to the Dearing recommendation, the funding council proceeded to offer colleges a choice between three funding options: indirect funding (franchising) through a HE institution; direct funding from HEFCE to an individual college; and funding through a consortium composed of colleges and one or more HE establishments (HEFCE, 1999). Colleges were able, if they wished, to continue with multiple funding routes. Nevertheless, the funding council exercised a strong steer in favour of collaborative arrangements since these might 'best support quality and standards'. The central concern was that the quality of the student experience should not vary. FE colleges were expected to deliver the same quality and standards of HE as the universities and colleges of HE.

The plural funding approach, together with new codes of practice on indirect funding partnerships, were introduced in 2000. In the previous year, HEFCE had assumed funding responsibility for all postgraduate and undergraduate education, irrespective of its location. This was another Dearing recommendation and it led to the re-definition of the HNC as prescribed HE. Those courses remaining in the non-prescribed category, such as higher-level vocational qualifications awarded by various external bodies, remained the responsibility of FEFC. As a result of these changes,

HEFCE became responsible for an additional 50,000 or more students at another 200 colleges. As a consequence of some colleges choosing to be funded indirectly or through consortia, the total number of colleges receiving funds directly from HEFCE reduced from a high of 270 in 1999 to 202 by 2001.

The transfer of funding responsibility also meant that a much larger number of colleges were brought under the QAA, many of which had little or no previous experience of its requirements and processes. In 2001, the Secretary of State announced a significant reduction of review activity in HE establishments but, for colleges of FE, a comprehensive programme of full-scale review would continue. In its report on the consultation exercise ahead of this change, the QAA repeated its concerns about quality and standards in a minority of colleges.

Here, as before, HE in FE was differentiated in ways that 'obscured and confused its identity on the one side and increased its complexity on the other' (Parry, 2003). Not only was this provision divided between two categories of HE (prescribed and non-prescribed) and four types of funding (direct, franchised, consortium and non-HEFCE), but its external quality assurance arrangements were different again: subject review for directly funded programmes; academic review (through the relevant HE institution) for its franchised programmes; and inspection or assessment of its non-prescribed HE when yet another body, the Qualifications and Curriculum Authority, had completed the accreditation of higher level vocational qualifications.

With little evidence of improved demand in the post-Dearing years, ministers came to doubt the capacity of existing forms of sub-degree provision to deliver further significant expansion. Ahead of the general election in 2001, New Labour used its election manifesto to announce a participation target of 50 per cent of 18 to 30 year olds in HE by the year 2010. To help deliver this target, the government invented a new two-year qualification – the foundation degree – on which any future expansion would be concentrated. Both were radical departures. The 50 per cent target was based on a different measure of participation than that used previously in government and, though criticised for not including older age groups, it opened the way to near universal access, when more than half the relevant age grade were engaged in some kind of higher and post-secondary education (Trow, 1974). The foundation degree was the first time that a short-cycle qualification carried the title 'degree', rather than diploma or certificate. It was also the first new major qualification in English HE since the introduction of the Diploma of Higher Education in the 1970s. Both were, however, consistent with the larger policy effort to shift demand away from the first degree and to ask colleges to take a central role in the delivery of future growth.

In turn, the foundation degree was one element in a wider government strategy to bring education and employment into closer relationship. By involving employers in its design and operation, by enabling students to apply their learning to specific workplace situations, and by guaranteeing arrangements for progression to the first degree, the new qualification would, it was anticipated, raise the value of work-focused qualifications and redress the historic 'skills deficit' at the intermediate level. Awarded by HE institutions with degree-awarding powers, the foundation degree was to be delivered 'typically' by FE institutions. In time, the foundation degree would subsume many of the other qualifications at these levels, including the higher national awards whose numbers had 'begun to fall away' (DfEE, 2000b; HEFCE, 2000a).

Foundation degrees were to be located at the upper end of 'a new vocational ladder' spanning secondary and post-secondary education (Blunkett, 2001). Here they would provide a vocational route into HE for those qualifying with upper-secondary qualifications or through the award of credits for appropriate prior and work-based learning. Employees looking to upgrade their skills were a key target group for the foundation degree, and its wide range of modes of delivery, including part-time, modular, distance and work-based study, were expected to be more aligned to 'earning and learning' than existing provision.

At the other end of the ladder, more vocational versions of secondary qualifications were to be introduced for 14 to 16-year-olds which would open a pathway to more advanced programmes that were predominantly vocational or which combined academic and vocational study. Having already established itself as the principal location for young people and adults to undertake qualifying programmes for entry to HE, the FE sector was poised to supply qualifications at each of the three main levels in the new vocational ladder.

Elaboration III: Indirect funding and a shared territory

The proposal for a vocational pathway offering progression through school, FE and HE, with links into the workplace and other qualification routes, coincided with a major reform of the infrastructure for 'post-16 learning'. This was intended to achieve a more integrated approach to lifelong learning but, as in 1988 and 1992, the Learning and Skills Act of 2000 reinforced a firm separation between the HE sector (untouched by this reform) and a radically restructured learning and skills sector. For FE colleges offering HE, the survival of sector divisions meant a continuing engagement with a dual structure and parallel bodies for post-compulsory education.

Following a cross-departmental review of post-16 education and training, the government proposed the establishment of a single body – the Learning and Skills Council (LSC) – to take responsibility for the strategic development, planning, funding and quality assurance of post-compulsory learning 'excluding higher education' (DfEE, 1999). Styled 'the most significant and far reaching reform ever enacted to post-16 learning in this country', the LSC assumed responsibility for FE colleges (from FEFC), for sixth forms in schools (from the local authorities), for government-funded training and workforce development (from the training and enterprise councils), and for adult and community learning (from local government). To meet its quality standards, the existing inspection systems responsible for schools, for colleges and for work-based learning were brought together within a single framework.

Where previously intense competition with other colleges was the order of the day, these institutions were now expected co-operate as well as compete with other organisations in the new, enlarged post-16 sector. Moreover, they found their core provision planned and co-ordinated locally, through a network of 47 local LSCs. Like FEFC at the beginning of its tenure, the LSC inherited responsibility for non-prescribed HE. Cross-sector collaborations, such as franchise and consortium partnerships, were largely unaffected by these measures. As before, colleges that provided HE in their own name or delivered courses on behalf of partner universities had still to deal with the funding, quality and information regimes of another sector.

The reform strategy for the whole of the learning and skills sector, including its more than six million 'learners' and over 4,000 providers, involved a new system of targets and performance management, strategic area reviews to assess the pattern of provision in each part of the country, and collaborative working between colleges and schools across the 14 to 19 phase of learning. To play to their strengths in this environment, individual colleges were pressed to demonstrate their distinctiveness and to cultivate a specialist focus: 'The need first and foremost for each college to identify what it is best at, and to make that field of excellence central to its mission' (DfEE, 2000a). In 2001, the first 16 'pathfinder' colleges were announced and, by 2004, half of general FE colleges were planned to have an established vocational specialism for which they were recognised as a centre of excellence.

Examples of financial mismanagement in some colleges, together with evidence of uneven quality and standards achieved in English FE, had made for a low-trust relationship between government and the colleges, especially under the two Blair administrations. To tackle a situation in which one in seven colleges required full re-inspection, the present government implemented a framework of targeted support and intervention to give under-performing colleges the opportunity to improve. To recognise and reward successful providers, it allowed these colleges greater autonomy and flexibility (DfES, 2002).

A concern about quality and standards in FE was evident again in the much-delayed White Paper on HE that unveiled plans for, among other things, a deregulation of tuition fees, a concentration of research in 'leading universities' and a steering of non-research-intensive universities 'towards other parts of their mission', such as knowledge transfer and teaching (DfES, 2003b). In renewing its commitment to increase participation 'towards' the 50 per cent target set for the end of the decade, the government underlined the role of the foundation degree in securing the bulk of this growth. Henceforth, it would become the standard two-year HE qualification in England. The White Paper proposals on foundation degrees, including a willingness to 'incentivise' both the supply of and demand for this qualification, were the third and latest stage in the post-Dearing experiment to alter the shape of demand for English HE.

When the first prototypes were approved in 2000, the foundation degree was expected to function both as a valued qualification in its own right, equipping students with intermediate skills that were increasingly demanded by employers, and as a staged qualification giving progression to honours degrees and to higher-level occupational awards. By the time of the White Paper, the requirement to provide 'guaranteed' arrangements for time-limited progression to at least one honours degree had been relaxed. As quickly realised, only if accepted and respected as an end qualification was the foundation degree likely to help close the 'skills gap' at the associate professional and higher technician levels. This was where skills were already in short supply and, according to official forecasts, would be in still greater demand in the next decade. This message was highlighted in the national skills strategy for England, published in the same year as the White Paper, where the reform of sub-degree qualifications in HE was set alongside measures to improve skills across all phases of education and learning (DfES *et al.*, 2003).

However, the special mission that Dearing had in mind for the colleges was a less discrete and protected one in the 2003 White Paper, although this goal had been eroded in the intervening years. FE would continue to play an 'important' role in serving the HE needs of local students, and foundation degrees would 'often' be delivered in these settings, but there was no intention of making short-cycle vocational HE exclusive to colleges. In contrast to Scotland, the sub-degree provision offered by the English colleges was a territory shared with establishments of HE, especially the post-1992 universities. Although the composition of this HE was different between the two sectors, it was still the case that more students were taught at the other undergraduate levels in the HE sector than in the colleges. Even when franchise students were included in the FE numbers, more than a third of HND students were still taught in the universities and HE colleges (Table 2).

Nor were colleges to be allowed a more independent role in the delivery of foundation degrees. According to the White Paper, only where 'niche' provision was delivered, or where there were no obvious HE partners, would colleges be able to apply for directly funded places. In future, these would be considered on a case-by-case basis and 'against criteria which will include critical mass, track record on quality and standards, and nature of provision'. The remainder, if they had not done so already, would need to combine with partner HE institutions since, it was claimed, this was a relationship that safeguarded quality.

> *Further education has strengths in providing ladders of progression for students, particularly for those pursuing vocational routes, and serves the needs of part-time students and those who want to study locally. Further education colleges make an important contribution to meeting local and regional skills needs, including through the higher education they provide. We want this significant role to continue and to grow. However, it will be important that any expanded provision is of the quality that we expect from higher education. We believe that structured partnerships between colleges and universities – franchise or consortium arrangements with colleges funded through partner HEIs – will be the primary vehicles to meet these aims and will best deliver benefits for learners. (DfES, 2003b, p. 62)*

All the same, when it came to the invitation to bid for additional

Table 2. Students undertaking higher education and higher level qualifications in higher education institutions (including Open University) and further education colleges by level and type of qualification, England, 2000/01 (thousands).

	Students taught at higher education institutions	Students taught at further education colleges	All students
Postgraduate	282.2	8.0	290.2
First degree	761.9	24.9	786.8
Other undergraduate	183.7	91.2	274.9
Higher National Diploma	24.4	39.6	63.9
Higher National Certificate	5.6	43.1	48.7
Diploma of higher education	47.1	1.7	48.8
Certificate of higher education	15.7	0.6	16.3
Other undergraduate diplomas and certificates	56.8	4.3	61.1
Professional qualifications at undergraduate level	19.7	0.2	19.9
Other qualifications at undergraduate level	14.4	1.8	16.2
Higher level qualifications	0.0	63.1	63.1
National vocational qualifications at levels 4 and 5	0.0	20.8	20.8
Other higher level qualifications	0.0	42.4	42.4
Institutional credit	237.5	0.1	237.6
All levels and types of qualification	1465.3	187.3	1652.6

Notes:
1. Figures for further education colleges include franchise students.
2. Postgraduate, first degree and other undergraduate qualifications comprise prescribed higher education.
3. Higher level qualifications comprise non-prescribed higher education.
4. Figures for institutional credit include all Open University students.

Sources: Further Education Funding Council, Higher Education Funding Council for England and Higher Education Statistics Agency

foundation degree places (some 10,000 full-time equivalent student places for 2004), FE colleges directly funded by HEFCE were still eligible to apply themselves for these numbers. Only colleges with small amounts of directly funded provision were advised to bid in collaboration with larger providers of HE. Equally, it was recognised that HE establishments might wish to deliver a proportion or perhaps the whole of the foundation programme. Here, as in its response to some of the Dearing recommendations, the funding council adopted a more nuanced position than that outlined in the White Paper. Not only did the funding council expect colleges to 'play a major role' in the delivery of foundation degrees, it insisted that, where no college was involved in the partnership, the bid 'should indicate why this was not possible or appropriate' and 'should explain the strategy for delivering the programme' (HEFCE, 2003a).

In the meantime, as announced in the White Paper, a new national network was established – Foundation Degree Forward – to support colleges in their indirect funding partnerships, as well as to help widen their choice of validating university. In addition, the network would act as a centre for foundation degree expertise and as a link with the occupational and professional bodies involved in drawing up frameworks for foundation degrees in new areas of the economy.

More generally, the government committed itself to remove 'unnecessary bureaucracy' that stood in the way of 'sensible partnerships' between the two sectors. Less than three years after the passage of the Learning and Skills Act, there was an acknowledgement that 'unnecessary difficulties for collaboration' were presented by the need to respond to two funding regimes and to juggle the requirements of two quality assurance and inspection systems. Greater integration of the two systems was anticipated, but no merger of the two funding councils, as was recently agreed in Scotland.

Asymmetries of position and policy silences

Apart from the requirement for English colleges to deal with dual and discordant regimes for its higher-level provision, the sector divisions maintained since 1988 have brought other consequences. Foremost among these was a situation where no one sector was able or willing to take ownership and leadership of college-based HE. No political lobby, no policy community and no serious public debate have been mobilised around HE in FE. Only the 'mixed economy group' of colleges, representing some 20 or so of the largest providers of HE, have tried to find a collective voice, but their influence has been slight and selective. Despite government attempts to generate integrated policy around notions of lifelong learning or the knowledge economy, sector interests and sector mentalities, allied to the pursuit of institutional advantage, have prevailed.

Responsibilities, relationships and boundaries

The responsibilities of the funding councils were, first, to their own institutions and, second, to the programmes they funded outside the sector. Their relationship with these other providers was operationally and proportionally 'different'. In case of HEFCE, this was explained in terms of function and capability:

> In addition to working with the 132 universities and HE colleges in the HE sector, we also have a direct funding relationship with over 200 further education colleges. The nature of our relationship with FECs is necessarily different from our relationship with HEIs. We do not have the same responsibility for the overall health and development of the institution in the case of FECs. That responsibility rests with the Further Education Funding Council (and in future the Learning and Skills Council) as the primary funder. Our role is only to fund one or more HE programmes, which will always be a minority of the institution's activity.
>
> There is also a question of proportion. We cannot realistically achieve the same depth of relationship with an FE college which may offer only a handful of HE places as with a university offering tens of thousands of places. (HEFCE, 2001, p. 23)

A similar relationship informed the funding of FE provision in universities and HE colleges by FEFC, and then the LSC, although this was always a smaller, simpler, and less sensitive activity for these bodies to manage. Except when mergers were proposed between FE and HE institutions, the FE courses supported in some 50 or so HE establishments rarely commanded much notice. HE students in FE and FE students in HE were minority populations in each sector, yet the former were at the centre of government policies to expand HE and achieve greater differentiation.

A second consequence of the way HE and FE were partitioned and positioned over these years was to allow the central authorities for HE considerable influence over the development of higher-level work in colleges, even if this was sometimes by way of decisions directed chiefly at the universities and colleges of HE. The central authorities for FE, it would seem, were willing to countenance this division of labour, as evidenced by their consistent coolness and regular resistance to HE being incorporated into the mission of colleges. The members of the mixed economy group were probably exempt from this policing since their HE was already substantial and much larger than most other FE establishments.

That college-based HE was a larger proportion of the HE sector (currently around 11 per cent) than that of the FE sector (then about 5 per cent), and that of its successor (now less than 1 per cent), was another reason why the policy and funding bodies for FE were content to let the Dearing committee make the recommendations it did. In this sense, the decision to exclude HE from the remit of the LSC was wholly consistent with the sector-led policy development since 1988. The only higher-level work that remained with the LSC was provision in the non-prescribed category, much of which was not conventionally regarded as HE.

The 1999 White Paper on post-16 learning justified this exclusion in terms of the unique scope of HE. It operated on a wider front than other sectors and its contribution was international and national as well as regional and local. However, the other justification for exclusion was more telling. To include HE would undermine one of the main aims in creating the LSC, which was 'to bring order to an area which is overly complex' and 'where there are critical issues to address about coherence and the quality of provision'. Behind this statement was a view that arrangements for HE were less of a problem than other parts of post-compulsory education and training where 'the system is failing a significant section of the community, often the most vulnerable and disadvantaged' and where there was a failure 'to match the needs of the local labour market'. Crucially, there were very large differences in performance and quality within the different parts of the system, especially in the retention and achievement levels recorded in FE colleges (DfEE, 1999).

Incorporation of the colleges had led to some innovation in course delivery and a substantial expansion of numbers amongst 16 to 19-year-olds and adults, but leaving aside its acquisition of national funding and inspection systems, FE was not transformed thereby into a cohesive national sector.

> The bureaucratic 'nationalisation' of the college sector has not rendered its historic diversity and 'lack of system' into a coherent whole, nor has it forestalled a continuing 'strategic drift' as regards its overall vision. (Green and Lucas, 1999, p. 223)

Again:

the history of the last two decades is one of the emergence of a more identifiable FE sector being blocked by competition between providers and growing territorial battles on its borders – with renascent school sixth forms on the one side, and an increasingly expansionist HE sector on the other. The boundaries between the FE and HE sectors are becoming weaker as the vision of a seamless lifelong learning provision dominates policy discourse. (Green and Lucas, 1999, p. 228)

As soon as they were transferred out of their own sector and into the strategic embrace, local and national, of the LSCs, the general FE colleges came under immediate pressure to focus their activity and acquire a centre of vocational excellence.

Difference, diversity and distinctiveness

Issues of identity and distinctiveness were significant as well for the HE carried by the FE sector. A third consequence of the combination of sector reforms and growth policies applied after 1988 was to introduce more diversity and considerable complexity into the HE provision offered by colleges. The overlap in the qualifications offered by institutions of HE and FE, especially at the sub-degree levels, was a long-standing feature of English HE. This local authority legacy continued into the era of mass expansion and, under the impact of franchising, a larger proportion of first degree and full-time undergraduate education was delivered by the colleges.

By the turn of the new century, franchise students accounted for nearly one-third of all those taught on courses of prescribed HE in FE. Where full-time students were still a minority on prescribed courses offered by colleges in their own right, they were a majority on programmes sub-contracted to them by partner universities. Where the HNC was the major prescribed qualification taught by colleges in their own name, the franchised contribution was centred on the first degree and HND (Parry, Davies and Williams, 2003). By 2002, there were 75 HE institutions and 289 FE colleges involved in indirect funding partnerships in England. In other words, over half of the total of HE establishments and around two-thirds of colleges were party to such arrangements.

As HEFCE acknowledged, these relationships necessarily implied 'a hierarchical relationship' since the franchising university or HE college was 'fully responsible' for the students and accountable for 'all aspects' of finance, administration and quality relating to these students. This was different, however, from HEFCE-approved funding consortia which recognised 'FECs as key and equal partners with HEIs' and where each institution remained responsible for the quality of the experience it provided for students (HEFCE, 2000b). There were just 13 such consortia in operation at this time.

A key dimension of the dependent relationship in franchise arrangements was the top-slicing and apportioning of public funds received by the HE partner. The proportion retained by the franchising university covered the costs of the services it provided and the remainder was passed to the college to fund the teaching function. The amount of funding retained and transferred was a private matter. Only in the case of funding consortia was there a requirement to provide public information about this relationship. A review of indirect funding arrangements undertaken for the funding council showed significant variation in the proportion of funds retained. Colleges reported top-slicing figures ranging from 8 per cent to 50 per cent, although a number were unclear about the exact proportion and about how it had been calculated. Their HE partners reported proportions between 3 per cent and 42 per cent. Most of the HEFCE-recognised funding consortia appeared to operate at a much lower figure than the average, usually around 10 per cent to 15 per cent (HEFCE, 2003b).

While colleges might express satisfaction with the operation of the partnership, the lack of transparency surrounding the division of funding was a frequent source of discomfort and tension. Nevertheless, franchise agreements were widespread and, along with those for consortia, they were designated the main vehicle for delivering the 50,000 foundation degree places that the government hoped to have available by 2006 (DfES, 2003a). Ahead of this planned growth, there were around 340 colleges delivering HE and higher-level qualifications, usually in small amounts, on the basis of direct, indirect and non-HEFCE funding. Such was the uneven distribution of provision that less than 60 FE establishments were responsible for half the total number of students studying at these levels. Even so, most colleges offering higher-level work had students in each of these funding categories.

In the time since Dearing proposed a strictly delimited and directly-funded role for FE colleges, their HE had become ever more various. One effect of this pluralism was to diffract the college contribution and fragment its profile, making it less easy for this provision to be understood by prospective students and by the agencies responsible for its operation and direction. Leaving aside the different conditions of service for academic staff in each sector, claims for the distinctiveness of HE in FE rest less on separate types of courses or qualifications and more on the character of teaching and learning in college environments. An FE tradition of student-centredness and 'personal pedagogy', along with the smaller scale and greater intimacy of teaching groups, serve as before to distinguish the college from the mass university.

In some areas of similar or shared undergraduate provision, the distinction between the teaching-only mission of the FE college and the research-informed teaching of the university has lessened. Depending on the size and scope of their HE, efforts have been made in a number of colleges to enable selected staff to devote most of their teaching to higher-level courses and to make modest allowance for them to undertake scholarship and sometimes research. Conversely, not all academic staff in teaching-intensive universities might be active in research, especially where their teaching was centred on sub-degree and work-focused programmes. Courses at these levels were at the lower end of the status hierarchy in HE establishments, whereas these same programmes were often at the premium end of the curriculum in colleges (Parry, Davies and Williams, 2004).

Concentration, dispersion and the region

A final consequence of the English preoccupation with dual sectors has been an absence of serious debate and deliberation about the HE mission of colleges. In enlisting the colleges to do service in the next phase of expansion, neither the Dearing inquiry nor subsequent elaborations of government policy were disposed to consider the sustainability of HE in FE. For Dearing, other matters – notably those to do with funding – dominated the work of the inquiry. For ministers, the imperative was to 'break' the pattern of traditional demand for undergraduate education and, equally bold, to bring a new flagship qualification to this task. Whether some or all colleges should be involved in this effort, and to what extent, were not among the questions that figured in the reform agendas of either sector.

Nevertheless, these were questions of some relevance to the access, quality and employability policies that underpinned the drive to the 50 per cent participation target and beyond. An argument for concentration, as articulated by some of the colleges with large and long-standing provisions in HE, had the staged development of the polytechnics as its preferred model. The critical mass and institutional maturity achieved by these establishments was a process managed by the state and supported by a national validating and degree-awarding authority. The latter was abolished by the 1992 Act but, rather than reinventing past structures, there was a case for central government and its agencies adopting a more direct role in building the capacity and protecting the HE mission of designated colleges. In a differentiated system, the scope of that mission might need to be controlled, as the Dearing report had recommended.

An argument for dispersal, on the other hand, played to the quasi-market and semi-regulated environments that existed at present. Furthermore, if changing labour markets and fluid knowledge–skill requirements demanded a rapid response model of HE, then colleges were well placed to deliver the kind of short-cycle, short-order or short-life qualifications that might be incorporated within the foundation degree framework. In a distributed and market-driven system, most if not all colleges might be in structured partnerships to deliver qualifications validated by HE establishments with degree-awarding powers. A key assumption in this model was that a funding relationship between universities and colleges would serve as a vehicle to assure, enhance and embed the quality and standards expected of HE. Missing from this formulation was the concept of the college as a developing and maturing institution, capable of taking increased responsibility and future ownership of the HE it delivered.

Policy silences were just one indication of the ambivalence that surrounded the idea of HE in colleges. A reluctance to recognise a college segment or sector of HE has been a characteristic feature of English expansion, even when poised to move from mass to near universal levels of participation. Rather than consider options that risked 'complicating significantly' the remit of the LSC (DfEE, 1999), or which highlighted the disparity in funding for HE and FE students (Piatt and Robinson, 2001), the government has looked instead to integrated strategies at the regional and sub-regional levels. While ministers have insisted on closer working between the funding councils, it has been through joint strategies aimed at local and regional collaboration that the two bodies have directed their main effort. The most recent of these has vocational and workplace progression, in and through HE, as its core purpose, with plans to develop 'lifelong learning networks' in each of the regions in England (LSC and HEFCE, 2004).

Given the recency of the decision to create the learning and skills sector, together with the sheer scale and scope of its activities, dual arrangements for college-based HE were set to continue into the foreseeable future. Of more immediate significance for colleges would be the de-regulation of fee levels for undergraduate education from 2006, with FE establishments deciding these for their own courses and HE institutions determining these for their franchised programmes. Short of intervention by government to protect the position of the foundation degree, these were conditions likely to give real meaning to the 'mixed economy' of HE in FE.

Acknowledgements

A version of Table 2 was first published in Parry *et al.* (2003) and is reproduced here by permission of the Learning and Skills Development Agency.

References

Abramson, M., Bird, J. and Stennett, A. (eds) (1996) *Further and Higher Education Partnerships. The Future of Collaboration.* Buckingham: Society for Research into Higher Education and Open University Press.

Blunkett, D. (2001) *Education into Employability: The Role of the DfEE in the Economy.* London: DfEE.

Cantor, L. M. and Roberts, I. F. (1972) *Further Education in England and Wales.* London: Routledge & Kegan Paul.

Cantor, L. M. and Roberts, I. F. (1986) *Further Education Today: A Critical Review.* London: Routledge & Kegan Paul.

Cantor, L., Roberts, I. and Pratley, B. (1995) *A Guide to Further Education in England and Wales.* London: Cassell.

Department of Education and Science (DES) (1987) *Higher Education: Meeting the Challenge*, Cm 114. London: Her Majesty's Stationery Office.

Department of Education and Science (DES) (1989) *Aspects of Higher Education in Colleges Maintained by Local Education Authorities: A Report by HM Inspectors, 277/89.* London: DES.

Department of Education and Science (DES) (1991) *Higher Education in Further Education Colleges: Franchising and Other Forms of Collaboration with Polytechnics, A report by HM Inspectors, 228/91.* London: DES.

Department for Education and Employment (DfEE) (1999) *Learning to Succeed: A New Framework for Post-16 Learning*, Cm 4392. London: The Stationery Office.

Department for Education and Employment (DfEE) (2000a) *Colleges for Excellence and Innovation: Statement by the Secretary of State for Education and Employment on the Future of Further Education in England*. London: DfEE.

Department for Education and Employment (DfEE) (2000b) *Foundation Degrees: Consultation paper*. London: DfEE.

Department for Education and Skills (DfES) (2002) *Success for All: Reforming Further Education and Training*. London: DfES.

Department for Education and Skills (DfES) (2003a) *Foundation Degrees: Meeting the Need for Higher Level Skills*. London: DfES.

Department for Education and Skills (DfES) (2003b) *The Future of Higher Education*, Cm 5735. London: The Stationery Office.

Department for Education and Skills, Department of Trade and Industry, Department of Work and Pensions and HM Treasury (2003) *21st Century Skills: Realising Our Potential. Individuals, Employers, Nation*, Cm 5810. London: The Stationery Office.

Further Education Funding Council (FEFC) (1996) *Vocational Higher Education in the Further Education Sector: National Survey Report from the Inspectorate*. Coventry: FEFC.

Further Education Funding Council (FEFC) (1997) *Learning Works: Widening Participation in Further Education*. Coventry: FEFC.

Green, A. and Lucas, N. (eds) (1999) *FE and Lifelong Learning: Realigning the Sector for the Twenty-first Century*. London: Institute of Education, University of London.

Higher Education Funding Council for England (HEFCE) (1995) *Higher Education in Further Education Colleges: Funding the Relationship*. Bristol: HEFCE.

Higher Education Funding Council for England (HEFCE) (1996) *Higher Education in Further Education Colleges: A Future Funding Approach*. Bristol: HEFCE.

Higher Education Funding Council for England (HEFCE) (1999) *Higher Education in Further Education Colleges: Guidance for Colleges on Funding Options*. Bristol: HEFCE.

Higher Education Funding Council for England (HEFCE) (2000a) *Foundation Degree Prospectus*. Bristol: HEFCE.

Higher Education Funding Council for England (HEFCE) (2000b) *Higher Education in Further Education Colleges. Indirectly Funded Partnerships: Codes of Practice for Franchise and Consortia Arrangements*. Bristol: HEFCE.

Higher Education Funding Council for England (HEFCE) (2001) *Higher Education and the Regions: HEFCE Policy Statement*. Bristol: HEFCE.

Higher Education Funding Council for England (HEFCE) (2003a) *Foundation Degrees: Invitation to Bid for Additional Places and Development Funds 2004–05*. Bristol: HEFCE.

Higher Education Funding Council for England (HEFCE) (2003b) *Review of Indirect Funding Agreements and Arrangements between Higher Education Institutions and Further Education Colleges*. Bristol: HEFCE.

Learning and Skills Council (LSC) and Higher Education Funding Council for England (HEFCE) (2004) *Lifelong Learning Networks: Joint Letter from the Learning and Skills Council and HEFCE*, 3 June 200

Matterson, A. (1981) *Polytechnics and Colleges: Control and Administration in the Public Sector of Higher Education*. Harlow: Longman.

National Committee of Inquiry into Higher Education (NCIHE) (1997a) *Higher Education in the Learning Society: Main Report*. London: NCIHE.

National Committee of Inquiry into Higher Education (NCIHE) (1997b) *Higher*

Education in the Learning Society: Report of the Scottish Committee. London: NCIHE.

Parry, G. (1996) 'Access education 1973–1994: from second chance to third wave', *Journal of Access Studies*, 11(1), pp. 10–33.

Parry, G. (1999) 'Education research and policy making in higher education: the case of Dearing', *Journal of Education Policy*, 14(3), pp. 225–41.

Parry, G. (2001) *Academic Snakes and Vocational Ladders*, Fourth Philip Jones Memorial Lecture. Leicester: NIACE.

Parry, G. (2003) 'Mass higher education and the English: Wherein the colleges?', *Higher Education Quarterly*, 57(4), pp. 308–37.

Parry, G. and Thompson, A. (2002) *Closer by Degrees: The Past, Present and Future of Higher Education in Further Education Colleges*. London: Learning and Skills Development Agency.

Parry, G., Davies, P. and Williams, J. (2003) *Dimensions of Difference: Higher Education in the Learning and Skills Sector*. London: Learning and Skills Development Agency.

Parry, G., Davies, P. and Williams, J. (2004) *Difference, Diversity and Distinctiveness: Higher Education in the Learning and Skills Sector*. London: Learning and Skills Development Agency.

Piatt, W. and Robinson, P. (2001) *Opportunity for Whom? Options for the Funding and Structure of Post-16 Education*. London: Institute for Public Policy Research.

Pratt, J. (1997) *The Polytechnic Experiment 1965–1992*. Buckingham: Society for Research into Higher Education and Open University Press.

Pratt, J. (2000) 'The Emergence of the Colleges', in A. Smithers and P. Robinson (eds) *Further Education Re-formed*. London: Falmer Press, pp. 13–25.

Scott, P. (1984) *The Crisis of the University*. Beckenham: Croom Helm.

Sharp, P. R. (1987) *The Creation of the Local Authority Sector of Higher Education*. Lewes: Falmer Press.

Trow, M. (1974) 'Problems in the transition from elite to mass higher education', in *Policies for Higher Education*. Paris: OECD.

Links between vocational education and training (VET) and higher education: The case of Germany

Thomas Deissinger

Introduction

The debate on parity of esteem between general and vocational education has been a long-standing topic of educational policy as well as of research within vocational education and training (VET). In Germany, the 1970s saw the emergence of the *Kollegschule* model in the federal state of Nordrhein-Westfalen based on a pedagogical concept which denied the different natures and educational values of apprenticeships and academic studies (Blankertz, 1972; Kutscha, 1989; Greinert, 2003, p. 134). It may be claimed from a historical perspective that the intended reform of VET, based on this concept and the co-related notion of 'double qualifications', failed because the tradition and the political and economic interests backing the German apprenticeship system proved too strong for a substantial change of VET policy at that time. Also, educationalists pointed to the politisation of the educational ideas behind this 'integration model' which apparently ignored the benefits of employer-led VET and workplace learning by denying the 'unique' quality of vocational training in comparison to school-based and/or academic studies (Zabeck, 1972).

Compared to other countries, there is no doubt that 'the continuance of tradition' in Germany has always been highly valued (Phillips, 1995, p. 61). This is especially true with respect to the Dual System of apprenticeship training since it owes much of its reputation to the fact that it has remained one of the most frequently (though not necessarily successfully) copied training systems in the world (Arnold, 1985; Kloss, 1995). The German education system in general, however, has recently come under fire in international studies on student performance (OECD, 2000; 2003). Similarly, the national 'Education Report' (*Bildungsbericht*) published in October 2003 (Avenarius *et al.*, 2003) claims 'serious' deficiencies in the country's school system by pointing to too many drop-outs, too few achievers of higher education (HE) entrance qualifications and too little support for students coming from poorer families. Nevertheless, there is still a strong belief that the apprenticeship system is faring much better than both the school system and the tertiary sector. In a recent press declaration the ministers of education of Austria, Switzerland and three German federal states[1] deplored the fact that international studies on education too often neglect the significance of vocational pathways for the 'ordinary school leaver'. In their plea to the OECD to 'accept and investigate the status of vocational education' they hold that the Dual System with its apprenticeship focus still offers well-accepted routes into skilled employment.

The function of the Dual System unequivocally refers to initial training of school leavers in a given range of 'declared trades' or 'recognised occupations' (Deissinger, 2001a). Although the dualism of 'learning venues' and legal responsibilities certainly is the striking feature of this 'German system' of vocational training (Greinert, 1994), its working principles also comprise at least three more aspects:

- Initial training through the apprenticeship system is a well-understood and socially accepted pathway into employment as it follows a traditional pattern deeply enshrined in the ancient mode of apprenticeship (Deissinger, 1994). This means that training is workplace-led and predominantly practical by stressing the importance of work experience during the training period. It also means that the system works in accordance with skill requirements defined 'around the workplace' (Harney, 1985; Deissinger, 1998).
- Despite its traditional basis and long history, the Dual System is determined by the involvement of the state which defines and protects both the nature and quality of occupational standards as well as the legal conditions of skilled apprenticeship (Raggatt, 1988). Therefore the German 'training culture' (Brown and Evans, 1994) is based on the notion that an apprenticeship should not only be dealt with as a contractual duty but should be based on an underpinning pedagogic understanding which sets it apart from 'normal work'.
- Since the state's function is to secure quality standards with respect

to in-company training in a predominantly formal manner, other social groups have a major say in the Dual System. The principle of consensus implies that public, private and semi-private institutions work together by using long-established modes of co-operation within the system and that employers and unions normally take the initiative with respect to training ordinances and their revision or modernisation (Benner, 1984; Deissinger, 2001a).

It is therefore plausible to refer to the German Dual System as an institutional realisation of a very specific 'apprenticeship culture' differing largely from the 'Anglo-Saxon' approach (Canning, Deissinger and Loots, 2000; Harris and Deissinger, 2003). The overall importance and acceptance of non-academic training has a clear implication for the *relationship between VET and HE*: as the various pathways represent both horizontally and vertically separated routes, transitions are only possible through detours. This means that an apprenticed person has indeed formal opportunities to upgrade his or her occupational qualification (for example by going for a technician or master craftsman qualification). The route into HE, however, requires at least a polytechnic entrance qualification (*Fachhochschulreife*).

On the other hand, there has been a transposition of principles typical of the VET system into HE. The result has been a kind of 'academic Dual System' which, despite its growing importance, is still a regional reform project since the emergence of the so-called vocational academies (*Berufsakademien*) has virtually remained restricted to four of the now 16 federal states of Germany (Baden-Württemberg, Berlin, Sachsen, Thüringen). This chapter discusses this special approach to 'linking up' VET and HE – which has also become a pivotal topic of the educational debate in the UK (UVAC, 2003) – against the background of the specific 'character' of the German VET system.

A world of its own: Institutional and functional patterns of VET in Germany

The Dual System of apprenticeship training

Apprenticeships in Germany have a strong historical dimension as they are based on the tradition of medieval craft training (Deissinger, 1994; NCVER, 2001). At the end of the nineteenth century the genesis of the modern vocational training system, due to substantial state intervention, led to a revitalisation of the ancient craft system. The Craft Regulation Act passed in 1897 (Schlüter and Stratmann, 1985, pp. 210 ff.) provided for craft chambers as institutions of public law authorised to hold examinations for journeymen and masters. The notion of the skilled craftsman became rooted within a framework of self-government (Zabeck, 1975). The 1897 Act also confined the technical qualification required for the training of apprentices to skilled journeymen. Indentures became general practice in the craft sector as well as the three-year training period. In 1908, by reviving the apprenticeship tradition of the pre-industrial age, the right to train apprentices was even restricted to craft masters (Stratmann, 1982).

The 'dual' character of the apprenticeship system in Germany emerged during the first two decades of the twentieth century when the vocational part-time schools replaced the continuation schools (although compulsion was only enforced in 1938) to accompany apprenticeships and to give young people education 'through the vocation'. From the mid-1920s, the chambers of industry and commerce established examinations for industrial workers (Greinert, 2003, pp. 80 ff.; Schütte, 1992, pp. 79 ff.). Despite its more systematic character industrial training copied the practices which developed in the craft sector, above all the 'occupational' orientation of training schemes (Deissinger, 1998).

Due to this strong historical base of the apprenticeship system, the vocational pathway in Germany is well established and well known. The Dual System with its 350 'recognised occupations' absorbs the majority of all 16–19 year-olds. The number of training places offered by employers over the last decades has always ranged between some 600,000 and 700,000 per annum, depending on economic conditions. Unlike in most other European countries, with the exception of Austria and Switzerland, apprenticeships in Germany exist in nearly all branches of the economy including the professions and parts of the civil service. Small- and medium-sized companies are significant contributors to training opportunities (Deissinger, 2001b).[2] Therefore apprentices come from different educational backgrounds, although most have an intermediate or lower secondary school certificate. In recent years, the number of grammar school leavers progressing from school to apprenticeship training has remained more or less stable at around 15 per cent, a phenomenon which places Germany in a low position in terms of the academic drift of young people by comparison to many other comparable countries.[3]

The training market in Germany 'has the character of a suppliers' market' (Greinert, 1994, p. 80). Once a training contract has been signed this means the principal financial responsibility of companies for the training process includes, in addition to training allowances, all direct and indirect costs such as training personnel, machinery, training administration, and social insurance contributions. The fact that the 'system is financed principally by employers' (NCVER, 2001, p. 38) reflects the principle of self-government re-affirmed by law in the late nineteenth century. Therefore, companies provide training opportunities on a totally voluntary basis. While the overall training quota in Germany is just about 30 per cent in the old and 27 per cent in the new federal states (2001), at 91 per cent large companies train to a very substantial extent. Craft sector training has a particularly strong tradition (Deissinger, 2001b) as some 530,000 young people out of the present total of nearly 1.62 million trained in the Dual System (2002) are apprenticed in a craft company under the supervision of a master craftsman (although with a decreasing tendency).[4]

The German apprenticeship system may be viewed as a system of training rather than a system of employment, in which the wages of apprentices reflect this emphasis on training, with German apprentices typically paid wages that are far lower than adult rates and apprentice rates in Australia or in the UK (NCVER, 2001, p. 39). Training allowances are the result of collective bargaining but are linked to the purpose of giving young people a basic start into their working lives without putting too much burden on employers. As the apprenticeship system is seen to be neither part of the school or education system nor a normal sphere of work, the 'system reference' is clearly training and recruitment for skilled work. The consequences of such a clear separation of pathways or subsystems of course implies that lots of expectations rest on the Dual System and frictions in the training market can hardly be compensated without additional activities on the side of the state. Despite its private character, public funding of vocational training in general is becoming increasingly important due to the critical situation in the labour and training markets. Among these funds, activities to promote either external training options or give incentives to employers are paramount (Berger and Walden, 2002). This tendency could lead to a creeping 'pluralisation' of the Dual System and certainly shows its dependency on sound economic framework conditions.

Whereas in other European countries, such as the UK, on-the-job training – even under the new Modern Apprenticeship Scheme (Ryan,

2001) – is complemented by off-the-job training on a more or less voluntary basis, in Germany it is mandatory. While there has been an ongoing discussion about the 'process character' of vocational training in the UK – including the scope for 'expansive participation' of companies in workplace-related training (Senker *et al.*, 2000; Fuller and Unwin, 2003), in Germany the State Education Acts provide an essential element of the legal framework for dual apprenticeships by making sure that school-leavers are kept within the educational system.[5] For each 'recognised skilled occupation' the state education ministries, in line with training regulations under the federal law, determine syllabi for the vocational and general subjects within a given occupation taught at the part-time vocational schools (Greinert, 1994). Also, German apprentices enter a special training contract subject to the 1969 Vocational Training Act (Deissinger, 1996). The company is obliged to impart the competences laid down in the training regulation or ordinance. The Vocational Training Act may be viewed as the final stage of a post-war public debate on the degree to which the Dual System as a whole should be submitted to state influence. As a compromise, the Act did not install a new training system including the vocational school, but mainly 'consolidated much previous practice under one Act' (Raggatt, 1988, p. 175). The Vocational Training Act is essentially a specified labour law since its central objective is the indenture between the apprentice and the training company. The Act therefore covers both the private and the public sphere of vocational training. The contribution of the state to systematising and standardising apprenticeships can be seen in three areas where legislation 'protects' vocational training against market forces: (i) the indenture which alone makes this Act 'the most comprehensive and detailed regulatory system for apprenticeship training in the Western world' (Raggatt, 1988, p. 175); (ii) the degree to which skill requirements of trainers have become formalised; and (iii) the issue of formal instruction and delivery of knowledge and skills that have to be imparted in the course of the training process.[6]

The system of vocational full-time schools

In 2002/2003, out of 2.7 million students in non-academic VET, some 1.7 million underwent training in part-time courses in the *Berufsschule* (i.e. in the Dual System). 452,300 attended an ordinary vocational full-time school (*Berufsfachschule*) with the option (depending on the type of school and the federal state, respectively) of entry-level vocational training in specified occupational areas, such as nursing or physiotherapy. The number of students attending three of the major sub-types in full-time VET (vocational foundation year; vocational preparation courses; ordinary vocational full-time schools) actually increased between 1993 and 2001 from 363,351 to 541,676. As companies feel insecure about the future demand for skilled employees and complain about the lack of training maturity among school leavers, the latter have to search for alternative pathways, a phenomenon which is aggravated by the regional and occupational imbalances in the training market including the difficult situation in eastern Germany. Therefore, both the number of students entering HE and the influx into vocational full-time schools have increased in recent years and are likely to rise in the forthcoming years (for all figures see Federal Ministry of Education and Research, 2003).[7]

Apart from the 'parking function' of specific types of vocational schools due to training market restraints (Reinberg and Hummel, 2001, p. 28) the relationship between the Dual System and the various subtypes within the system of school-based vocational education and training appears to be ambivalent. This means that vocational schools basically serve three functions (Deissinger and Ruf, 2003; Feller, 2000; Kell, 1996; Reinisch, 2001):

- The first function is *vocational preparation* (mostly one to two years), which means making young people competent to apply successfully for an apprenticeship. The skills dimension of this type of course is normally enriched by the achievement of a lower or intermediate school qualification.
- A second objective of VET is *FE* (mostly two to three years), which means leading young people to achieve a higher school qualification. This includes both the university and the polytechnic entrance qualification or, for students from the lower secondary schools, the option to go for an intermediate school qualification.
- Finally, schools provide for *vocational training* (mostly two to three years) which means leading young people to achieve a portable labour-market-relevant occupational qualification either outside the Dual System or through an apprenticeship. This option is sometimes coupled with the opportunity to go for a higher schools qualification (normally a polytechnic entrance qualification).

It is the vocational training function which makes the system of school-based VET complex and opaque (above all in relation to the Dual System) as vocational full-time schools run courses which lead to qualifications either within or outside the scope of the Vocational Training Act. Besides, some of the schools deliver entry-level training based on specialised federal regulations, such as in the area of health occupations. In particular, the ordinary full-time vocational schools (*Berufsfachschulen*) accommodate a range of different students and aspirations. Among the major sub-types are both schools leading to a full occupational qualification and institutions which only partly focus on occupation-relevant competences, as they deliver either school qualifications (such as the intermediate secondary school leaving certificate) or concentrate on vocational preparation (Feller, 2000). Certainly one of the biggest problems is the lack of acceptance from the labour market of most vocational qualifications obtained in school-based, full-time courses against the background of an over-mighty Dual System (Euler, 2000).

The Baden-Württemberg Ministry of Education currently seems to be intent on finding ways to increase the labour-market relevance of school-based qualifications. This in particular affects the vocational colleges (*Berufskollegs*) and the acceptance and portability of the (school-based) assistant qualification. One of the didactical tools supposed to help to achieve this goal is the ongoing implementation of practice firms in each of the state's vocational colleges (Deissinger and Ruf, 2003). This could eventually result in a new policy to strengthen the vocational qualification function of schools in general and to cope with the growing number of school leavers who want to step into VET as a pathway into HE. The status of vocational full-time schools therefore differs from the Dual System, but also from the system of HE as students in full-time VET normally hold qualifications below the level of the Abitur (the university entrance qualification). In contrast to the apprenticeship system, schools currently focus more on access qualifications than on portable labour market-relevant skills, while in relation to universities and polytechnics they form a subsystem opening up 'second chances' for young people. This localisation of vocational schools implies that there is – as mentioned earlier – both a horizontal and a vertical segregation in institutional terms which tends to preserve the different 'system references' typical of pre-vocational education in schools, apprenticeships in the Dual System, vocational full-time courses, and the tertiary sector.

Linking up two worlds: Higher vocational training in the vocational academies

The context: Germany's system of higher education

Although nowadays 'vocational' in many fields, such as engineering, medicine, or business administration, the German HE system is deeply rooted in the German university tradition influenced by Wilhelm von Humboldt's idea of general humanistic education (Blankertz, 1982, pp. 89 ff.; Menze, 1991). This tradition can still be identified if one looks at the administrative structure of Germany's universities characterised by the principle of self-administration, the freedom of teaching and research, and the common belief among German professors that a university should in the first place be a venue for scientific research serving both scholars and students. Hence the notion of a university qualification at that time was not predominantly linked to preparing students for specific occupations, with the exception of medicine, law, and theology. It was only in the twentieth century that degrees – above all the Diploma (*Diplom*) – became more clearly labour market relevant. During the 1960s and 1970s this development was accelerated by the quantitative expansion of the tertiary sector and the emergence of the 'mass university' (Baumert *et al.*, 1979, pp. 212 ff.)[8] as well as by the foundation of new HE institutions, in particular the polytechnics (*Fachhochschulen*), which up to the present day are seen as an attractive alternative to a purely academic preparation for occupations such as engineer, manager or social worker (Diploma FH). The polytechnics emerged from institutions specialising in practice-related vocational education, notably from the former schools of engineering.

With the increasing differentiation of the HE system, accompanied by an extension of secondary HE, more and more young Germans[9] now have the opportunity to attend one of the institutions of the German tertiary system comprised of:

- universities;
- polytechnics, including public administration colleges;
- comprehensive universities (merging university and polytechnic under one roof);
- the distance learning university in Hagen;
- theological colleges;
- colleges of art and music;

- colleges of education (especially in Baden-Württemberg); and
- vocational academies (especially in Baden-Württemberg).

Indeed only about a third of German HE institutions bear the title of 'university'. Hence the situation is different from the UK where former polytechnics became universities. In Germany, there still is a clear binary divide between universities and polytechnics and, in particular, the vocational academies are affected by this difference in status and denomination as they belong to the tertiary system but cannot be treated as 'proper' institutions of HE in a comprehensive legal sense. Somebody entering the civil service as a graduate from a polytechnic or vocational academy gets a lower entrance salary and is normally barred from the highest career track in public institutions. Another interesting example of differentiation in status among Germany's HE institutions is the so-called *Pädagogische Hochschule* (college of education) in the federal state of Baden-Württemberg, which offers teacher training for primary as well as lower and intermediate secondary schools, but not for employment in vocational or grammar schools which requires a university degree (Baumert *et al.*, 1979, pp. 225–7). All non-university courses in poly-technics, colleges of education, and vocational academies stretch over three years, whereas university studies normally cover four to five years of academic learning. One major difference can also be seen in the fact that polytechnics, vocational academies and colleges of education require compulsory practical courses, internships, or even an apprenticeship placement as part of the academic training scheme.

Since 1976, the Federal Government, through the Framework Act of Higher Education, has been empowered with a general competence to enact stipulations governing the development of the HE system in Germany as well as major organisational principles such as the staff structure and admission procedures. Responsibility for filling this framework with life, however, lies with the *Länder* (federal states), which, according to the German Constitution, also administer the school system and the post-academic and further training of teachers. Academic staff, therefore, are civil servants of the respective federal state which also bears the running cost of academic institutions.

Currently, 2.02 million (2003/2004) young people are enrolled as students in the German HE system (with 70 per cent studying at a university) as against some 1.58 million (2003) in the Dual System of initial vocational training.[10] Admission to an HE institution in Germany is not necessarily dependent on the final school-leaving certificate, the

Abitur (the German equivalent to an A-level, granting the right to university study in all subjects). Both secondary general and vocational schools offer polytechnic entrance qualifications or a minor version of the university entrance degree (normally from a vocational upper secondary school or a specialised grammar school), which only opens up a limited range of subjects at a university. Whereas enrolment at a polytechnic demands a polytechnic entrance qualification, universities, vocational academies, and colleges of education may only be attended with an *Abitur*.

The concept of 'premium apprenticeships': The success story of the vocational academies

Courses at a vocational academy (VA), or *Berufsakademie*, have the character of a 'premium apprenticeship' because they involve companies in a similar way as the Dual System. In Baden-Württemberg the ten *Berufsakademien* currently provide vocational training for nearly 17,000 students, with the co-operation of some 4,000 firms offering training placements, mostly in the field of commerce and technology/engineering.[11] The concept goes back to 1974 when the first pilot schemes were set up as an alternative to traditional university courses. The VA thus can look back on 30 years of expansion. The number of academies has increased from two (Stuttgart and Mannheim) to eight. The number of school leavers in Baden-Württemberg taking up a VA course grew with the general development of the VA system itself. This expansion, while helping to solve the problem of too many well-qualified school-leavers and too few study places, has added a remarkable dimension to specific subjects: business administration alone attracts two thirds of the students and, within this sector, 'management in industry' is the most popular course.

The official website of the VA in Baden-Württemberg depicts this special type of 'tertiary training' as follows[12]:

> *The Berufsakademie concept*
> From the start, the Berufsakademie was conceived as a radically new kind of practice-oriented higher educational institution. The involvement of companies as active partners in the educational process results in highly qualified and experienced graduates. The Berufsakademie – University of Cooperative Education thus offers an attractive alternative to traditional university education.

Advantages
- Berufsakademie graduates are highly regarded by employers
- Students attain an impressive level of academic and practical achievement
- Courses of study involve interlocking study and work periods
- Programs are flexible and innovative
- There is active cooperation between the Berufsakademie and training companies

Main Objectives
- To unite the resources of state institutions of higher education and professional training facilities in a joint effort
- To respond to employers' demands for a more work-oriented approach to higher education
- To offer school leavers an attractive alternative form of higher education
- To reduce the time students spend in higher education: three years at the Berufsakademie, as opposed to an average of six years or more at traditional German universities
- To share the ever rising cost of higher education between employers and the state

In 1982 the Law on Vocational Academies (*Berufsakademiegesetz*) established the vocational academy as a proper institution in the Baden-Württemberg's tertiary sector (Reinert, 1999, p. 6). Drawing on the results of the trial phase, not only were the organisational structure and training concept barely modified, but the concept worked out in the starting phase as a whole was purposely left unchanged. The legal definition (article 1 I BAG) characterises vocational academies as institutions offering 'both a theoretical and a practice-orientated apprenticeship. They fulfil this task through the combination of state academies and apprenticeship placements (Dual System).'

Nevertheless, the VA is not of a primary vocational training nature, but is a tertiary sector, university-like institution.[13] The law (article 1 II BAG) states that vocational academies 'are part of the tertiary educational system. They constitute an alternative to polytechnic and university studies ... Successful completion of the three-year course of training and education at the vocational academy is the equivalent of a degree awarded upon completion of comparable courses by state-run polytechnics'. Quite apparently, the law refers to a functional comparability of VA and polytechnic. Against this background, the label 'University of Cooperative Education' which has been introduced by the Baden-Württemberg Ministry of Science, Research and Arts in its marketing strategy (Reinert, 1999, p. 9) is a totally misleading denomination as it suggests a factual as well as a legal parity between the two institutions. This wrong perception has a clear political implication since the VA, as a 'newcomer' to the HE system of Germany, over the years has had to fight a fierce battle to establish its reputation even alongside the polytechnics and also faced resistance coming from most of the other federal states of Germany (Deissinger, 1995, pp. 432–3). The Baden-Württemberg 'Equality Order' decreed in 1989[14] gave the VA parity status to polytechnics as an 'equal' institution only within the tertiary sector of this federal state.[15]

In 1995, the Conference of German State Ministers of Culture (*Kultusministerkonferenz*) finally resolved to accord full recognition to the *Berufsakademie*. This means that the VA now confers entitlements identical to those attached to polytechnic degrees. In consequence, the VA now falls under the regulations of the European Council issued in 1988 (89/48/EWG) with respect to degrees in HE (Green, Hartley and Usher, 1991, pp. 163 ff.; Zimmermann and Deissinger, 1995, pp. 454 ff.). In the meantime, the state law on VAs has been modified to grant access to postgraduate doctoral studies to VA graduates. Nevertheless, the legal status of the VA still separates it from the classical university, as it is a three-year course and does not lead into the highest stratum of the civil service, and it undoubtedly introduces a new structural facet to HE policy not common to the polytechnics either. It is in fact the tertiary position of the VA in the educational sector which results in peculiarities that do not distance it from the university. The teaching staff are subject to the same professional requirements as at the universities in general and the polytechnics in particular. VA graduates get a degree comparable to a polytechnic or university degree. The only difference is an extra 'BA' in the title. Studies are divided into semesters as at the university. On the other hand, the didactical programme in the fields of business administration and social work is orientated less around the (more or less general) functional principle of importance to the universities, as it is focused on the 'branch principle' (Table 1). This obviously tends towards the training structure of the Dual System.

One of the peculiarities of the VA is the possibility to go for an intermediate professional certificate before reaching the Diploma, which is not typical of a university degree or for the majority of training courses in the Dual System. Once again, the structure of the VA teaching staff is in stark contrast to that of a university: the vast majority consists of part-time educators, in particular of senior managers or trainers from the apprenticing firms (Zabeck and Deissinger, 1995, p. 7). This is a feature which is not compatible with the Dual System either, as schoolteachers and trainers here have separated responsibilities for their respective parts of the training arrangement.[16]

Table 1. Study structure of the vocational academy indicating layering of courses.

Employment		
Diploma in Business Administration (BA)	*Diploma in Engineering (BA)*	*Diploma in Social Work (BA)*
Semester 6: dual training		
Semester 5: dual training		
Business Assistant	*Engineering Assistant*	*Educator*
Semester 4: dual training		
Semester 3: dual training		
Semester 2: dual training		
Semester 1: dual training		
Business Administration	*Engineering*	*Social Work*
ABITUR (university entrance qualification) plus TRAINING CONTRACT		

Source: www.ba-bw.de

The organisational structure of the VA is the framework of its daily *curricular arrangement*. The following points are seen as vital by the partners:

- *Practical orientation with simultaneous scientific methods of training.* This is about the connection of two didactical principles with the aim of smoothly integrating the VA graduates into the working world. The practical side of the training process should increase the mobility and flexibility of the graduates not just in industry in general but also internally in the firm.
- *Dual structure of learning.* The training concept transposes the organisational principle typical of the Dual System of initial training onto the tertiary sector. The co-operation between educational academy and apprenticing firm aims at making the process of learning more efficient and brings theoretical and practical work as well as work experience together.

- *Curricular combination of theory and practice.* The study regulations of the academy and those of the apprenticeships are fitted into one another. This is guaranteed by the aforementioned subject-specific expert commissions composed of representatives from the state, academies and firms.
- *Co-operation of state and industry.* The influence of the 'participating fields of practice' is seen as a major pillar of the VA system as it defines the bodies governing the 'education alliance' (committee, expert commissions, co-ordination committees). This may be rated as a clear transposition of the 'principle of consensus' from the Dual System into the VA system.
- *Complex structure of teaching staff.* The part-time staff of the academy is made up of university and polytechnic lecturers, vocational school teachers and trainers from industry. Thus practical experience is embodied in the firm as well as in the academy.
- *Layering of training courses.* An intermediate examination can be taken after two years – similar to some training courses within the Dual System – which counts as a professional qualification (business assistant, engineering assistant, educator). The qualifications at the end of the course are degrees (Business Administration Diploma, Engineering Diploma, Social Work Diploma). Hence, the second training phase which lasts a further year is based on a clear professional or functional specialisation also underlined by the total of 44 existing courses.

All these traits correspond with a specific advantage for the VA student when it comes to finding a job after completion: 64 per cent of students/trainees are taken over by the training company.[17] The 'realistic' character and labour market relevance of vocational academies was already confirmed by a study by Zabeck and Zimmermann (1995): both integration into the job and integration into the apprenticing firm were reported to be working well, although unemployment rates were not significantly lower than among university and polytechnic graduates. Also, in general students viewed the training schemes as interesting and motivating and companies reported satisfaction with the motivation and performance of their trainees. Interestingly, though, identification among students was rather with the 'profession' or 'occupation' than with the company, which is a typical trait of the Dual System (Deissinger, 1998). It is against this background that the VA has been able to become a comparatively successful model of HE. Therefore it ought to be seen as an attractive alternative to university education rather than as a clone of a purely academic preparation for employment.

This high share is also typical for a number of apprenticeships in the German apprenticeship system therefore underlining one of the most significant common characteristics of the non-academic and the academic 'Dual System', which may be seen in the substantial interest of employers to invest into but also benefit from formal initial training based on the vocational principle (Deissinger, 1998).

Conclusion

Despite the fact that the discussion about the parity of general and vocational education was a major topic in post-war Germany, the links between vocational and higher education in Germany are not associated with a policy intent to create an artificial equivalence of qualifications or pathways leading to them. Quite contrary to what is going on in the educational debate in the UK, bridges are not built by opening direct progression routes for non-academically trained people into HE, but rather by linking up 'philosophies'. On the other hand, this means that the vocational bias enters HE in an institutional and didactical way similar to dual apprenticeships. A second aspect to this relationship may be seen in the specific function of vocational full-time schools which, because of the more or less 'exclusive' status of the apprenticeship system, work as a 'second chance pathway' into FE and HE. Hence there still is a clear separation and segregation of functions with obvious implications for both the apprenticeship system and the tertiary sector.

Modernisation of the Dual System occurs predominantly 'internally' and not in the sense of a change of paradigm or underlying principles. However, challenges have turned out to be less soluble than in the past, above all when it comes to the training market with its volatility and its dependence on the state of the national economy (Deissinger and Hellwig, 2004). Also, alternative approaches to VET, such as the vocational academies, or the likely expansion of more or less 'vocationalised' university or polytechnic courses looming with the Bologna reform of university systems within Europe put strain on the apprenticeship system. Apart from that, the Dual System still does not build bridges to the academic world, for example, through 'double qualifications', prominent in the VET systems of France, Austria and even Switzerland (Deissinger,

2001c; Gonon, 2001; Gruber, 2001). As to the future prospects of the Dual System, another crucial question might be whether the rapidly expanding services sector, including data processing and innovative customer-orientated services, will be willing or able to follow its 'philosophy' of training, i.e. above all the *vocational principle*. The future appeal of apprenticeships will also depend on other nations' experiences with more 'open' or 'market-oriented' approaches to VET and their functional links, both in quantitative and in qualitative terms, to national and international labour markets. As the prime concern of vocational training policy in Germany stays focused on initial training there can be no doubt that the training market still is and will remain the biggest challenge. And it is also obvious that the overall decline in apprenticeship intakes over the years is due to the supply side of the training market and not to young people's appreciation of the Dual System in general (Reinberg and Hummel, 2001, p. 25). After long years of substantial support from employers, Germany now seems to join all those countries that have always been desperate to convince the private sector of the benefits of skill formation.

There is no doubt that the German HE system will look different in a few years' time on account of impending pressures from European harmonisation policies. Partly because of its strong position in the last two decades in the tertiary sector of one of the largest federal states, the VA is the brand leader among special training programmes in HE. This important position of the VA in educational policy, coupled with its now 'improved' legal status, has led to a heterogeneous but still limited system of HE options below the university level: it becomes manifest not only in the debate around qualification titles and the conferring of degrees but also in the decision of some federal states to position alternative post-secondary qualifications well below that of a university or polytechnic, a decision which Baden-Württemberg never has been prepared to accept. That the debate over the VA has affected and is still affecting many interests is evident. Against this background the VA can be considered to be a pragmatic 'instrument' of HE policy (Zabeck and Deissinger, 1995, p. 24).

This has a clear implication for the perception of the 'character' of the German education and training system. As the focus is not on 'integrating' pathways and 'inclusive' approaches – which certainly was the 'big topic' for a comparatively short timespan during the 1960s and 1970s (Deutscher Bildungsrat, 1974) – but instead on upgrading vocational training and establishing vocational principles within HE, the German system seems to be far away from becoming a 'unified system'

(Greinert, 2003; Pilz, 2003). One of the reasons for this – apart from the fact that a country's VET system certainly has to be understood 'in relation to other societal institutions such as its labour market and economy, its industrial relations system and its system of government' (Raffe, 1998, p. 391) – seems to be the traditional understanding of a separate vocational pathway as something which deserves to be 'unique' and valuable in itself. It may be criticised that this fosters the organisation of general and vocational qualifications 'according to separate criteria and systems of assessment' and stands for 'limited possibilities for progression between them' (Young, 2003, p. 228). On the other hand, it may be argued that general and vocational education, in the German case, are interdependent systems and that the interaction between them helps to stabilise the 'vocational pathway' much more than in other countries.

Despite problems related to the training market there are no signs that the apprenticeship system representing this strong belief in the importance of vocational qualifications has entered a stage of degradation. Modernisation of existing training schemes remains a crucial topic, which may be interpreted as a clear concession towards 'internal modernisation', instead of changing the foundations and principles of the system. It may also be argued that the reform of the Vocational Training Act (Euler and Pätzold, 2004) – with its focus on bringing closer together the spheres of school-based and dual vocational training – is likely to be accompanied by a policy of building new bridges from company-based training to HE. Whether this will lead to strengthening the vocational route, however, remains to be seen.

Notes

1 See Gemeinsame Pressemitteilung der Schweizerischen Konferenz der kantonalen Erziehungsdirektoren, der Länder Österreich, Baden-Württemberg, Hessen und Bayern zur OECD-Studie Bildung auf einen Blick (*Pressemitteilung des bayerischen Kultusministeriums*, No. 288, 17 September 2003).

2 In 2002, the task of providing all applicants with a training place was associated with major challenges. At 572,227, the number of new training contracts was down 42,000 on the previous year and had thus sunk to an unexpected level. The reasons for this decline may be seen in the following factors: the weak economy; insecurities about the future demand for skilled employees; lack of training maturity among school leavers; regional and occupational imbalances in the training market; and, above all, with respect to situation of the former East Germany. Therefore, both the

number of students entering HE and the influx into vocational full-time schools have increased and are likely to rise in the forthcoming years (for all figures see: *Federal Training Report 2003*, online at: www.bmbf.de).

3 Quite unambiguously, the present federal government has underlined its will to increase the number of school leavers going on to higher education. This policy, clearly in the wake of assessment studies such as PISA (Programme for International Student Assessment), could lead to a gradual undermining of trust in and contentment with the Dual System.

4 In terms of the financial burden, companies shoulder the lion's share of training cost: in 2000, companies invested nearly € 28 billion into the Dual System. The average training outlay per apprentice is currently rated at € 16,435 p.a. (Beicht and Walden, 2002). As a result, the cost argument can be found amongst the most important reasons that companies report for not entering training.

5 Everybody under the age of eighteen not in HE or further education (FE) is compelled to attend the local part-time vocational school (*Berufsschule*) on a sandwich or day-release basis. Everybody commencing an apprenticeship is required to stay on at school until the end of the training period (Elser and Kramer, 1987).

6 The Act not only stipulates the rights and duties of trainees and training companies, but also prescribes the personal and technical skills of training personnel. For this purpose, a distinction is made between the trainer and the person or firm taking on apprentices. 'Personal aptitude' means that a person must not have broken the law. These preconditions are basically deemed sufficient for hiring an apprentice. However, a person engaging in apprenticeships also has to prove the competence for instructing the apprentice at the training site, called the 'technical aptitude', unless there is a training officer having the necessary personal and technical qualifications to provide the training. Therefore the trainer, besides 'personal aptitude', must have technical (i.e. occupational) and pedagogical abilities and knowledge, which means that he/she has to be an expert in the occupation as well as in educational and psychological skills, including the application of appropriate teaching and instruction methods. Since 1972, courses for trainers, normally offered by the chambers as the 'competent authorities' (Weber, 1985, pp. 60–4), have followed a uniform pattern based on the Vocational Training Act. This regulation is currently at stake as the federal government desperately seeks to liberalise the Dual System and attract more companies to take on apprentices.

7 For figures see: destatis.de/basis/d/biwiku/schultab8.htm. Between 1998 and 2002 the share of school leavers entering HE rose from 28 per cent to 35 per cent, which is still below the OECD average of 47 per cent. See: Gemeinsame Presseerklärung von BMBF und KMK, 16 September 2003 (www.bmbf.de/presse01/934.html).

8 A clear indication is the fact that between 1975 and 1988 the number of students rose by 75 per cent (Friedeburg, 1989, p. 428).

[9] The share of students with a working class background rose from 6 per cent in 1963 to 13 per cent in 1976, in a timespan which can be seen as the triggering period of educational expansion in Germany (Baumert *et al.*, 1979, p. 218).

[10] The share of female students is 47.4 per cent, the share of foreigners 11.7 per cent (2002/2003). The Federal Statistical Office reports an average age of students in Germany of 26.2 years (see: www.destatis.de/basis/d/biwiku/hochtab2.php; http://bibb.skygate.de/Z/B/30/99600000.pdf; http://www.destasis.de/basis/d/biwiku/beruftab1.php).

[11] See: www.ba-bw.de.

[12] See: www.ba-bw.de.

[13] The legal status of the VA in Baden-Württemberg makes it an 'independent institution of cooperation between state and apprenticing firms, operating neither under the school nor university statutes' (Erhardt, 1993). With its dual structure of learning and the co-operation between state institutions and firms, the VA lies somewhere between initial vocational training and university studies. Hailbronner (1993, p. 12) characterises the VA as a 'higher vocational training institution', while Erhardt (CDU, 1994) paints the picture of a 'flagship of the dual vocational training system'. However, as the schooling part of the institution, the state academy, is not a school according to the state school law and thus not a vocational school in the normal sense of the Dual System partnership, despite the integrated practical part of the training taken in co-operating firms, VA training does not come under the Vocational Training Act (Deissinger, 1996). This is also because this particular type of training is outside the conditions of article 28 of the Vocational Training Act ('principle of exclusiveness').

[14] Order of the Ministry of Science, Research and Arts on the Equality of Diploma Qualifications from the vocational academies in Baden-Württemberg with those of the Polytechnics, 10 April 1989. See: *Wissenschaft und Kunst*, 6, 12 June 1989, p. 202. The order is based on article 1 II, No. 2 BAG.

[15] Although stressing the unique system of training in the VA the Science Council of Germany (*Wissenschaftsrat*) maintained in 1994 that VAs were at par with existing institutions of HE. The Science Council had been asked by the state of Baden-Württemberg to set up a working group with the task of giving recommendations based on analyses 'expert and free from bias' (Wissenschaftsrat, 1994, p. 4). Such a position was taken by the Science Council in Schwerin on 20 May 1994. Summed up, the Science Council took a 'positive view of the VA training structure'. In their opinion, the VA offered a 'differentiated training course from that of a polytechnic, but in the sense of the professional qualification, a comparable training to that of a polytechnic'. The 'most important strengths' of the VA were seen in the 'three-year long training course, the focus on practical work and the scientific basis of the syllabus, which secure an easy transition to the workplace, as well as the

social skills emerging from the dual concept of training' (Wissenschaftsrat, 1994, p. 89).

[16] It should also be noted that the VA's matriculation process has its own regulations: only those who have already found an apprenticeship placement after their school examinations are eligible for a place at the VA. The "training contract" caters for the registration procedures for students at the educational academy, which is the responsibility of the firm, the guarantee of time off during the apprenticeship to visit classes, and adherence to examination requirements and training guidelines (article 8 I BAG).

[17] See: www.ba-bw.de

References

Arnold, R. (1985) 'Das duale System – Ein Modell für den Aufbau leistungsfähiger Berufsbildungssysteme in Entwicklungsländern?', *Zeitschrift für internationale erziehungs- und sozialwissenschaftliche Forschung*, 2, pp. 343–69.

Avenarius, H. *et al.* (2003) *Bildungsbericht für Deutschland: Erste Befunde* (Zusammenfassung). Online at: www.dipf.de/bildungsbericht/bb_zusammenfassung.pdf

Baumert, J. *et al.* (1979) *Das Bildungswesen in der Bundesrepublik Deutschland*. Reinbek: Rowohlt.

Beicht, U. and Walden, G. (2002) 'Wirtschaftlichere Durchführung der Berufsausbildung – Untersuchungsergebnisse zu den Ausbildungskosten der Betriebe', *Berufsbildung in Wissenschaft und Praxis*, 31(6), pp. 38–43.

Benner, H. (1984) 'Zum Problem der Entwicklung betrieblicher Ausbildungsordnungen und ihrer Abstimmung mit schulischen Rahmenlehrplänen', in: W. Georg (ed.) *Schule und Berufsausbildung*. Bielefeld: Bertelsmann, pp. 175–87.

Berger, K. and Walden, G. (2002) 'Trends in public funding for in-company training in Germany', in: G. Burke and J. Reuling (eds) *Vocational Training and Lifelong Learning in Australia and Germany*. Adelaide: National Centre for Vocational Education Research, pp.135–49.

Blankertz, H. (1972) 'Kollegstufenversuch in Nordrhein-Westfalen – das Ende der gymnasialen Oberstufe und der Berufsschulen', *Die Deutsche Berufs- und Fachschule*, 68, pp. 2–20.

Blankertz, H. (1982) *Die Geschichte der Pädagogik: Von der Aufklärung bis zur Gegenwart*. Wetzlar: Büchse der Pandora.

Brown A. and Evans, K. (1994) 'Changing the training culture: Lessons from Anglo-German comparisons of vocational education and training', *British Journal of Education and Work*, 7, pp. 5–15.

Canning, R., Deissinger, T. and Loots, C. (2000) 'Continuity and change in apprenticeship systems: A comparative study between Scotland and Germany', *Scottish Journal of Adult and Continuing Education*, 6(2), pp. 99–117.

CDU-Landtagsfraktion Baden-Württemberg (1994) *Redebeiträge anlässlich der Fachtagung zum Thema "Zukunft und Perspektiven der Berufsakademien" im*

Plenarsaal des Landtags. Unpublished manuscript, Stuttgart.

Deissinger, T. (1994) 'The evolution of the modern vocational training systems in England and Germany: A comparative view', *Compare: A Journal of Comparative Education*, 24, pp. 17–36.

Deissinger, T. (1995) 'Eine bildungspolitische Forderung im Spiegel der aktuellen Rechtslage: die überregionale Anerkennung der Berufsakademie Baden-Württemberg', *Recht der Jugend und des Bildungswesens*, 43(4), pp. 429–42.

Deissinger, T. (1996) 'Germany's vocational training act: Its function as an instrument of quality control within a tradition-based vocational training system', *Oxford Review of Education*, 22, pp. 317–36.

Deissinger, T. (1998) *Beruflichkeit als "organisierendes Prinzip" der deutschen Berufsausbildung.* Markt Schwaben (Eusl).

Deissinger, T. (2001a) 'Entwicklung didaktisch-curricularer Vorgaben für die Berufsbildung in Deutschland', in: B. Bonz (ed.) *Didaktik der beruflichen Bildung.* Baltmannsweiler: Schneider, pp. 71–87.

Deissinger, T. (2001b) 'Vocational training in small firms in Germany: The contribution of the craft sector', *Education and Training*, 43(8/9), pp. 426–36.

Deissinger, T. (2001c) 'Zur Frage nach der Bedeutung des Berufsprinzips als "organisierendes Prinzip" der deutschen Berufsausbildung im europäischen Kontext: Eine deutsch-französische Vergleichsskizze', *Tertium Comparationis*, 7(1), pp. 1–18.

Deissinger, T. and Hellwig, S. (2004) 'Initiatives and strategies to secure training opportunities in the German vocational education and training system', *Journal of Adult and Continuing Education*, 10(2), pp. 160–74.

Deissinger, T. and Ruf, M. (2003) 'Wissenschaftliche Evaluation des Übungsfirmenkonzepts in Baden-Württemberg – Skizzierung des Forschungsvorhabens', *Wirtschaft Plus – Magazin für Wirtschaft und Bildung*, 1, pp. 5–8.

Deutscher Bildungsrat (1974) *Empfehlungen der Bildungskommission: Zur Neuordnung der Sekundarstufe II. Konzept für eine Verbindung von allgemeinem und beruflichem Lernen.* Bonn.

Elser, W. and Kramer, O. (1987) *Grundriss des Schulrechts in Baden-Württemberg.* Neuwied: Luchterhand.

Erhardt, M. (1993) 'Rechtsgrundlage und Rechtsgestalt der Berufsakademie', in: Unabhängige Kommission Berufsakademie (ed.) *Materialienband zum Bericht zur Fortentwicklung der Organisation der Berufsakademie Baden-Württemberg.* Stuttgart.

Euler, D. (2000) 'Bekannt, aber nicht anerkannt – zur Weiterentwicklung der Berufsausbildung in schulischer Trägerschaft', in: G. Zimmer (ed.) *Zukunft der Berufsausbildung. Zweite Modernisierung unter Beteiligung der beruflichen Vollzeitschulen.* Bielefeld: W. Bertelsmann, pp. 71–88.

Euler, D. and Pätzold, G. (2004) 'Gelingt mit der Novellierung des Berufsbildungsgesetzes der Sprung von der Krisenverwaltung zur Reformgestaltung?', *Zeitschrift für Berufs- und Wirtschaftspädagogik*, 100(1), pp. 1–6.

Federal Ministry of Education and Research (2003) *Report on Vocational Education and Training for the Year 2003*, Part I. Online at: www.bmbf.de/pub/bbb2003_en.pdf

Feller, G. (2000) 'Ausbildung an Berufsfachschulen – Ein differenziertes und flexibles Qualifikationssystem', in: F. J. Kaiser (ed.) *Berufliche Bildung in Deutschland für das 21. Jahrhundert.* Nürnberg: Bundesanstalt für Arbeit, pp. 439–50.

Friedeburg, L.v. (1989) *Bildungsreform in Deutschland: Geschichte und gesellschaftlicher Widerspruch.* Frankfurt a.M.: Suhrkamp.

Fuller, A. and Unwin, L. (2003) 'Learning as apprentices in the contemporary UK workplace: Creating and managing expansive and restrictive participation', *Journal of Education and Work*, 16(4), pp. 407–26.

Gonon, P. (2001) 'Neue Reformbestrebungen im beruflichen Bildungswesen in der Schweiz', in: T. Deissinger (ed.) *Berufliche Bildung zwischen nationaler Tradition und globaler Entwicklung*. Baden-Baden: Nomos, pp. 63–77.

Green, N., Hartley, T. C. and Usher, J. A. (1991) *The Legal Foundations of the Single European Market*. Oxford: Oxford University Press.

Greinert, W. D. (1994) *The "German System" of Vocational Training: History, Organization, Prospects*. Baden-Baden: Nomos.

Greinert, W. D. (2003) *Realistische Bildung in Deutschland: Ihre Geschichte und aktuelle Bedeutung*. Hohengehren: Schneider.

Gruber, E. (2001) 'Entwicklungen der Berufsbildung in Österreich', in: T. Deissinger (ed.) *Berufliche Bildung zwischen nationaler Tradition und globaler Entwicklung*. Baden-Baden: Nomos, pp. 79–101.

Hailbronner, K. (1993) 'Rechtsfragen einer staatlichen Anerkennung der Berufsakademien des Landes Baden-Württemberg nach §§ 70 HRG, 89 FHGBW', in: Unabhängige Kommission Berufsakademie (ed.) *Materialienband zum Bericht zur Fortentwicklung der Organisation der Berufsakademie Baden-Württemberg*, June, pp. 1–76 (original page numbering).

Harney, K. (1985) 'Der Beruf als Umwelt des Betriebs. Vergleichende, historische und systematische Aspekte einer Differenz', in: Verbände der Lehrer an beruflichen Schulen in Nordrhein-Westfalen (eds) *Die Relevanz neuer Technologien für die Berufsausbildung*. Krefeld, pp. 118–30.

Harris, R. and Deissinger, T. (2003) 'Learning cultures for apprenticeships: A comparison of Germany and Australia', in: J. Searle, I. Yashin-Shaw and D. Roebuck (eds) *Enriching Learning Cultures. Proceedings of the 11th Annual International Conference of Post-compulsory Education and Training*, Volume Two. Brisbane: Australian Academic Press, pp. 23–33.

Kell, A. (1996) 'Berufliche Schulen in der Spannung von Bildung und Beruf', *Zeitschrift für Berufs- und Wirtschaftspädagogik*, 92, pp. 6–18.

Kloss, G. (1995) 'Vocational education: A success story?, in: D. Phillips (ed.) *Education in Germany: Tradition and Reform in Historical Context*. London: Routledge, pp. 161–70.

Kutscha, G. (1989) *Bildung unter dem Anspruch von Aufklärung: zur Pädagogik von Herwig Blankertz*. Weinheim: Beltz.

Menze, C. (1991) 'Wilhelm von Humboldt und die deutsche Universität', *Vierteljahresschrift für wissenschaftliche Pädagogik*, 67, pp. 471–84.

National Centre for Vocational Education Research (NCVER) (2001) *Australian Apprenticeships: Facts, Fiction and Future*. Adelaide: NCVER.

OECD (2000) *Measuring Student Knowledge and Skills: The PISA 2000 Assessment of Reading, Mathematical and Scientific Literacy*. Paris: OECD.

OECD (2003) *Education at a Glance*. Paris: OECD.

Phillips, D. (1995) 'Lessons from Germany? The case of German secondary schools', in: D. Phillips (ed.) *Education in Germany: Tradition and Reform in Historical Context*. London: Routledge, pp. 60–79.

Pilz, M. (2003) 'Wege zur Erreichung der Gleichwertigkeit von allgemeiner und beruflicher Bildung. Deutsche Ansatzpunkte und schottische Erfahrungsbeispiele',

Zeitschrift für Berufs- und Wirtschaftspädagogik, 99(3), pp. 390–416.

Raffe, D. (1998) 'Conclusion: Where are pathways going? Conceptual and methodological lessons from the pathways study', in: OECD (ed.) *Pathways and Participation in Vocational and Technical Education and Training*. Paris: OECD, pp. 375–94.

Raggatt, P. (1988) 'Quality control in the dual system of West Germany', *Oxford Review of Education*, 14(2), pp. 163–86.

Reinberg, A. and Hummel, M. (2001) 'Die Entwicklung im deutschen Bildungssystem vor dem Hintergrund des qualifikatorischen Strukturwandels auf dem Arbeitsmarkt', in: A. Reinberg (ed.) *Arbeitsmarktrelevante Aspekte der Bildungspolitik*. Nürnberg: Bundesanstalt für Arbeit, pp. 1–62.

Reinert, J. (1999) '25 Jahre Berufsakademie: Ein innovatives Bildungsmodell hat sich durchgesetzt', in: Conference of Directors of Vocational Academies (ed.) *Berufsakademie Forum 1999*. Stuttgart: BA Stuttgart, pp. 4–9.

Reinisch, H. (2001) 'Formen und Funktionen beruflicher Vollzeitschulen in Deutschland – aufgezeigt am Beispiel des Bundeslandes Niedersachsen', in: D. Frommberger, H. Reinisch and M. Santema (eds) *Berufliche Bildung zwischen Schule und Betrieb. Stand und Entwicklung in den Niederlanden und Deutschland*. Markt Schwaben: Eusl, pp. 155–76.

Ryan, P. (2001) 'Apprenticeship in Britain: Tradition and innovation', in: T. Deissinger (ed.) *Berufliche Bildung zwischen nationaler Tradition und globaler Entwicklung*. Baden-Baden: Nomos, pp. 133–57.

Schlüter, A. and Stratmann, K. (eds) (1985) *Quellen und Dokumente zur betrieblichen Berufsbildung, 1869–1918*. Köln: Böhlau.

Schütte, F. (1992) *Berufserziehung zwischen Revolution und Nationalsozialismus. Ein Beitrag zur Bildungs- und Sozialgeschichte der Weimarer Republik*. Weinheim: Deutscher Studien Verlag.

Senker, P. *et al.* (2000) 'Arbeiten, um zu lernen: ein ganzheitlicher Ansatz für die Erstausbildung Jugendlicher', *CEDEFOP Berufsbildung*, 20, pp. 45–58.

Stratmann, K. (1982) 'Geschichte der beruflichen Bildung. Ihre Theorie und Legitimation seit Beginn der Industrialisierung', in: H. Blankertz (ed.) *Enzyklopädie Erziehungswissenschaft, Bd. 9.1: Sekundarstufe II – Jugendbildung zwischen Schule und Beruf*. Stuttgart: Klett-Cotta, pp. 173–202.

University Vocational Awards Council (UVAC) (2003) *Review and Development of Graduate Apprenticeship. A National Higher Education and Employment Bridging Programme*. Bolton: UVAC/HEFCE.

Weber, R. (1985) *Berufsbildungsgesetz und Berufsbildungsförderungsgesetz*. Bergisch-Gladbach: Heider.

Wissenschaftsrat (1994) *Stellungnahme zu den Berufsakademien in Baden-Württemberg*. Schwerin.

Young, M. (2003) 'National Qualifications Frameworks as a global phenomenon: A comparative perspective, *Journal of Education and Work*, 16(3), pp. 223–37.

Zabeck, J. (1972) 'Berufsbildung zwischen Gesellschaftskritik und Traditionalismus', in: R. Löwenthal *et al.* (eds) *Schule '72*. Köln, pp. 123–37.

Zabeck, J. (1975) *Die Bedeutung des Selbstverwaltungsprinzips für die Effizienz der betrieblichen Ausbildung. Untersuchung im Auftrage des Ministers für Wirtschaft, Mittelstand und Verkehr des Landes Nordrhein-Westfalen*. Mannheim.

Zabeck, J. and Deissinger, T. (1995) 'Die Berufsakademie Baden-Württemberg als Evaluationsobjekt: Ihre Entstehung, ihre Entwicklung und derzeitige Ausgestaltung sowie ihr Anspruch auf bildungspolitische Problemlösung', in: J. Zabeck and M. Zimmermann (eds) *Anspruch und Wirklichkeit der Berufsakademie Baden-Württemberg. Eine Evaluationsstudie.* Weinheim: Deutscher Studien Verlag, pp. 1–28.

Zabeck, J. and Zimmermann, M. (eds) (1995) *Anspruch und Wirklichkeit der Berufsakademie Baden-Württemberg. Eine Evaluationsstudie.* Weinheim: Deutscher Studien Verlag.

Zimmermann, M. and Deissinger, T. (1995) 'Zur Forderung nach überregionaler Gleichstellung der an der Berufsakademie Baden-Württemberg erworbenen Abschlüsse mit Fachhochschul-Diplomen. – Eine Darstellung und kritische Würdigung der aktuellen Diskussion', in: J. Zabeck and M. Zimmermann (eds) *Anspruch und Wirklichkeit der Berufsakademie Baden-Württemberg. Eine Evaluationsstudie.* Weinheim: Deutscher Studien Verlag, pp. 441–76.

The further education system in Ireland

Dermot Coughlan

Introduction

Prior to considering the Irish further education (FE) sector it is necessary to examine how it relates to the other sectors within the Irish educational system. The principal point to note is that the system is very centralised, managed and indeed controlled by the central government's Department of Education and Science. There are four distinct levels within the overall structure. The primary sector is quite discrete and defined as the schooling for those aged between 4/5 and 12/13. Similarly, the secondary sector, which covers those aged from 12/13 to 17/19, is equally well defined. The increase in the difference in finishing age is due to the fact that the secondary system allows for a voluntary 'transition year' programme between the junior and senior cycles within the secondary sector.

The third grouping is the university sector and this is clearly delineated as there are just seven universities governed by statute (Government of Ireland, 1997). The fourth stream within the system is the sector which is the focus of this chapter, namely FE. This area of the Irish educational offer is without question the most complex of the groupings. This complexity arises as a result of the range of the providers and the level of the provision. It ranges in terms of qualifications awarded from level 1 to level 6 in the National Qualifications Authority of Ireland (NQAI, 2003a) Framework ranging, which covers levels 1–10 (see Figure 1). In terms of providers FE is offered by institutions that range from private training organisations to institutes of technology (ITs) (also significant players in the higher education (HE) sector). The formal cross-over between ITs and universities formally happens at level 7 (from which point the generic term 'third level' refers to all subsequent provision) within the Framework, but in practice there other points of convergence below this level. For instance ITs, in addition to their range of HE offerings (i.e. the awarding of certificate, diploma, degree and postgraduate qualifications), in association with *Foras Áiseanna Saothar* (FÁS) also participate in the system of apprentice education in Ireland. To complete the picture it should also be noted that the ITs are also providers of accredited programmes under agreement/license with bodies such as City & Guilds Society. Clearly, therefore, they also play a pivotal role in the area of further and vocational training. This permeability between the sectors can cause some confusion to the outside world, but despite this complexity it is very evident from the findings of the Report of the Expert Working Group (Council of Directors of the ITs, 2003), which examined the future position and roles of the FE sector, that it is a key player in the educational infrastructure.

The ITs first came on stream as regional technical colleges in the early 1970s. Since then they have, as stated by Professor Pat Fottrell in his foreword to the report, played a major role in transforming the education and economic opportunities for large sections of Irish society. In 2003 the ITs accounted for approximately 40 per cent of enrolments and 53 per cent of first admissions to HE. If one then considers the amount of other non-accredited programmes delivered by the sector (particularly in the evenings) its role in FE is even more considerable.

Having given this brief overview of the Irish educational system I will now revert to the primary focus of the chapter which is the FE sector and its role in providing access to or delivery of HE. From the foregoing discussion it is clear that addressing the issue of FE in Ireland is a somewhat difficult task as the definition of what constitutes FE can and does depend to a large extent on whom you ask to define it. For this purpose I am defining the FE sector through the use of the NQAI designation of level 1 through to level 6.

Context

The one statement that can be made without too much fear of contradiction is that the FE sector in Ireland covers a broad spectrum of activity. It incorporates much of what in some other countries might be referred to as vocational training. This includes specific vocational training for industry delivered by a range of different bodies covering different sectors of the economy such as general apprenticeship training, training for the hotel and hospitality industry, the fishing industry, and the agriculture

Figure 1. Irish National Framework of Qualifications.
Source: National Qualifications Authority of Ireland (NQAI)

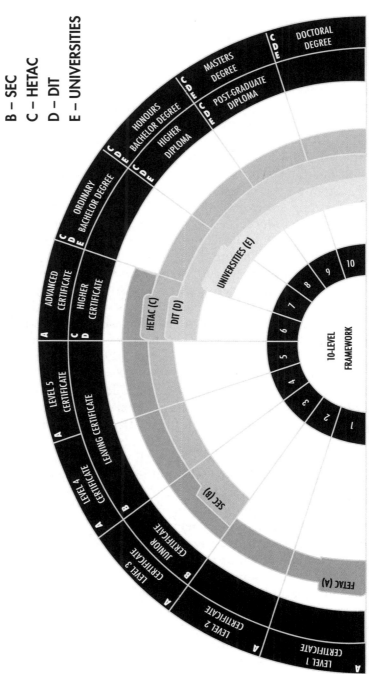

A – FETAC
B – SEC
C – HETAC
D – DIT
E – UNIVERSITIES

sector. During the course of this chapter I will deal with all of these sectors with the exception of hospitality.

The lack of definition of FE could be attributed (apart from some specific instances) to its being a relatively new element of the educational system in Ireland. As was noted by Maguire (2003) the FE system in Ireland has only begun to develop as a distinct sector since the mid-1990s. As evidence to support this assertion she noted that the Green Paper *Education for a Changing World* (Department of Education and Science (DES), 1992) did not even use the term. By 1995 however when the White Paper on Education *Chartering our Education Future* (DES, 1995) was published the sector was given a complete separate section. In theory the FE system has been designed to give the learner a continuum of learning by providing a series of different pathways to other forms of education. Whether it has succeeded in achieving this will be addressed later. I will operationally use as the definition of FE the sector between secondary and higher education. During the course of this chapter I will address its role in providing a pathway across and between the other sectors.

The new-found interest in FE is also noted by Gleeson (1998) who observed that the scale of developments in Irish education during the 1990s had been the most intense since Ireland had gained its independence. As evidence of this he lists a series of developments ranging from the OECD Examiners' report of 1991 to the new Education Act of 1998 (Government of Ireland, 1998). Since then there have been other significant developments. These include the *White Paper on Adult Education* (DES, 2000) and the *Report of the Taskforce on Lifelong Learning* (Department of Enterprise, Trade and Employment, 2001).

For a nation that is recognised internationally as a leader in many aspects of education why is the FE system of such a recent vintage? Equally, it has to be asked why, following a number of low-key initiatives, it has become centre stage.

The answer to these questions, and indeed to others which could be asked of the education system in general, lie in the manner in which successive governments have charted the Irish economic revival which became to be known as the *Celtic Tiger*. For the outside observer it can be difficult to comprehend Ireland's phenomenal economic recovery, development and the sustaining of its progress from a period in the mid-1980s when its unemployment was running at in excess of 20 per cent and inflation in double digits, to its current state which boasts of almost full employment, and an inflation rate of 3 per cent. Ireland has experienced a period where its growth rate for long periods was in double digits and has outstripped those of all the leading world economies. The growth rate has dropped somewhat in recent times but it is still one of the strongest economies within the expanded European Union.

The bedrock for these economic advances is in the development of the consensus and partnership approach to wage bargaining, which went far beyond the traditional boundaries associated with such negotiations and resulted in agreements which have paved the way for this economic boom. I will address some of the issues associated with these national programmes, but a more fulsome account is given by Gleeson (1998) in his account of consensus and policy making in Ireland. Murphy and Coughlan (2003) also refer to the role that these national economic programmes have had in the development of education within Irish society.

National pay agreements have been a key feature of industrial relations in Ireland since the early 1970s and, while important in their own right, it was not until national pay bargaining was extended to embrace the philosophy of social partnership that the real benefits accrued. Since the inception of pay agreements, education, including the FE sector, has been a fundamental element of all of the state's economic and social policy strategies and programmes. While there are some commentators, such as Turner (2002), who would argue that the inclusion of education as a key element of the agreements has not led to a reduction on the impact of issues associated with equity and inclusiveness, few would argue against the fact that its inclusion has brought education to centre stage. A key impact has been that the various individual social partners and in particular the employers' association, the Irish Business and Employers' Confederation, now devote significant time, attention, and resources to having coherent policies on issues pertaining to education at all levels.

As the finishing touches are being put to this chapter it has been announced that the social partners have again reached agreement on another national partnership agreement, the *Sustaining Progress – Social Partnership Agreement* (Government of Ireland, 2003). Education is again afforded a primary role in the programme. While the section dealing with education does not deal with the FE sector per se, the fact that education is again afforded its own chapter in this agreement proves that education in general is seen as a central tenet of government policy and as a sector which will ensure the continued development of the Irish economy.

Having now outlined how FE has emerged from the wings to take centre stage I will address some of the key developments contributing to the renaissance. I will in the first instance examine the functions of some specific state bodies and their respective roles in the provision and development of the FE sector in Ireland.

Teagasc – The Irish Agriculture and Food Development Authority

Farming is an area where the role of FE has an interesting past, is currently very vibrant and, based on the published plans of the authority governing its development, will have an exciting future. While it is not always credited with a great commitment to education the farming sector in Ireland has a proud tradition in the area of training and development. With its roots in systems and institutes that pre-date Ireland's independence the system has taken these roots and has developed into a flourishing set of crops. The current body governing charged with its ongoing development is titled *Teagasc*.[1]

As is evidenced by even the most cursory review of the history of the Irish Public Service it is very much based on systems established when Ireland was ruled by England. For instance, when the Department of Agriculture was established some 100 years ago it assumed responsibility for the educational and research centres then in place. These were very much state bodies with a national remit, but were augmented by local educational providers, which were generally referred to as County Committees of Agriculture. These committees employed agricultural instructors who, as early as the 1930s, understood what flexible delivery meant and provided their training programmes at times that suited the differing farming cycles.

The next major phase of development came with the establishment of a number of dedicated agricultural colleges. These colleges linked with the County Committees of Agriculture to provide a comprehensive training programme for young farmers and programmes that today would be referred to as upskilling for established farmers. These colleges, in keeping with the modern phenomenon of Public Private Partnerships, ran in tandem with a number of private colleges who also provided programmes.

In 1980 the training and education of the farming sector was removed from the central government department and transferred to a new semi-state organisation, the national advisory and training body (ACOT). It took over the functions and personnel of the five state colleges and it also assumed responsibility for the state funding of the private colleges. In 1981 the first major review of agricultural training was published. The report's principal finding was that the training and development of the farming sector was unorganised and uncoordinated. The first step to correcting this was the introduction of the Certificate in Farming, which at that time became the standard qualification for all new entrants to farming, and this, coupled with the work of the Farm Apprenticeship Board, formed the foundation of all that followed in later years.

1988 saw the next major development with the establishment of Teagasc, the Agriculture and Food Development Authority, which was granted overall responsibility for the provision of research, training and advisory services to the agriculture industry. This brought all of the work of the various agencies involved in farming under the one umbrella.

Due to many factors the agricultural sector has declined significantly over the past few years and, consequently, the numbers employed directly in the sector has dropped considerably. According to Teagasc data (Browne, 2003) the numbers of young people enrolling in Teagasc courses has declined by around 40 per cent in recent years. As a consequence actions were deployed to minimise the impact of this dramatic downturn and to ensure an adequate supply of appropriately qualified people to take up careers in farming. Teagasc overhauled its entire educational structure and introduced a programme for the national certification of all courses and the upgrading of some courses to third-level status, thus ensuring that its work must be considered in any review of the Irish FE system.

This new course structure for the agricultural and related sub-sectors came into being in 2002. The national awarding bodies, namely the Higher Education and Training Awards Council (HETAC) and the Further Education and Training Awards Council (FETAC), now accredit all Teagasc courses.

According to Teagasc statistics, a total of 327 students accepted Central Applications Office offers for third-level certificate and diploma courses in agriculture and horticulture in 2003. This compares with an enrolment of 237 in 2001, the first year these courses were introduced. This represents an increase of almost 40 per cent, demonstrating student interest in these courses. While the programmes covered by HETAC are clearly outside the FE framework this does not diminish Teagasc's role in FE.

Recently published figures from Teagasc, for instance, show that a total of 700 students enrolled in first-year vocational certificate courses in ten Teagasc colleges and at local Teagasc training centres in 2003. Courses covered many aspects of agriculture, horticulture, horse production and forestry. The number of enrolments across all years of study is in excess of 3000. FETAC accredits all courses.

Like its predecessors in the past, Teagasc is committed to the concept of flexible delivery, with a number of vocational training courses run at local Teagasc training centres being held at night and at weekends, and containing significant distance learning components. The next phase has also adopted the latest developments in blended learning and there are now a number of the modules available on an e-learning basis in a pilot phase.

FE programmes which do not carry formal accreditation are also offered widely. In its *Annual Report* for 2002, Teagasc stated that over 9,500 adults attended courses runs by Teagasc in 2002. These courses covered technology and business management, rural viability, information technology, environmental protection, food safety, alternative enterprises and advanced management.

Bord Iascaigh Mara (BIM) – Irish Sea Fisheries Board

BIM, which was established in 1952 under the Sea Fisheries Act of that year, is the Irish State agency with responsibility for developing the Irish sea fishing and aquaculture industries. While it has many responsibilities within its remit, it is its role in education and training that I will concentrate upon.

Like the agricultural sector, the fishing industry up to very recently was a very traditional one. It was primarily composed of small operators fishing from small vessels, based in various locations around the coast of Ireland. In recent years, however, due to the influence of European Union intervention this profile has changed significantly. As a consequence BIM recognised that there would be a different range of skills and education required of those who wished to be part of the modern fishing industry.

To spearhead this requirement, BIM developed an integrated training plan for the Irish seafood industry covering the period 2000 to 2006. In his introduction to this initiative the minister with responsibility for BIM in 2000, Frank Fahy, stated that the objective of the plan was to expand the skills base and increase the availability of trained workers for the industry. He highlighted that the aim of the plan was to achieve a structured training system to support clear career paths in all sectors of the industry. It would, he said, also address the skills deficit by fostering a lifelong approach to learning and improve access through the provision of flexible modular courses delivered locally, emphasising that the programmes would be accredited by FETAC.

In the report BIM (2000) espoused a very cohesive policy and approach based on what it referred to as 'the four main pillars of the European Employment Strategy'. This new strategy BIM declared:

> Will ensure that the courses BIM will deliver to the seafood industry will for the first time be integrated within a national framework of education and training, recognised throughout the EU. There will be a strong emphasis on work based learning, allowing trainees to access modules to suit their requirements over a period of time. Strategic alliances will be formed with other educational and training establishments to facilitate progression paths for trainees from BIM's further education courses to the higher education sector.

These grand statements were, however, backed with significant funding which resulted in a significant investment in the National Fisheries College located in the north west of Ireland. This was augmented by a major expansion of the Regional Fisheries Centre in the south west of the country. In addition, BIM brought into service two mobile coastal training units which would travel to various locations throughout the country providing access to training programmes, in keeping with local fishing patterns.

The quantifiable impact of the programme, three years into its planned life cycle is shown in Table 1.

Table 1. Training Programmes in Fisheries, 1999–2003.

Year	No. of courses	Number of attendees
1999	25	1930
2001	27	1334
2003	23	1681

Source: BIM Annual Reports 1999–2003

It is important, however, to avoid judging success solely on the number of individuals trained. It is more important that the overall underlying philosophy within the organisation has as its raison d'être the development of the individual through FE and training. It is evident from BIM's strategic plan for the period 2000–2006 that it is not solely concerned with numbers.

BIM's movement to have all of its programmes accredited through the various agencies and its commitment to engage with a range of other players in the FE sector is a clear indicator that it will not be happy with increased numbers alone. Its current plans to pilot innovative training techniques within the new structure established by the NQAI, coupled with the aim of fostering a lifelong learning approach to provide a continuum of learning, clearly establishes BIM as a major force in the development of the FE system within Ireland.

The Training and Employment Authority (FÁS)

The previous sections dealt with bodies which are industry specific and, consequently, their influence is somewhat limited. In this section, I will deal with the work of FÁS[2] whose remit is so wide that it is clearly one of the most influential players in the FE sector in Ireland. There are many reasons why the work of FÁS has to be included in any review and, while different elements of its role and responsibilities will receive different levels of emphasis from different sectors of the economy, most parties will agree that it is a key player in the national framework of FE. Historically, it would have been its role in the area of apprenticeship training which would have merited its inclusion in a review of the Irish FE system, but recent developments have resulted in it taking a much wider role across the sector. I will attempt to address most of these roles, but the FÁS remit has developed so much that it would be impossible to give a full overview of all its activities.

FÁS came into existence in 1988, through the enactment of the Labour Services Act (Government of Ireland, 1987) and the new body was the amalgamation of three existing statutory bodies, namely AnCO – The Industrial Training Authority, The National Manpower Service, and The Youth Employment Agency. These three bodies had been responsible for and administered the principal training and employment services provided by the State.

Though a statutory body, FÁS is a constituent part of the Department of Enterprise, Trade and Employment, a fact which will be very important later when I refer to certain tensions which exist between this government department and the Department of Education and Science.

Since 1988 there have been many developments which have led to FÁS assuming additional responsibilities; for instance, in 2000, as part of government policy to mainstream services for people with disability, responsibility for vocational training and employment for this group transferred to FÁS.

Before addressing its role in the area of apprentice training, it is important to outline some of its other functions. The primary function of FÁS is the provision of an integrated scheme of training or retraining for employment, through a direct offering or through sub-contracting to other bodies. Probably the most interesting development on this front is the development and launch of an e-learning initiative in this broad area. Through what is titled FÁS Net College, it provides distance learning and development opportunities in areas such as business courses, Office applications, Web design/programming, technical support courses, health and safety and soft skills/personal development courses and apprentice-ship modules. The apprentice system of education is one of the oldest forms of education provision, dating from the earliest days of the master and apprentice system, through the medieval guilds and subsequent developments up to the modern era with its connection to the formal education system. The system requires that the progress of the apprentice through all phases of the apprenticeship be recorded by FÁS. The numbers currently engaged in apprenticeship training and the sectors of the economy, which are in growth and in decline, is evident from the following section of the FÁS 2003 annual review, and is shown in Figure 2:

> At the end of December 2003 there were 26,853 apprentices at various stages of their apprenticeship. This is an increase on the 2002 figure of approximately 3%. 7,337 new apprentices registered in 2003 compared to 6,933 in 2002. This represents a 6% growth in apprentice registrations.

The intake of new apprentices into the building sector increased by 20 per cent overall compared to 2002. The main increases in new registrations were in the trades of Plumbing, Bricklaying, Carpentry/Joinery and Plastering, with the Plastering trade showing an increase in registrations of 44 per cent. The intake into some trades within other sectors was down on the 2002 figures. Engineering trade intake, for example, was 800 compared to 900 in 2002 and a peak of 1,200 in 2000. Numbers in the motor, electrical, furniture and printing sectors were also lower. (FÁS, 2003)

Figure 2. Number of apprentice starters per year.

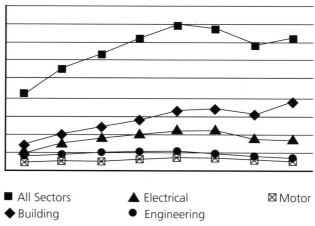

■ All Sectors   ▲ Electrical   ⊠ Motor
◆ Building   ● Engineering

Source: FÁS (2003).

As previously mentioned, the role of FÁS has changed through the years to meet the changing needs of the Irish economy. This has resulted in its involvement in a large number of training initiatives, which to a greater or lesser extent can be classified as FE. Not all of this provision is accredited. For instance, the building industry is coming under ever increasing scrutiny in the area of health and safety and FÁS has instituted a number of training programmes to meet some of the needs of the industry. It has devised and it delivers a number of short courses to meet such needs.

More relevant to this chapter are developments which are placing FÁS more and more in the FE sector and which reflect an increasing desire among individuals and employers to have training and development recognised and accredited. Thus FÁS offers more complex programmes for other sectors in conjunction with universities and other educational providers, and these are most certainly FE initiatives. To gauge the level of activity in this area I refer to the FÁS review of its activities for 2003. This report shows that about 22,000 unemployed persons completed FÁS training courses during 2003. In terms of training programmes, 10,800 completed training courses providing specific employable skills, while 3000 were early school leavers in Community Training Workshops. The remainder were on core or foundation skills courses leading either to employment or FE/training. About 58 per cent of these were female and about 10 per cent were persons with a disability. Follow-up surveys of

FÁS trainees show that 70 per cent are in employment or FE/training, and only one in five unemployed, a year after leaving FÁS. Including both completions and those still in training at the end of the year, FÁS provided training for 34,000 unemployed clients in 2003. FÁS also provided training for 2,700 company employees in its training centres and nearly 12,000 persons attended night courses.

In running programmes, FÁS works in co-operation with other bodies; for example the Retail Management Practice Certificate is operated in conjunction with the Irish Business and Employers' Confederation and the University of Ulster, and the Quality in Fish Processing programme is run in conjunction with BIM.

FÁS continues to make a major investment in safety training, in co-operation with the construction industry. A total of 132,000 workers obtained the Safe Pass certificate in 2003, making the total number of Safe Pass holders 315,000 to date. In addition, about 10,000 construction workers obtained construction skills certification in skills related to their employment.

The key to the success of FÁS is in its ongoing evaluation of its activities and how they meet the needs of the individual, employers and the economy generally. In its published plans for 2004, for instance, FÁS states that it will conduct a number of research studies to help inform training and education policy and planning. The first ever forecasts of employment broken down by occupation on a regional basis will be published by FÁS and the Economic and Social Research Institute early in 2005. Studies of skill needs and developments in the financial services, healthcare, software, and digital media areas will also be completed. FÁS has also agreed to support the OECD in undertaking an Irish country study of policies towards older workers. It is an organisation with a strategic view of the role of FE and training in sustaining Ireland's competitive advantage and will ensure through its actions that it will be a pivotal player in the future of the FE sector in Ireland.

Post-Leaving Certificate programmes

Having dealt with the institutions which play a major role in the Irish FE sector, in what some might refer to as work-based education, I will now concentrate on areas which some might refer to as mainstream or formal FE. One of the newest and fastest growing areas within the FE system in Ireland is what is referred to as Post-Leaving Certificate courses (PLCs).

These programmes are focused primarily on those students who have completed the senior cycle in the secondary system. Their objective generally lies in the provision of skills to meet the needs of the economy, but they also have a subsidiary goal of facilitating progression to further training and education, and to foster a culture of entrepreneurship, innovation, and adaptability amongst the students. According to the White Paper on education, *Charting Our Education* (DES, 1995), these courses were to be founded with a strong general education philosophy but would be directed towards:

- Technical knowledge – the development of the vocational skills needed for a particular discipline
- Personal development – the fostering of interpersonal skills, computer familiarisation and mathematical and literacy skills together with adaptability, initiative and a positive attitude to learning
- Work experience – providing the student with work experience, including structured on-the-job training, where feasible, which gives relevance to the skills she/he has learned and an appreciation of an adult's role in working life. (DES, 1995)

Recently published figures give a clear picture pertaining to the level of participation in this latter section of FE and of the phenomenal growth rate in the sector. From a base of 12,000 in 1989, it rose to 18,000 in 1995, and by 2003 in excess of 28,000 people were participating in these programmes. In the past this provision was designed as stand-alone courses, which were used as an entrée to the labour market and carried little or no recognised accreditation. They were first introduced in the mid-1980s and were viewed, using the sporting analogy, as the 'bronze medal' for school leavers, the gold being a place at university and the silver a place in an institute of technology. This description is not meant to laud the university sector or to denigrate the others. It is rather a reflection of the very overt snobbery associated with the educational system in Ireland. The programmes are generally of one- or two-year duration, offering general education and vocational training. They also encourage general skills, thus enhancing the employability of those who undertake the programmes.

The PLC provision has developed so extensively over the past few years that the report of the Expert Working Group (Council of Directors of the ITs, 2003) examining the future position and role of the ITs devoted an entire to chapter to this area. In this chapter the working group state:

> *The Post-Leaving Certificate (PLC)/Further Education (FE) sector has become an important provider of vocational education in Ireland during the last ten years. With a current enrolment of some 25,000 students throughout the country, the sector is providing valuable short course training (mainly one year) leading to fifty types of National Vocational Certificate award. In the main, certification is granted in disciplines which parallel to some extent, provision in the ITs. The courses are designed, specifically, to provide direct entry into the labour market on completion. However, more and more course design is being structured to cater for progression possibilities and to facilitate lifelong learning. The Links Scheme, implemented by the ITs since 1994, provided a coherent route into higher education from PLC courses.* (Council of Directors of the ITs, 2003)

Having noted the importance of the provision, the report goes on to make very clear recommendations as to how the link between the FE sector and the ITs should be developed. These recommendations include:

- The ITs need to articulate a vision that encompasses the highest possible level of cooperation with the PLC sector. This should aim to support course development, staff development and quality assurance/quality improvement in further education.
- ITs should look seriously at the possibility of closer regional association with PLC colleges through developing the concept of 'Associated Colleges'.
- All FETAC Level 11 awards (of whatever type) should be accepted as meeting minimum entry requirements.

While there are many instances of acknowledgement of the PLC provision, this is probably the most significant.

The Further Education and Training Awards Council (FETAC)

Post-Leaving Certificate programmes are only one element of FE and the entire activity within the sector is now under the control of FETAC, which, in addition to overseeing the entire sector, also validates the programmes. The true benefit of the FE system in Ireland is its twofold mission of (a) preparing people for the work environment, and (b) acting as a framework which provides educational links to the HE system.

A large proportion of the students coming to the FE sector come directly from the secondary system. Notwithstanding this fact, it is worth noting that 40 per cent of the people who undertake programmes are adults or mature students. Interestingly, while FETAC programmes are being undertaken by individuals who have failed to get a university or institute of technology place, there is an emerging trend (unfortunately not yet documented) of FETAC programmes being also used by graduates who wish to make a career change.

In addition to the individuals who pursue programmes of general education leading to an FETAC award, there are a number of specialised areas where other national bodies have arranged for FETAC to accredit their training programmes. These initiatives take place in areas such as the aforementioned fishing industry, the hospitality or tourism industry, and the agricultural sector.

The FE sector is one of the most important emerging forces within the Irish educational system. The key to this development is the vast array of programmes carrying FETAC accreditation. According to FETAC (2004), in its first report covering the period 2001–2003, the number of awards issued rose from 37,292 in 2001 to 81,770 in 2003. These figures are all the more impressive when viewed in the light of the fact that up until very recently the proportion of the population of Ireland with education only to primary level was 27 per cent (NDP, 2000). Recent reports show that this figure has risen dramatically and, according to Collins and Williams (1998) and McCoy *et al.* (2000) from the 1997 and 1998 *Annual Schools Leavers Surveys*, the number of students leaving with no qualifications is falling significantly.

The development so far under this new structure is an amazing achievement. It should be noted that FETAC was established only in June 2001 and in accordance with its most recent publication has made over 130,000 awards for programmes undertaken in over 200 locations throughout Ireland. In 2003 FETAC published a strategic plan for the period 2003–2006 in which it set out a clear vision and framework for its future work. It aims to develop a more progressive, inclusive and flexible award system for the education and training sector in Ireland. It is, according to FETAC, the outcome of a partnership process involving FETAC staff, FETAC council members, learners and key stakeholders.

This inclusive approach has already brought about a result which provides a solid infrastructure through which FE and training is delivered, its quality assured and benefits guaranteed. FETAC is, according to its strategic plan, working hard to implement the strategy in conjunction with the NQAI. And it is to this initiative which I will shortly turn my attention.

The emergence of the FE sector from the margins to centre stage in Ireland in the recent past is strongly linked to the establishment of FETAC and the energy that it has put into the development of the sector. Probably the most disappointing aspect of the development of FETAC is the slowness of the university sector to engage with it. As an example of this reluctance to engage, it is necessary to consider FETAC's Higher Education Links Scheme. This is a mechanism which enables learners who have achieved a FETAC (NCVA Level 2) award to apply for a place at a range of HE institutions. In 2004 there were over 2,000 of these places available on approximately 300 courses. In the FETAC guide to these courses, published in 2004, only four universities are listed as participating institutes and, with the exception of University College Cork, the offers are very limited. Of the 300 courses the universities account for only 19, and of these University College Cork contributes 13. There is little doubt that University College Cork is to be commended for its initiatives in this area, but even so it must also be borne in mind that the overall numbers involved are small.

The report of the Expert Working Group reviewing the future role of the ITs, as highlighted earlier, devoted a chapter to discussing the links between the FE sector and the ITs and outlined a set of recommendations to effect change. On the other hand, the Skilbeck Report (Skilbeck, 2001), which examined similar challenges faced by the university sector, offered little in relation to this issue. Although the topic was addressed in the chapter headed 'Differentiation and Diversification', regrettably the report did not make any firm recommendation on the matter.

National Qualifications Authority of Ireland (NQAI)

The significant developments that have taken place since the advent of FETAC, irrespective of how much energy FETAC had expended, would have generated little if it was not done in tandem with the establishment of the NQAI. This body has put considerable efforts into the development of a coherent qualifications strategy for Ireland. The NQAI was established on 26 February 2001 following the enactment of the Qualifications (Education and Training) Act, 1999 (Government of Ireland, 1999), which sets the following three principal objectives for the Authority:

- The establishment and maintenance of a framework of qualifications for the development, recognition and award of qualifications based on standards of knowledge, skill or competence to be acquired by learners;
- The establishment and promotion of the maintenance and improvement of the standards of awards of the further and higher education and training sector, other than any existing universities;
- The promotion and facilitation of access, transfer and progression throughout the span of education and training provision. (Government of Ireland, 1999)

According to the authority itself, it will achieve these objectives through actions on two fronts:

- Through the establishment and maintenance of a framework of qualifications which will facilitate the development of procedures for access, transfer and progression throughout education and training;
- In undertaking this work it will liase closely with the Further Education & Training Awards Council and the Higher Education Training Awards Council on their validation, award making and quality assurance processes. (NQAI, 2004)

NQAI did not linger too long and got straight to work on developing the strategy and a programme of action to achieve its aims and objectives.

The impact NQAI has had on the educational system within Ireland even within its short period of existence has been immense. It has been achieved by its concentration on two key issues: the establishment of a National Framework of Qualifications, and the promotion and facilitation of access, transfer, and progression. The first of these objectives was its principal focus and it was achieved by shifting the focus of the award system away from the providers of education and planting it firmly in the domain of the learner. The second key initiative, which has been the other cornerstone of NQAI's success, has been its policy of openness and ongoing and deep consultation with all of the stakeholders.

By refocusing the system back towards the learner, NQAI feels that the result will be a more diverse learner community throughout FE and HE and training. The number of adults in the educational system will be significantly increased, there will be more learners taking programmes on a flexible and part-time basis, and there will be a greater range of work-based education and learners with specific or special needs. However, NQAI has pointed out that to accommodate this new generation of learners, the current providers will have to adapt and change significantly because these new participants will require new mechanisms to enter FE. In addition, the practice of recognising prior learning and prior experiential learning will have to be extended significantly within the educational system to accommodate new learners, and the current relatively rigid manner in which awards are achieved will also have to be examined. The notion of signing on for nothing other than a four-year degree programme, for instance, will have to be modified significantly. The recognition and subsequent creation of a ladder of learning to facilitate these new learners will have to be implemented.

To facilitate the move to this newer and more flexible system and mechanisms, the NQAI has defined, developed, and now published the National Framework of Qualifications. In doing this, the NQAI has established what they refer to as:

> the single, nationally and internationally accepted entity, through which all learning achievements may be measured and related to each other in a coherent way and which defines the relationship between all education and training awards. (NQAI, 2003a)

In designing and developing this framework the underpinning strategy has been the creation of what I referred to previously as the 'continuum or ladder of learning'. Or, as NQAI has put it:

> the learner should be able to enter and successfully participate in a programme, or series of programmes leading to an award, or series of awards, in pursuit of their learning objectives. The National Framework of Qualifications and associated programme provision should be structured to facilitate learner entry, and to promote transfer and progression, so that learners are encouraged to participate in the learning process to enable them to realise their ambitions to the full extent of the abilities. (NQAI, 2003b)

NQAI, in publishing this new framework, recognises that there are much broader issues to be addressed than those of the formal educational system. The framework's overall aims are to facilitate the cultural, economic, political-democratic, and social participation of citizens in society as a whole and in their community by measuring, as appropriate, relevant learning achievements in this regard and relating them to each other. Thus it has set itself the goal of creating a programme of active citizenship which has, as its fundamental basis, the creation of mutually supporting objectives of personal fulfilment, democratic participation, social inclusion, adaptability, and accessibility. To explain the system, reproduced below is an outline produced by NQAI itself:

> *The National Framework of Qualifications is a radical development in Irish education and training. This learner-centred framework, which is transparent and readily understandable, relates all education and training awards made in Ireland to each other. In doing so, it brings coherence to the awards system. It establishes clearly-defined standards about the quality of awards and about what a learner can be expected to achieve for each award. The Framework is designed to bring about change. It introduces a new approach to the meaning of an award, that an award will recognise learning outcomes 'what a person with an award knows, can do and understands' rather than time spent on a programme. It also shifts the emphasis of the awards system from the maintenance of existing systems and structures to meeting the needs of learners. The need for a more flexible and integrated system of qualifications arises from the national objective of moving towards a 'lifelong learning society', in which learners will avail of learning opportunities at various stages throughout their lives. The diffuse nature of the existing qualifications systems does not easily support portability of recognition for learning. The strong separation of responsibility for education and training across a range of government Departments has been reflected in the separation of qualifications systems, with linked but separate arrangements for schools, further education, ITs, universities and a variety of training organisations. Another reason for change is the need for learners, employers and others to be able to compare Irish qualifications more easily and accurately with those from other countries. This is particularly important in the European context, where the Bologna and Copenhagen Declarations signal a move towards greater compatibility and comparability of qualifications. These Declarations*

concern European cooperation in higher education and in vocational education and training. (NQAI, 2003c)

The framework having been created, the next crucial phase in the development of the work of the NQAI was the establishment of a process for access, transfer and progression.

Access, transfer and progression

The real added value to all of the developments outlined previously will be if a system of transfer and progression is put in place to facilitate the learner as they attempt to navigate their way through the continuum of learning. Systems of transfer and progression have been in place for some time but they have been limited and not altogether transparent or user friendly. There had always been a system of transfer and progression from the FE sector to the ITs, and to a more limited extent there is a system in place for movement between the ITs and the university sector. This arrangement, while lauded on the one hand, was rounded criticised on the other as elitist and discriminatory, since the universities only took the highest performing students and in some instances gave little or no credit for the prior learning. This factor is highlighted in the *Final Report and Recommendations* of the Commission on the Points System (1999). The NQAI (2003b) has, through its publication of *The National Framework of Qualifications*, espoused a vision for a national system of recognition of awards:

> *The learner should be able to enter and successfully participate in a programme, or series of programmes, leading to an award, or series of awards, in pursuit of their learning objectives.*

The NQAI, in its technical paper dealing with this issue, states that this vision will be realised through actions that it, HETAC and FETAC will take. Interestingly, while all other sectors of the educational system will be expected to draft new procedures to achieve the desired outcomes, the university sector is only obliged to consider these procedures and their implementation will be reviewed by the NQAI.

Conclusion

Developments in the area of FE in Ireland have taken on a new momentum in recent years as the government has put in place a structure and institutions which have the power and the resources to effect change. These changes have come about not just through the desire of government to address issues, but through the commitment of social partners to have education as a central plank of the successive National Partnership Agreements, thus ensuring that the role of education in the social and economic development of the country is recognised.

The rate of change is, to say the least, phenomenal, and it now appears that a new system of awards is planned for the FE and training sectors of the educational system. The new system, when complete, will allow for a direct link to be established between PLCs, programmes delivered by FÁS, CERT, Teagasc, and the ten-level NQAI system. The stated aim of the new system is to make it easier for students, employers, and third-level institutions to judge the value of courses and awards.

The strides being made are exceptional and have significant benefits attached to them, but there are some negatives in the system. As evidenced by some major differences in the White Paper on Lifelong Learning and the Report of the Taskforce on Lifelong Learning there are certain tensions between the Departments of Education and Science and Enterprise, Trade and Employment. Whether real or perceived these issues need to be addressed and resolved. There is little doubt, however, that FE in Ireland has a bright and exciting future. Its true potential, though, will only be achieved if the current level of State commitment to and funding of the sector is maintained and increased. The momentum generated in the recent past will be hard to stop and so the prediction for the future has to be one of measured optimism.

Notes

[1] As this is the title most commonly used in Ireland to describe the organisation, I will use it throughout the chapter. The word 'teagasc' is an Irish language word which bears no relationship to the English title of the organisation. The word translates in English to 'the teaching', which in the context of this article seems most appropriate.

[2] It is my intention during the course of this section to use the term FÁS, an acronym for Foras Áiseanna Saothair, which is the Gaelic title for the authority. The acronym

'FÁS' is a word in its own right in the Irish language, which very appropriately translates to 'growth' or 'to grow', and hopefully the full significance of my decision to use FÁS will be justified at the conclusion of this section of the chapter.

References

BIM (Irish Fisheries Board) (2000) *An Integrated Training Plan for the Irish Seafood Industry 2000–2006*. Dublin: Bord Iascaigh Mhara (Irish Fisheries Board).

BIM (Irish Sea Fisheries Board) (1999–2003) *BIM Annual Reports 1999–2003*. Dublin : Bord Iascaigh Mhara (Irish Sea Fisheries Board).

Browne, P. (2003) *The Challenges Facing the Teagasc Education & Training Programme in National Conference on Agriculture Education* (Conference Proceedings). Dublin: Teagasc.

Collins, C. and Williams, J. (1998) *1997 Annual School Leavers Report*. Dublin: Department of Enterprise, Trade and Employment, Department of Educaiton and Science and the ESRI.

Commission on the Points System (1999) *Final Report and Recommendations*. Dublin: Stationery Office.

Council of Directors of the ITs (2003) *ITs and the Knowledge Society – Their Future Position and Roles*, Report of the Expert Working Group. Dublin: Council of Directors of the ITs.

Department of Education and Science (1992) *Education for a Changing World, Green Paper on Education*. Dublin: Stationary Office

Department of Education and Science (1995) *Charting Our Education Future, White Paper on Education*. Dublin: Stationery Office.

Department of Education and Science (2000) *Learning for Life, White Paper on Adult Education*. Dublin: Stationery Office.

Department of Enterprise, Trade and Employment (2001) *Report of the Taskforce on Lifelong Learning*. Dublin: Stationery Office.

Foras Áiseanna Saothair (FÁS) (2003) *FÁS Annual Report & Financial Statements 2003*. Dublin: FÁS.

Further Education and Training Awards Council (FETAC) (2003) *Strategic Plan 2003–2006*. Dublin: Further Education and Training Awards Council.

Further Education and Training Awards Council (FETAC) (2004) *First Report 2001–2003*. Dublin: Further Education and Training Awards Council.

Gleeson, J. (1998) 'A Consensus Approach to Policy-Making – The Case of the Republic of Ireland', in: I. Finlay, S. Niven, and S. Young (eds) *Changing Vocational Education and Training: An International Comparative Perspective*. London: Routledge.

Government of Ireland (1987) *Labour Services Act (1987)*. Dublin: Stationery Office.

Government of Ireland (1997) *Universities Act*. Dublin: Stationery Office.

Government of Ireland (1998) *Education Act*. Dublin: Stationery Office.

Government of Ireland (1999) *Qualifications Education and Training Act (1999)*. Dublin: Stationery Office.

Government of Ireland (2003) *Sustaining Progress: Social Partnership Agreement 2003–2005*. Dublin: Stationery Office.

Maguire, T. M. (2003) *Engendering Numeracy in Adults Mathematics Education with a*

Focus on Tutors, Ph.D. Thesis, University of Limerick, v. – M0010160LK.

McCoy, S. *et al.* (1999) *1998 Annual School Leavers Survey of 1996/97 Leavers*. ESRI with Department of Enterprise, Trade and Employment and Department of Education and Science, Dublin.

Murphy, M. and Coughlan, D. (2003) 'University Continuing Education in Ireland', in: M. Osborne and E. Thomas (eds) *Lifelong Learning in a Changing Continent*. Leicester: NIACE.

National Qualifications Authority of Ireland (NQAI) (2003a) *Policies and Criteria for the Establishment of the National Framework of Qualifications*. Dublin: National Qualifications Authority of Ireland.

National Qualifications Authority of Ireland (NQAI) (2003b) *A Framework for the Development, Recognition and Award of Qualifications in Ireland: Policies, Actions and Procedures for Access, Transfer and Progression for Learners*. Dublin: National Qualifications Authority of Ireland.

National Qualifications Authority of Ireland (NQAI) (2003c) *A Framework for the Development, Recognition and Award of Qualifications in Ireland: The National Framework of Qualification – An Overview*. Dublin: National Qualifications Authority of Ireland.

National Qualifications Authority of Ireland (NQAI) (2004) *Role and Functions of the Authority*. Online at: http://www.nqai.ie

OECD (1991) *Review of National Policies for Education: Ireland*. Paris: OECD.

Skilbeck, M. (2001) *The Universities Challenged: A Review of International Trends and Issues with Particular Reference to Ireland*. Dublin: The Higher Education Authority.

Teagasc (2002) *Annual Report*. Dublin: Teagasc.

Turner, T. (2002) 'Corporatism in Ireland: a comparative perspective', in: D. D'Art and T. Turner (eds) *Irish Employment Relations in the New Economy*. Dublin: Blackhall Publishing.

New Zealand tertiary education: Patterns and pathways

Helen Anderson

Introduction

The New Zealand tertiary education system is a perplexing arrangement of both discrete and overlapping elements which have each settled into position through a mixture of history, convention, politics, and sometimes shaped by insightful and innovative policy, research, and practice. There is a multiplicity of points of initiative across the sector, within institutions and at the level of the individual teacher – responding to the need to deliver excellence and engagement with the 'knowledge society' on the one hand, and addressing access and equity on the other, and if there was a third hand it would be dealing with articulation between institutions and sectors. This devolved approach produces much creative and inspired practice but leaves the system lacking in more than broad-brush direction and the parts of the system sitting awkwardly in relation to each other.

The origins of this somewhat fragmented system are found in political and economic trends. The traditional university-dominated, minimal participation sector of the 1970s when full employment was taken for granted gave way to neo-liberal government impetus during the 1980s and 1990s when the economy was more prone to frights. This produced a market-driven approach to sector development: functions expanded, fees increased, student loans appeared, and participation grew (Maani, 1997). With the advent of the coalition government now in its second term, participation has continued as a catch cry but there have also been attempts to increase direction. The current government has instituted reviews which have signalled an intent to provide more precisely articulated goals and priorities that may eventually be linked to funding (Ministry of Education, 2002; TEAC, 2000, 2001a, 2001b, 2001c).

Unlike the English, Australian or American systems, for example, the

New Zealand approach does not have a national set of articulations beyond generic entry qualifications for university degree study. Localisation is prominent and institutions carry multiple roles. Thus, students are advantaged in an ad hoc way and their pathways through post-compulsory education are frequently not well defined; this is particularly so if students have not benefited well from compulsory (secondary) education.

The New Zealand tertiary sector

The New Zealand post-compulsory education sector (described as the 'tertiary' sector) is made up of seven universities accounting for 36.1 per cent of the student population in 2002. The traditions and conventions of New Zealand universities have their origins in the British system, evolved into a recognisably local expression with the exception of one university of technology, which was originally a polytechnic. There are 19 polytechnics whose functions can be broadly described as providing applied studies with a vocational brief and traversing levels from postgraduate to beginner. The polytechnics are split between rural and urban localities and make up 35.2 per cent of the 2002 student population. The phenomenon of the late 1990s has been the growth of private training establishments (PTEs). Under marketisation during the 1990s (Fiske and Ladd, 2000) these institutions grew rapidly (18.6 per cent of all tertiary students in 2002). PTEs competed for public funding of tertiary study at the pre-degree level under a government-driven intent to create an education industry and to expand participation while employment became increasingly tied to qualifications. Within this trend grew a further element to the tertiary sector. *Wānanga* are institutions designed to provide tertiary education for Māori (New Zealand's indigenous people) (NZ Waitangi Tribunal, 1999). They show the greatest increase in participation. Wānanga included 11.8 per cent of all students in 2002. The smallest group in the sector (3.7 per cent of students in 2002) is colleges of education (teacher education) and their student numbers continue to decline. (All statistics are from Scott, 2003.)

Issues of equity and access

The traditions of 'equality of opportunity' are well grounded in the rhetoric of New Zealand education and are derived from the post-colonial view of the 'level playing field' as the fundamental concept in the expression of fair competition regardless of family status. While this is a long-held tradition it is also a long-held myth. The New Zealand education system was founded on the British traditions of availability to those who were seen to best benefit from academic training. A separate native schools system was set up to cater for Māori according to the needs projected for them by government. Within this tradition, students in compulsory education were rigorously examined to ensure that a narrow group of students progressed to secondary and tertiary education. The evidence of these well-worn tracks is apparent in the secondary schools today, to the extent that they are still referred to as traditional or mainstream when they cater for only a small proportion of students, less than 30 per cent of school leavers (Scott, 1996).

For the student who is well suited by the compulsory sector provisions and consequently achieves to expectation and gains a university entrance qualification, the pathway into tertiary study is clear and largely barrier free. Entrance to both university and polytechnic is well pathed for those who hold one of the university entrance equivalences; these students' aspirations are well supported by expectations, information, and across sector articulation. However, the greater number of potential students do not have a university entrance qualification. They are unqualified or partially qualified school leavers or mature students. Their pathways into tertiary studies are much less evident and are not necessarily supported by expectations, information, or systems of articulation, that are anything other than ad hoc (Butterworth and Butterworth, 1998; Maani, 1997).

A feature of the New Zealand tertiary system is open access for over 20 year-olds. In practice this is a limited benefit as significant numbers of faculties impose additional entry requirements. However, where it is in operation there remain the issues of preparedness and the high cost of failure both to the institution and the students. While this offers a 'dab' at opening access, it lacks finesse as a mode of increasing successful participation.

Very recent changes in participation rates demonstrate the effectiveness of the Wānanga and PTEs in increasing participation at the sub-degree level for traditionally under-represented minority groups. At this level Māori now participate above their population proportion for over 15 year-olds and *Pasifika* are just at their population proportion (Scott, 2003). Pasifika refers to those groups who are either born in the Pacific Islands which are proximate to New Zealand, or who are New

Zealand born but have a generational link with Samoa, Tonga, The Cook Islands, Nuie or Tokelau Islands. However, both Māori and Pasifika groups remain under-represented in degree studies. The question to be asked is whether this increased participation will result in any alteration of the relativities of participation by level of study. The absence of sector-wide articulation mitigates against this except in local instances of excellent practice.

A further issue is the way data is collected in New Zealand education. While participation statistics are freely available, retention and success statistics are not. This information is only available where institutions have systems to collect it and it is available at the institution level, not at the national level. Evidence from institutions indicates that attrition rates for Māori and Pasifika groups are significantly higher than for Asian and Pakeha (European New Zealanders). Thus, the pathways for many students across the education sectors are frequently barrier laden and may lead to unexceptional achievement for those students described as non-traditional (Anae *et al.*, 2002; Benseman, Nichol and Anderson, 2003).

This is a situation which cannot remain if a small country like New Zealand is to participate economically and socially in the international context. A tertiary system which operates a closed discourse exempts itself from the innovation and change that arrives with unfamiliar cultures and the consequent challenges to comfortable ways of thinking. Instances of excellent practice abound, but not by across-sector policy and resourcing.

Assessment and qualification reforms

Post-World War II, the New Zealand education system offered a set of provisions that were based on clearly defined sectors with formal examinations at key exit points. The system took a more egalitarian approach by finally abolishing native schools (1969) but the examinations had a clear gate-keeping function with regard to progression (Simon and Smith, 2001).

Apart from the introduction of a nominally internally assessed year 12 qualification in the 1970s the system remained examination driven into the late 1980s. At this point reform accelerated (Butterworth and Butterworth, 1998; The University of Waikato, 1988). The reforms that followed were in part driven by a perception that the lack of articulation in and across the education sectors was impacting on the transferability of qualifications outside of the traditional examinations. A large number of independent qualifications were developing, generally with an industry base where academic qualifications seemed irrelevant. This was also a time of growing unemployment, and keeping school leavers in the education system and off unemployment benefit was evident as a motive. A national qualifications framework was developed to house competency-based unit standards. This system was intended to provide universal levels descriptors across the secondary and tertiary systems, provide more accessible learning for those failing formal examinations, and to exert some pressure on independent groups such as universities and industry groups to conform to a national system (TAMU, 2003).

The outcome was the continuation of the two-tiered system, which placed greater value on academic, examination-based qualifications. The less-valued vocational/trade/technology disciplines took to unit standards as a way of providing a qualification base, if a less valued one. The proliferation of qualifications which ensued exacerbated the lack of coherence in the secondary–tertiary interface and in the interfaces between various tertiary providers. The educational needs of some groups were met, but not by design.

These experiences did not spell the end to system reform. The next iteration was the introduction of achievement standards at years 11, 12, and 13 of the secondary system in an attempt to standardise qualification structures and assessment styles in the secondary school (Black, 2002). This initiative, National Certificates in Education Achievement (NCEA), offered at three levels, is current with year 13 joining the system in 2004. Achievement standards offer a mix of internal and external assessments and are assessed against predetermined standards rather than through the previous system of competitive examinations. The intent of this initiative is to identify the standards required of all students, while still acknowledging excellence through the establishment of pass, merit, credit standards. Entry to tertiary study is now described by the number of credits obtained with some subject requirements identified for specialised disciplines (Ministry of Education, 2003b). This attempt to 'flatten' the system was set alongside the unit standards already developed and placed on the framework. This has been done by allowing unit standards credits to be accumulated alongside the achievement standards toward the three generic national certificates (Ministry of Education, 2003b). While this seems to have some merit in terms of coherence, there are frequent complaints that the unit standards are easier than the achievement standards, that the levels for each are mismatched and, critically, articulation with tertiary providers works best for those who are headed on the academic, university degree path.

Pressures to maintain a competitive system came from many directions. The universities opposed a simplified achievement standards approach with no distinctions, as did a range of secondary schools, notably including those serving areas of high socio-economic status. The results slips for students now show a percentage and a rank indicator, as well as credits. While NCEA has shifted the description of achievement from competitive grades to numbers of credits and some commonality of descriptors is emerging, entrance qualifications to tertiary study under the new system are still bedding in and it may take some time for the impacts of the reformed assessment and qualifications procedures on articulation to become evident (TAMU, 2003).

Student support systems

There are two main forms of student support in the New Zealand tertiary education system. Most students are eligible for student loans to pay for fees and living expenses which are interest free during the time of study, to be repaid after study is complete and the student's income reaches a regulated threshold. Student allowances are available, subject to income testing. A very small group of students are provided with fee-free tertiary study and an associated allowance contingent on groupings of factors including minimum prior qualifications, age, and ethnicity. Further, students who are recipients of a single-parent benefit are eligible for fee relief. The support systems are relatively non-discriminating with regard to issues of access and equity and produce a very high take up of repayable student loans across all groups, with 56 per cent of eligible students taking loans in 2001 and rising (Ministry of Education, 2001). Non-repayable students allowances reached 17 per cent of students enrolled in formal tertiary education in 2001 (Ministry of Education, 2001).

Initiatives to increase articulation

Curriculum alignment

During the 1990s there was significant development in secondary schools of curriculum provisions for a wider group of students than the traditional preparation for the university stream. These developments were innovative and wide-ranging in content and form. At the same time, polytechnics widened their offerings in response to the changing nature of education and training needs, a shift to much higher participation in tertiary education, and tertiary education was opened to market forces. These changes in both sectors occurred rapidly and frequently without across-sector co-ordination (Butterworth and Butterworth, 1998), and affected the disciplines that are variously described as 'non-traditional' or vocational. These disciplines carry less prestige in the curriculum but offer a significant contradiction in terms of economic value by including such areas as travel and tourism, and technology, which are at the forefront of national development.

These changes generated greater opportunities for tertiary education and workforce participation for many students and acted as barriers for others, simply because of the fragmented development of the curriculum and attendant qualification offerings at the interface of the secondary–tertiary sectors.

The key issues are the link between education, employment, and access to income, and the flow-on effects for economic and social development. Consequently, it is critical that students stay at secondary school to obtain the highest qualification within their reach, and then make a transition to tertiary education with as few barriers as possible.

Curriculum alignment refers to collaboration between secondary schools and tertiary providers with regard to curriculum pathways. The first step is to identify curriculum strands which are common to both. This is followed by definition of the pathways between schools and tertiary institutions. Next, anomalies and misalignments are identified. The resolution of these anomalies is then negotiated to remove barriers to progression to tertiary study. The basic principle of negotiation is that the curriculum interface between schools and tertiary institutions becomes aligned and clearly communicated for mutual benefit. While the need for such projects raises issues, the effects are entirely positive in terms of student benefit and the reconstructing of relationships between secondary and tertiary teaching staff.

Projects to establish effective curriculum alignment are one of the most 'common sense' initiatives in recent times. They are also one of the most potent reminders of failure to develop constructive national policy at critical moments in sector development. The front end research for these projects has identified extraordinary misalignments between secondary schools and their local tertiary providers so that any sense of articulation between the sectors beyond the traditional 'school to university' track is banished and clearly in need of change (Anderson, 2003).

Strategies such as Gateway, Modern Apprenticeships, and STAR programmes are developments intended to clarify pathways from school to further study and work. That these activities have suffered from ad hoc implementation and a lack of coherent alignment across the relevant curricula is beginning to be recognised and may have their effectiveness increased as a result.

Bridging education/foundation studies

The story of the New Zealand tertiary education system is frequently one of sparkling innovation driven by the system's lack of functionality with regard to pathways to accommodate the diversity of students' learning histories and aspirations. Bridging education fits into this category, and serves to capture the talent that is evident across groups who have not been well fostered in the secondary system.

Bridging education is the term used in New Zealand to describe educational programmes for students who want to access tertiary education but do not have the traditional credentials/qualifications required for entry. Bridging education is a relatively new field in New Zealand but a substantial literature of practice, theory and research has been developed internationally. The New Zealand literature is growing and there are substantial examples of successful practice (Anderson, 2001a, 2001b, 2002; Ministry of Education, 2000, 2001).

Bridging education has had a presence in the New Zealand tertiary education system for at least 25 years. One of the first programmes was the University of Auckland's New Start Programme, followed in the mid-1980s by Manukau Institute of Technology's Introduction to Higher Education, and now called Foundation Education (Coltman, 2002). More recently, a survey of bridging provisions (Benseman and Russ, 2001) identified pro-grammes in most of New Zealand's tertiary education institutions (TEIs) and growing provision in the newer private training enterprise (PTE) sector. These programmes are designed to provide opportunity for adults who are underprepared and/or second chance learners to access tertiary study as part of a pathway to meet their career goals. These programmes offer academic and life skills preparatory work where student's career goals are beyond their current skills and qualifications.

In the last three years, tertiary institutions in Auckland have begun to work together to share practice, to increase the profile of bridging education, and to make submissions to the Ministry of Education and related commissions to increase awareness of bridging education and to have it included in Ministry policy development. These efforts have been very successful and bridging education has become a significant part of policy development as both 'Bridging' and 'Foundation Skills' and is discussed at length in the TEAC reports (2000/01) and in *The Tertiary Education Strategy* (Ministry of Education, 2002).

Further acknowledgement and support of the bridging function in tertiary education depends on the development of a literature, which extends beyond the current programme based and anecdotal writings which have provided the first layer of an academic framework. The Benseman and Russ (2001) survey was the first attempt to scope the field and there has been some work on theory development. Advancing the field now depends on shifting the focus of the literature to research, which will identify and quantify the economic and social impacts of bridging education in a rigorous way within the New Zealand context.

Adult and community education

Many secondary schools, as well as polytechnics and universities, offer informal, non-assessed programmes for mature students. These programmes vary from hobby and interest classes through to technology and language classes. There has been a significant tradition of this kind of learning in New Zealand and its value has been acknowledged by ring-fenced ministry funding amounting to 2 per cent of the system resource (Working Group, 2003b). Adult and community education (ACE) reflects an egalitarian tradition which sits outside formal education and has education for all as its premise. It also functions as a pathway for adults returning to or commencing study in the formal context.

Institutional co-operation

Although not common, there are some innovative agreements between institutions to provide shared or complementary qualifications. A prominent example of this is the agreement made between a suburban polytechnic located in one of New Zealand's least affluent localities and a city university. In this agreement three of the universities degrees are taught on the polytechnic site. The interesting element in terms of articulation is that students progress from the polytechnic bridging programme on to university degree programmes by agreement between the institutions on the level of achievement and curriculum content on the bridging programme. In other examples, first year university degree papers are located at remote polytechnics to enable students to begin their degree studies close to home and then transfer to the university locality when progress is assured.

Shifts in policy

There have been several policy initiatives implemented recently or under development which come from the Minister of Education's determination to 'steer' the system in a way more positively linked with the economic needs of the country, while protecting diversity, flexibility and responsiveness.

The Minister of Education has issued a set of education strategies which reflect the government's intent to provide direction for the tertiary system. These strategies include a focus on foundation learning and the participation of Māori and Pasifika. Subsequently, a set of priorities from within the strategy has been published to identify elements requiring immediate attention (Ministry of Education, 2003c).

The most prominent of these initiatives is the requirement for institutions to develop charters and profiles. In their early stages these are intended to provide a frame for rationalising and articulating the tertiary system through documentation which describes the institutions 'mission' and priorities within national guidelines. There have been signals that these may be linked to funding in the future (Working Group, 2003c).

Policy development work is underway on the identification and strengthening of foundation learning, including reviewing funding categories (Ministry of Education, 2003a). There is also ongoing work on an incentive component in institutions' funding eligibility for the completion of qualifications (Working Group, 2003a).

These moves signal clear steps away from a market-driven sector and an intent to manage the balance of provisions as well as clarifying the pathways across and into the tertiary sector. There is no overt sign of a shift from the parallel provision of unarticulated programming but there is an overt attempt to make tertiary study more accessible, particularly to groups who have not traditionally participated.

Conclusion

Steve Maharey, the government minister responsible for tertiary education, addressed the inaugural conference of the New Zealand Association of Bridging Educators 2001. He noted that on taking office he was faced with a system that lacked policy and research to inform direction regarding the bridging and foundation functions of the tertiary system (Anderson, 2001b). On his return in 2002 he described a raft of proposals intended to build capability and direction with regard to pathways for students entering and traversing the system (Anderson, 2002). There remains the problem of achieving the delicate balance between rationalising the system into a coherent and articulated set of provisions and pathways, without losing the existing capacity to startle with innovation and surprise with insight into the difficult task of creating equity, access, and expansion of the talent pool to meet the needs of a small country participating in the economic and social community of the world.

References

Anae, M., Anderson, H., Benseman, J. and Coxon, E. (2002) *Pacific Peoples and Tertiary Education Issues of Access*. Report to the NZ Ministry of Education. NZ: Ministry of Education.

Anderson, H. (2001a) 'Bridging Education: A critical element in New Zealand's educational future. Where have we been and where are we going?', in: H. Anderson (ed.) *Bridging Education in New Zealand. Proceedings of the Inaugural Conference of the New Zealand Association of Bridging Educators*. NZ: Manukau Institute of Technology.

Anderson, H. (ed.) (2001b) *Bridging Education in New Zealand. Proceedings of the Inaugural Conference of the New Zealand Association of Bridging Educators*. NZ: Manukau Institute of Technology.

Anderson, H. (ed.) (2002) *Bridging Education in New Zealand. Proceedings of the Inaugural conference of the New Zealand Association of Bridging Educators*. NZ: Manukau Institute of Technology.

Anderson, H. (2003) *Secondary Tertiary Curriculum Alignment Update January 2003 Technical Report*. NZ: Manukau Institute of Technology.

Benseman, J., Nichol, J. and Anderson, H. (2003) 'Recruitment is but the first step: lessons in retention from access strategies in New Zealand', in: L. Thomas, M. Cooper and J. Quinn (eds) *Improving Completing Rates Among Disadvantaged Students*. London: Trentham Books.

Benseman, J. and Russ, L. (2001) 'Mapping the territory: a national survey of Bridging Education', in: H. Anderson (ed.) *Bridging Education in New Zealand. Proceedings of the Inaugural conference of the New Zealand Association of Bridging Educators*. NZ: Manukau Institute of Technology.

Black, P. (2002) *Report to the Qualifications Development Group on the Proposals for the Development of the NCEA*. Online at: www.minedu.govt.nz

Butterworth, G. and Butterworth, S. (1998) *Reforming Education: The New Zealand Experience 1984–1996*. NZ: Dunmore.

Coltman, D. (2002) *Annual Report*. NZ: Manukau Institute of Technology.

Fiske, E. B. and Ladd, H. F. (2000) *When Schools Compete*. Washington, DC: The Brookings Institution Press.

Maani, S. A. (1997) *Investing in Minds: The Economics of Higher Education in New Zealand*. Wellington: The Institute of Policy Studies, Victoria University.

Ministry of Education (2000) *New Zealand Tertiary Education Sector: Profiles and Trends*. NZ: Ministry of Education.

Ministry of Education (2001) *New Zealand Tertiary Education Sector. Profiles and Trends*. NZ: Ministry of Education.

Ministry of Education (2002) *The Tertiary Education Strategy*. Wellington: Ministry of Education.

Ministry of Education (2003a) *Funding Review Paper 5*. Online at: www.minedu.govt.nz

Ministry of Education (2003b) *NCEA Communications*. Online at www.minedu.govt.nz

Ministry of Education (2003c) *Statement of Tertiary Priorities 2003/04*. NZ: Ministry of Education.

New Zealand Waitangi Tribunal (1999) *The Wānanga Capital Establishment Report*. Wellington: GP Publications.

Scott, D. (1996) *The Currie Commission: A Report on Education in New Zealand*. Unpublished Ph.D. thesis, The University of Auckland.

Scott. D. (2003) *Participation in Tertiary Education*. NZ: Ministry of Education.

Simon, J. and Smith, L. T. (2001) *A Civilising Mission*. NZ: AUP.

TAMU (2003) *NZQA Functions and Responsibilities*. Online at: www.minedu.govt.nz

TEAC (2000) *Shaping a Shared Vision*. Wellington: Tertiary Education Advisory Commission.

TEAC (2001a) *Shaping the Funding Framework*. Tertiary Education Advisory Commission.

TEAC (2001b) *Shaping the Strategy*. Wellington: Tertiary Education Advisory Commission.

TEAC (2001c) *Shaping the System*. Wellington: Tertiary Education Advisory Commission.

The University of Waikato (1988) *Structure of Tertiary Education in New Zealand: An Alternative to the Hawke Report*. Hamilton: University of Waikato.

Working Group (2003a) *Papers of the Performance Element of the Student Component Working Group*. Online at www.minedu.govt.nz

Working Group (2003b) *Paper 3 of the Funding Category Review*. Online at: www.minedu.govt.nz

Working Group (2003c) *Report of the Charters and Profiles Working Group*. Online at: www.minedu.govt.nz

Complementarity or differentiation? The roles of further education colleges and higher education institutions in Scotland's higher education system

Jim Gallacher

Introduction

Scotland now has a mass higher education (HE) system, with an Age Participation Index of 51.5 per cent.[1] However, the HE system is an increasingly complex and differentiated one, and the sector which is known as the further education (FE) colleges sector now makes a significant and distinctive contribution. This has reflected a change in the role of these colleges from one in which 'non-advanced' vocational education and training provision (VET) was central, to a situation in which many of the colleges have increasingly become 'community colleges', providing for a wide range of educational needs in the communities which they serve. Within this context there has been an increasing emphasis on the role of widening access to education for groups traditionally excluded from post-compulsory education, and on supporting policies designed to promote social inclusion. At the same time the former 'polytechnic' or more vocationally oriented higher institutions have been integrated into the university sector, to create a more unified system of higher educational institutions (HEIs). As a result, Scotland now has a tertiary system in which distinctions between the vocational and academic sectors have become more blurred. There are strong links between the FE colleges (FECs) and HEIs, and the FECs are increasingly seen as a route into degree-level study for many students. However, despite an increasing policy interest in strengthening the links between the two sectors (Scottish Executive, 2003a; Scottish Parliament, 2002), these developments have been largely unplanned, and their impact continues to be uneven. As a result, some critics have described these developments as creating an academic ghetto, in which opportunities for disadvantaged 'non-traditional' students continue to be limited (Field, 2004; Osborne *et al.* 2000). In this chapter we will consider the extent to which we now have in Scotland two systems which complement each other, or an increasingly differentiated HE system, and the implications of these issues for policy regarding post-compulsory education and training.

The growth of HE within the Scottish FE colleges

During the last 15 to 20 years there has been a steady growth in HE provision in Scotland's FE colleges. This is demonstrated by the figures presented in Table 1. It can be seen from this table that while students enrolled on FE level or 'non-advanced' courses continue to represent by far the majority of students in this sector, HE level provision has grown more rapidly over this period, and it now comprises a far higher proportion of provision than in the past. This reflects the changing role of these colleges, which has been referred to above and will be discussed further below.

It can be seen from Table 1 that while the total number of students enrolled in FE colleges increased by 118 per cent over the period 1985/6 to 2000/01, the numbers participating in HE programmes increased by 141 per cent. These students are mainly enrolled on Higher National

Table 1. Students enrolled in FE colleges by level and mode.

	1985–86	1990–91	1995–96	2000–01
FE level courses				
F/T	30,374	27,500	30,709	41.444
P/T	114,817	199,600	194,130	188,495
HE level courses				
F/T	6,996	9,431	25,328	31,293
P/T	23,029	23,722	35,390	41,168
Total	175,216	260,253	285,557	302,400

Note: These figures exclude students registered on non-vocational courses.
Source: SOEID (1998) and SFEFC (2001)

Certificates (HNCs), Higher National Diplomas (HNDs), and other vocationally oriented programmes validated by the Scottish Qualification Authority (SQA). These can be seen as short-cycle programmes; an HNC is a one-year programme for full-time students, while an HND is a two-year programme. Many of these programmes continue to have strong vocational focus; however, a number are increasingly academic in content, an issue which will be discussed further later on.

As a result of this growth, FE colleges are now major providers of HE at undergraduate level in Scotland. In 2001/02 29 per cent of all HE level undergraduate students in Scotland were enrolled in FE colleges (Scottish Executive, 2003b).[2]

This growth has been associated with wider changes in the role and function of FE within the post-compulsory sector. These changes have led to an enhanced status for the FE sector, and within the present political climate FE colleges in Scotland are clearly viewed as key institutions in widening access, promoting social inclusion and providing opportunities for lifelong learning (Scottish Office, 1999; Scottish Parliament, 2002).

A number of major developments which have helped bring about significant change in the FE sector over the last 15 years can be identified. In the post-World War II era colleges had become increasingly important providers of education and training for a wide range of employees, particularly at craft or technician level in many industries. Most of these courses were provided on a part-time evening, day release, or block release basis, and led to a range of vocational qualifications. However, as many of the traditional industries have diminished in size and importance, and in some cases completely disappeared, the provision of training for employees in these industries has become far less important. As a result, colleges have had to seek new markets. This process, while they continued to have a strong interest in vocationally oriented education, was increasingly focused on different target groups.

This concern to find new markets also coincided with a movement within government policy in the 1980s and early 1990s to introduce market principles to education, and to give 'customers' a more central role in influencing the type of programmes provided within colleges. This led to proposals in the early 1990s to remove colleges from local authority control, and establish them as free-standing corporate bodies with their own budgets and employing their own staff. This was presented in the 1991 White Paper as an important means of giving them 'freedom to innovate and respond quickly to the needs of their customers' (Scottish Office, 1991, p. 27, 7.3), and was seen as an alternative to the situation in which the local authorities had a major influence over the development of provision. The funding system also changed at this time, with colleges now working on the basis of independent budgets, provided initially through the Scottish Office, and more recently through the Scottish Further Education Funding Council (SFEFC), plus any other sources they could identify, such as the European Social Fund (ESF), Scottish Enterprise, through the local enterprise companies (LECs),[3] and income from private industry for courses which they provided. The necessity to secure an adequate flow of funds from a variety of sources, and through targeting a wide range of student groups, became a major priority for many colleges as they struggled to maintain their financial security in this competitive economic climate. One impact of these changes has been rapid growth in certain types of provision when it was felt that the market would support this growth. One area of particular significance in this respect has been the growth of new areas of HE provision, through Higher National Certificates (HNCs) and Higher National Diplomas (HNDs), including the growth of new areas of full-time HND and HNC provision.

This growth in HE provision in the FE sector has also been supported by a number of related developments. One of these was the establishment of the Scottish Vocational Educational Council (SCOTVEC). Within this new organisation the provision of vocational education and training was substantially re-shaped. The modular National Certificate system was introduced in 1985 to create a more flexible and responsive system for non-advanced vocational education, while a new structure for HNCs, and HNDs was introduced based on a unitised framework of provision.

These new structures were designed to provide colleges with greater flexibility to develop provision which was responsive and relevant to local markets as well as providing vocational qualifications which would be recognised and valued at the national level. This system provided by SCOTVEC, and more recently the Scottish Qualifications Authority (SQA), which has now replaced it, has enabled colleges to work within a national system of development, validation and certification, and to develop their own programmes of HE which are distinct from and independent of the HE institutions. This appears to have been an important factor in encouraging and sustaining the rapid growth of higher national (HN) provision in the FE sector during the 1990s. This was also supported by a funding system within the Scottish Office which encouraged growth within the FE sector during the early 1990s, and the provision of financial support for students which encouraged the development of full-time HNCs and HNDs in addition to the part-time programmes which had traditionally been an important part of vocational education and training.

Another element contributing to the growth of HE within colleges was the growing emphasis on widening access to FE and HE, which emerged in the second half of the 1980s. This led to the establishment of the Scottish Wider Access Programme (SWAP) in 1987. SWAP brought together the universities, colleges, and local authorities to work collaboratively in developing and providing programmes which would enable adult returners to prepare for and gain access to HE. Colleges were given a key role as the providers of access courses. As a result of SWAP, and similar developments, work with adult returners became an important priority for many colleges in the late 1980s and early 1990s, and there was a large growth in the numbers of adult returners who were participating in a variety of programmes.

This interest within the colleges in widening access and providing opportunities for adult students to return to education was further reinforced by the impact of a series of major reports and policy documents which appeared in the late 1990s. While some of these were published (Kennedy, 1997) or commissioned (NCIHE, 1997a, b) before the Labour Government came to office, they can all be seen as part of the growing emphasis on establishing a 'learning society', and the conditions which will promote 'lifelong learning' which this government emphasised in its educational policy (Fryer, 1997; Scottish Executive, 2003a; Scottish Office, 1998). Within this lifelong learning agenda colleges have been recognised as having a central role in Scotland, and more generally within the UK.

In the context of these policy developments the NCIHE report *Higher Education in the Learning Society* (Dearing Report), and the Scottish sub-report (the Garrick Report) further reinforced the importance of the FE in developing HE in the 'learning society' (NCIHE, 1997a, b). In particular, the Garrick Report emphasised the importance of the links between colleges and HEIs in the development of HE, and recommended that 'colleges and HEIs should actively collaborate to enhance and publicise access and articulation routes into degree programmes for students at further education colleges' (NCIHE, 1997b, p. 49, section 4.62 and Recommendation 7). In these reports we can therefore see an emphasis on the role of colleges in the development of a mass system of HE for the UK. In particular the role of these colleges in widening access, and the importance of working in collaboration with other educational providers and other agencies to provide sub-degree level, vocationally relevant HE is emphasised.

In addition to these external factors encouraging the growth of HE provision, there was also evidence that many adult students who returned, initially to undertake relatively short part-time courses, gradually progressed to more demanding full-time provision at HE level (Gallacher *et al.*, 1997). This encouraged colleges to see this as an important area of work, and acted as a further incentive for colleges to develop HN provision to meet this demand.

What is the role of the FE sector as a provider of HE in Scotland?

The type of HE level provision in the Scottish FE colleges is distinctive, and reflects the history of provision within this sector. Firstly, it can be noted that most of this provision is short-cycle HE, based on HN units, while only 3 per cent of students are enrolled on undergraduate degree programmes, which have been developed in co-operation with the universities (Table 2). Almost two-thirds of HE students in FE colleges (46,164) are enrolled on HNC or HND programmes. A further 15 per cent (10,840) are enrolled on a variety of certificate and diploma programmes, a number of which are professional development awards (PDAs). These awards are linked to professional development in a wide range of occupations including childcare, construction, graphic design, and management. Many of them make use of HN units. A further substantial group of students (15 per cent) are not registered on any programme, but are taking only one or more HN units.

HN programmes also continue to be distinctive in the range of programmes which are provided. As might be expected, given their origins, there is a strong vocational orientation in these programmes. Some indication of this can be seen in Table 4 which lists the top ten HNC and HND programmes on the basis of entries for these awards in 2001. While these are only ten of the numerous HNC or HND programmes available, they do account for almost 50 per cent of all entrants (53 per cent of HNCs and 45 per cent of HNDs). However, it can also be noted in Table 4 that, in addition to the strongly vocationally oriented programmes, Social Sciences is now included in the top ten programmes for both HNCs and HNDs. These programmes have a more academic orientation, and many students use them as a stepping-stone towards a degree programme. This use of HN programmes, as academic rather than vocational qualifications, is also increasingly true for a number of other

Table 2. Students on undergraduate HE level courses in Scottish FE colleges 2000–01.

Type of course	Number of students	Percentage of all HE level students in FECs
First degree	2324	3
Professional body qualification	1304	2
Scottish Vocational qualifications Levels 4 & 5	908	1
HND or equivalent	19,358	27
HNC or equivalent	26,806	37
Other HN level Dips or Certs	10,840	15
HN Units only	10,921	15
Total	72,461	100

Note: The data presented in this table are drawn from the SFEFC Infact Database, available through the SFEFC website: http://www.sfefc.ac.uk/infact/

Source: SFEFC (2002)

programmes, such as Business Administration. This reflects an important change in the use of the HN courses by many students, and will be discussed further below.

Table 3. Top ten HNC and HND programmes on the basis of entries, 2001.

HNCs		HNDs	
Computing	1708	Business Administration	752
Social Care	1318	Computing: Support	571
Child Care and Education	1253	Computing: Software Development	528
Business Administration	999	Accounting	505
Administration and Information Management	988	Social Sciences	436
Accounting	796	Administration and Information Management	431
Social Sciences	534	Beauty Therapy	352
Management	341	Sports Coaching with Sports Development	321
Engineering: Mechatronics	336	Travel with Tourism	308
Engineering: Electronics	323	Graphic Design	255

Source: SQA (2002)

While there are some similarities between the range of programmes provided in the FE colleges and those provided in the HEIs, there are also important differences. With respect to similarities, Business and Administrative Studies is the single largest subject group within the HEIs, with 16 per cent of all students, and Social Studies and Engineering and Technology, with 11 per cent and 8 per cent respectively, are also important subject groups (SHEFC, 2002). When differences in the range of programmes offered are considered it can be noted that the second largest subject group within the HEIs is Subjects Allied to Medicine with 12 per cent of all students, and Humanities and Languages together account for 9 per cent of all students. However, no similar programmes exist within the FE sector. Similarly, the HEIs are the sole providers of programmes in the professional areas of medicine and dentistry.

An important feature of HE provision in the FE colleges is the extent to which part-time provision remains the dominant mode, despite an important growth in full-time provision over the past ten years or so (Table 4). It can be seen from the data presented in Table 4 that 57 per cent of all undergraduate HE students in FE colleges are part time, and on this basis it can be calculated that while students in FE colleges account for 29 per cent of all Scottish HE undergraduates, they account for 61 per cent of all part-time undergraduate students.

Within the FE sector part-time study is particularly common among students on HNCs (58 per cent) and students studying for other certificates and diplomas (86 per cent). This reflects the continuing tradition of undertaking study while in employment, as part of continuing professional development. However, it must be noted that only 14 per cent of FE students on HE level courses are studying through a block release or day release arrangement, and only 1 per cent are recorded as being on programmes which are based on the assessment of work-based learning. A substantial number of these students (20 per cent) are

Table 4. Undergraduate students in HE in Scotland, 2001–02, by mode of attendance and sector.

	HEIs	FECs	Total
Full-time	122,602 (78%)	27,592 (43%)	150,194 (68%)
Part-time	33,936 (22%)	36,032 (57%)	69,968 (32%)
Total	156,538	63,624	220,162

Source: Scottish Executive (2003b)

attending at the evenings or weekends, while 10 per cent are studying through some distance or open learning mode (SFEFC, 2002). It should also be noted that in both the FEC and HEI sectors many part-time students are not completing programmes which lead to qualifications such as HNC/Ds or degrees, but are undertaking study which may only consist of one or two units or modules, or a short course of some kind.

However, while these part-time programmes remain a strong feature of HN provision within the colleges, the recent growth of full-time HN courses must also be noted. Table 1 indicates that the numbers enrolled on full-time HE level courses increased by 347 per cent over the period 1985/6 to 1999/00, while the overall growth of HE level provision was only 141 per cent. This growth has been particularly concentrated in HND programmes, where 90 per cent of students are full time. However, there has also been an important growth of full-time HNC programmes, where 42 per cent of students are now full time (SFEFC, 2002).

Social characteristics of HE students studying in Scottish FE colleges

FE colleges also differ from the HEIs in terms of the social characteristics of the students they attract, and in this respect an important issue is the role of the colleges in providing opportunities for a wider cross section of the community to participate in HE. This is illustrated in Table 5, which shows that a higher proportion of students in the colleges are older than those in the HEI sector. In 2000–01 55 per cent of HE students in FE colleges were aged 25 or older, while only 32 per cent of these students were under 21. By contrast, only 27 per cent of undergraduate students in HEIs were over 25, while 45 per cent were under 21 (Scottish Executive, 2003b). These differences in the age profiles partly reflect the large numbers of part-time working students in the FECs. In both the FEC and HEI sectors, as could be expected, the proportions of older students among those who are studying part time are far higher than among those studying full time. Thus 73 per cent of all part-time students in FECs are aged 25 or over, while 84 per cent of part-time students in HEIs are also in this age group.

The age profile of these college students, and particularly the ones on full-time programmes, reflects interesting issues about the role of the colleges as providers of opportunities for study at HE level. In the first place it can be noted that, while the role of the colleges with respect to

Table 5. Undergraduate students in HE in Scotland, 2000–01, by age, mode of attendance, and sector.

	Full-time		Part-time		All undergraduates	
	HEIs	FECs	HEIs	FECs	HEIs	FECs
20 & under	54%	55%	4%	15%	45%	32%
21–24	32%	15%	11%	12%	28%	13%
25–29	6%	9%	14%	15%	7%	13%
30 & over	8%	21%	70%	58%	20%	42%
Total number of students	116,253	31,293	26,378	41,168	142,631	72,461

Source: Scottish Executive (2003b)

older students has been emphasised, a majority of the students (55 per cent) on full-time programmes are aged 20 or under. Relatively little is known about these students, or their reasons for opting for an FEC rather than an HEI. However, there is evidence that school leavers entering HN courses in FECs are less well qualified than entrants to HEIs (Ticklin and Raffe, 1999). There is also some evidence that relatively high percentages of school leavers who enter HE from areas of social deprivation, and from schools with low levels of participation in HE, are likely to participate in courses in FE colleges (Forsyth and Furlong, 2004).

When the role of the colleges with respect to older students is considered, there is evidence that the colleges are providing a route back into education for many older students who do not have traditional educational qualifications. It appears that many of these students progress in a gradual and often tentative way, from shorter courses to longer courses as their confidence and commitment gradually increases (Gallacher *et al.*, 1997; Gallacher *et al.* 2000). This can also be seen in the fact that 75 per cent of students who are only registered for one or more HN units, rather than a programme which will lead to a recognised qualification, are aged 25 or older. It seems likely that many of these students may be taking one or two units as part of a process of re-engagement with education. However, further research is required to establish exactly who these students are and why they are pursuing this type of study.

Another distinctive aspect of the profile of HN students is the extent to which they are drawn from areas of social disadvantage. The work of Gillian Raab and her colleagues at Napier University is the main source of data on this issue (Raab, 1998). This study involved establishing Standardised Participation Ratios (SPRs) for the areas in which people lived. Areas were identified on the basis of an Education Advantage Score. This is a census-based score based on two census indicators: the proportion of heads of households in social classes 1 and 2; and the proportion of adults with post-school qualifications. Postcode sectors were ranked on this score and divided into seven equal categories, where 7 represents the most educationally advantaged (Raab, 1998, p. 38). SPRs are based on a calculation where 'a ratio of 100 represents the national average. This means that the number of people participating in HE from a locality is equal to the number we would expect, averaged for the whole of Scotland, taking into account the age structure of the population in that locality' (Raab, 1998, p. 6). A figure of over 100 means a higher than average SPR. A figure of less than 100 means a lower than average SPR.

While it can be seen from Table 6 that there is a clear overall gradient between advantaged and disadvantaged areas, it can also be seen that this is even more pronounced among participants in HEIs, while participation in FE colleges is much closer to what might be expected as a national average. Participation rates in FE colleges for those from the most disadvantaged areas are about twice as high as those found in the HEI sector. Scottish FE colleges would therefore appear to have a key role in widening access to HE. This evidence of differential participation rates between sectors can also be observed in UK national data (see, for example, UCAS, 1999).

Table 6. Standardised participation ratios by educational advantage score category for Scottish domiciled students (not postgraduate) 1996–97.

| Advantage Score Category | All | In HEIs | | In FE colleges | | |
		Full-time	Part-time	Full-time	Part-time	Distance learning
1 = low	55	42	41	85	76	44
2	79	66	67	100	104	72
3	89	82	73	105	100	94
4	99	98	88	108	95	112
5	116	117	112	108	118	125
6	130	143	131	109	110	132
7 = high	164	203	238	86	104	149

Source: Raab (1998)

Table 7. Percentages of students from areas of deprivation on HN programmes or units in FE colleges participating in 2000–01.

	HND or equivalent	HNC or equivalent	HN Units only
Undefined	5	3	5
Band 1: Not deprived	13	13	19
Band 2: Below average deprivation	17	17	16
Band 3: Average deprivation	17	18	14
Band 4: Above average deprivation	23	24	29
Band 5: High deprivation	25	25	17

Source: SFEFC (2002)

More recent confirmation of the continuing role of the FECs in attracting students from areas of deprivation can be seen in the report produced by Raab and Small (2003) and in the data gathered by SFEFC (Table 7). This shows that almost 50 per cent of participants in HNC and HND programmes come from areas within the two most deprived bands. While an almost equally high percentage of students taking only HN units (46 per cent) come from these areas, there is also some evidence that a somewhat higher proportion of these students do not come from deprived areas. As we have indicated above there is little systematic knowledge about these students and their reasons for participation in these units, and further investigation of this issue is clearly required.

The final issue which can be considered with respect to the role of colleges as providers of opportunities to enter HE is the qualifications of the students at the point of entry to these courses. Once more the situation is complex, and more evidence would be useful. The SFEFC Infact database indicates that for all entrants to HNCs only 11 per cent had three or more Highers (the usual minimum requirement for entry to degree courses), while 18 per cent of entrants to HNDs had this level of qualification. For the school leaver group there is some evidence that the proportion is somewhat higher, although still relatively low. In addition, data available from the Scottish School Leavers Survey indicates that the proportions of school leavers entering these types of courses with three or more Highers fell from 77 per cent in 1984 to 40 per cent in 1993. Over the same period the proportion with only one or two Highers rose from 18 per cent to 42 per cent (Ticklin and Raffe, 1999). With respect to older students, the role of the colleges in providing entry routes for students who do not have traditional qualifications has already been noted.

The data presented here shows that the FE colleges are now providing opportunities for students to participate in HE which are in many ways different from those provided within the traditional university sector. There is also considerable evidence that the colleges are having considerable success in their mission of widening access, and creating opportunities for students to participate who are in many ways different from the traditional student group, and who do not have traditional qualifications. However, it is also necessary to consider the experience of students within their programmes, and where their studies lead to.

Completion and progression for HN students

To date there have been no systematic studies of the experience of HN students on their college courses. It is therefore difficult to comment on the experience of these students, other than to report anecdotal evidence that they appreciate the relatively small classes in which they work, and the regular close contact with tutors. Studies of this kind are now planned, and it is hoped to provide more systematic evidence on these issues in future papers. However some work has now been undertaken on completion and withdrawal rates.

Attempting to establish completion and withdrawal rates for HN programmes is difficult, since data in this form are not currently published by SQA or SFEFC. This partly reflects a number of difficulties with the existing data. A major problem here is the difficulty in establishing completion rates for cohorts of part-time students who may take several years to complete their programme of study. This would require a tracking process for which current reporting systems do not appear to be designed. However some indication of completion rates based on the numbers of students enrolled in the FE colleges is available from data collected from the colleges by SFEFC (*Examination Results and First Destination Statistics*). These data are reported in Table 8.

While it is difficult to draw any firm conclusions at this point about completion and withdrawal rates for HN programmes, it can be noted that the initial indicators are that completion rates are relatively low for these students. However, it is useful to put these programmes in context. In the first place there is evidence of wide variations in withdrawal and completion rates between different HE institutions. Data published by HEFCE indicates that while the figure for progression after year of entry

Table 8. Qualification results for final year group award enrolments 2000–01.

Qualification	Total	Passed	Did not complete	Fail	Other
HND	14,168	7,595 (54%)	4,256 (30%)	1,988 (14%)	329 (2%)
HNC	20,785	12,052 (58%)	5,320 (26%)	2,946 (14%)	467 (2%)
Other advanced diploma/certificate	3,612	2,767 (77%)	360 (10%)	398 (11%)	87 (2%)

Source: SFEFC (2003)

for full-time undergraduates in all Scottish institutions was 87 per cent, there was considerable variation between institutions, and while some institutions had a 96 per cent progression rate, in others the progression rate was only 77 per cent (HEFCE, 2002). Furthermore, unpublished data indicates important variations within institutions. While these differences are associated with a complex range of factors, those universities which are able to be highly selective in their choice of students, and have a student group which is relatively homogeneous with respect to their academic background are likely to have higher progression rates. It is also of interest to note that progression rates for mature students are in general lower than those for younger students. Thus the overall Scottish progression rate for mature students is 83 per cent, while one institution has a progression rate of only 68 per cent for this group, and three others have progression rates of 76 per cent or 78 per cent. While separate data is not published for part-time students, there is also evidence that progression rates for these students are also lower. These differences in progression rates reflect a wide range of factors, including preparation for study, cultural and social issues, and domestic, work and financial commitments (Callender, 2003; Davies *et al.*, 2002; Osborne *et al.*, 2001). Given the characteristics of HN programmes, and the students who participate in them, which have been discussed above, it might therefore be expected that progression rates will be lower than in institutions with a more homogeneous intake. Nevertheless, the importance of ensuring that students who undertake a programme of study have a good chance of success must be recognised, from the point of view of both the students and the wider society. If completion rates are relatively low, as they appear to be on the basis of the very limited evidence available, this points to the need for this problem to be recognised, and appropriate measures to be taken to address this issue.

What do HN students do after completing their programmes?

It has been noted above that while the HNC and HND programmes in which students participate at the FE colleges have their origins as vocational programmes, they are increasingly used by many students as progression routes to degree-level study. There have been no major national studies of this question of progression after completion of HNC/Ds, however there is some evidence on the basis of which some conclusions can be drawn. When considering this issue one of the first points which must be borne in mind is the high proportion of part-time students on these programmes. It has been noted previously that 57 per cent of all HN-level students in FECs are part time. Many of the students on these part-time programmes will already be in employment, and will continue in this employment, or move on to other positions when their studies have been completed. However, little systematic data is available for this group.

With respect to the full-time students, some limited information is available regarding their progression to employment or further study. This is available from the First Destination study which colleges are required to undertake. Since this depends on obtaining responses from graduates/diplomates, the data is not comprehensive, and the results must be viewed with caution. They do, however, present an interesting picture (Table 9). When these data are considered it is perhaps interesting to note that a fairly high percentage of these students (56 per cent) for both HNC and HND progress into further study, and a lower proportion (31 per cent) are reported as having progressed into any form of employment. It should of course be noted that a substantial number of HNC students may well progress to HND.

The extent to which these HN programmes are either a route to further study or to employment will vary between programmes. This is reflected in data published by SFEFC which indicates considerable

Table 9. First destination of full-time students completing HNC/Ds.

	HNC	HND
Full-time study	56%	56%
Permanent home employment	31%	31%
Believed unemployed	5%	6%

Source: Scottish Executive (2004)

variations, by subject group, in the percentages of students who gain HN Group Award and progress to further study. Thus in 2000–01 this data shows that 82 per cent of students on HNDs in biosciences, 72 per cent in social studies, but only 42 per cent in engineering, proceeded to further study or training. While all of this data is limited, and must be treated with care, it can be seen to indicate a growing differentiation in the role of HN programmes and qualifications. Some will continue to be largely vocational in orientation, with high numbers of part-time students, while others will have an increasingly important role in preparing students for further degree level study as well as possible preparation for the job market.

While there is no systematic study of links between the FE and HE sectors, there is again some data which gives some indication of the patterns which are emerging. SHEFC report that 3703 entrants to Scottish HEIs in 1999–00 had HNC/Ds as their highest qualification at entry (SHEFC, 2002). Given that the figures reported above indicate that about 13,000 students complete full-time HN programmes, and that it seems likely that many of the 6300 students on HNC programmes will progress to HND programmes, a figure of 3703 entrants to degree programmes could well be a fairly large proportion of all students completing full-time HNC/D programmes who are not progressing to another HN programme. A study by Gallacher *et al.* (1997), which is based on students from 13 HN programmes in six FE colleges throughout Scotland, indicated that 65 per cent of the HN students, whom the researchers were able to track, proceeded to degree study. However, more detailed investigation would be required to establish accurate national figures regarding progression from HN to degree programmes. It is, nevertheless, clear that many students, and particularly full-time students, who begin their studies in FECs wish to carry on to complete degree level study in universities. However, it is also clear that the opportunities for progression of this kind are often limited, and are unevenly spread between different institutions.

In Table 10 the Scottish universities are divided into three categories. The 'ancient universities' are the four oldest, dating back to the fifteenth and sixteenth centuries. These continue to be the most prestigious universities, and they enjoy a high level of demand for their places. The group described as the '1960s universities' were established at the time of expansion of the British university sector in the 1960s following the Robbins Report, while the 'post-'92 universities' are the former polytechnic-type institutions which were designated as universities, under

Table 10. Students entering HEIs in Scotland for whom HNC/D or similar was highest qualification on entry, 1999–2000.

	Number of entrants with HNC/D as highest qualification	Percentage of all entrants
Ancient universities	303	3%
1960s universities	568	8%
Post-'92 universities	2,665	25%
Art/ music colleges	167	13%
Total	3,703	13%

Source: SHEFC (2001)

the terms of the 1992 Further and Higher Education Act, at the time of the abolition of the binary line in Britain.

Table 10 has been compiled on the basis of data published by SHEFC. It indicates that despite the fact that the 'ancient universities' admitted more than 10,000 students, only 303 entered on the basis of an HNC or HND. While it has been noted above that FE colleges have had considerable success in widening access, the outcome is that the progression routes available to students after study in FE colleges are still limited, and the main opportunities exist in the post-'92 sector.

A similar conclusion is reached by Osborne and McLaurin in a study which attempts to identify former FE students who have progressed into HEIs. The technique used in this study is known as probability matching. On the basis of this study they concluded that there was a total of 5135 students (at all stages of their programme) in HEIs in Scotland in 1999–2000 who had entered with an HNC/D as their highest entry qualification. While 71 per cent of these students were in post-'92 universities, only 8 per cent were in 'ancient' universities and 19 per cent were in the 1960s universities (Osborne and McLaurin, 2002).

A number of factors can help explain these patterns. Studies have shown that links which have been established to facilitate transfer between FECs and HEIs in Scotland are much more likely to exist between the FE colleges and the post-'92 universities than the older universities (Alexander *et al.*, 1995; Maclennan *et al.*, 2000; Osborne *et al.*, 2000). The 'post-'92 universities' have generally made widening access and developing links with the FE colleges a much more central part of their mission. However, it must also be noted that this has been in a context in which the older universities, and particularly the 'ancients', are for the most part 'selecting' universities, while in many cases the post-'92 universities are 'recruiting' universities (Maclennan *et al.*, 2000). This distinction refers to the situation in which the older universities can, for the most part, select students from a pool of traditionally well-qualified applicants. By contrast, a number of departments within the post-'92 universities need to be more active in recruiting suitable students, and FE colleges can be a valuable source of recruits. In this context there has been greater interest in the post-'92 universities in establishing articulation agreements between the universities and the FE colleges which facilitate transfer of students from HNC/Ds to degree programmes. Articulation arrangements, which are the most common form of link between HNC/Ds and degrees in Scotland, can be described in terms of a continuum ranging from formal agreements with guaranteed places which enable students to progress to the next year of study, to informal arrangements with no guaranteed places, and where progression is a more open question. Within this continuum there will be considerable variations in the agreements, both within and between institutions. (Alexander *et al.*, 1995, p. 31). In a number of cases 2+1 or 2+2 degree programmes have also been established in which the final one or two years of a degree are built on an HND programme which students have completed in an FE college. The outcome of all of these developments is that opportunities for progression from HNC/D study in an FE college to a degree are much more likely to be in the post-'92 university sector. While there is considerable evidence, although mainly of an anecdotal nature, that many students are happy with the options open to them, especially as the post-'92 universities are more likely to make special arrangements to address the problems associated with transition from an HNC/D programme to a degree, there is also concern that this is limiting choice for these students, which may have consequences for their later careers (Field, 2004).

FE/HE links: complementarity or differentiation?

The data presented here show that HN provision within the FE colleges is now a major aspect of the HE system in Scotland which makes a very distinctive contribution to this system. A relatively high proportion of these students are older, many are part time, although full-time HN programmes have grown considerably, particularly at HND level. The courses still have a strong vocational orientation, although many students now use them to progress to further study, before entering employment. These courses also attract a high percentage of students from areas of social deprivation, and make a valuable contribution in widening access to HE.

The model of development is also interesting in that links with HEIs are generally on the basis of articulation between HNC/Ds and degrees, rather than franchising of degree programmes. This reflects the opportunities for FE colleges to develop their own HE-level programmes under the auspices of the national system provided by SCOTVEC, and more recently SQA. This enabled FE colleges to develop work in this sphere independently from the HEI sector, and has contributed to the strong growth which has emerged. It is perhaps of interest to note that by comparison with England the emphasis has been on collaboration, rather than partnership. This has enabled the FE colleges to define and pursue their own priorities. A partnership relationship can be a more difficult one if the institutional priorities of the partners diverge in various ways. This is especially the case when the partnership is not one of equals, in which the HEIs are dominant in terms of both quality arrangements and funding. Furthermore, for many HEIs their links with FE colleges are seen as relatively marginal to the mainstream business of the institution.

The growth of HN provision in Scotland has also been associated with a blurring of the distinction between vocational and academic forms of provision as HNC/Ds are increasingly used by students to prepare them for transition to degree study, as well as being used for more traditional vocational preparation.

However, the difficulties associated with the provision of HE in the FE colleges and the relationships between FE colleges and HEIs in Scotland must also be recognised and addressed.

Completion and progression rates for students on HNC/D programmes appear to be relatively low. This may be associated with the student group who enter these programmes, and the fact that a considerable proportion have limited qualifications of a traditional nature. The factors associated with this need further investigation, and one issue which has already been highlighted by representatives of the FE sector is the relative levels of funding for work in the FECs and HEIs. While it is difficult to directly compare funding for HE level work within the two systems, written evidence submitted by the SFEFC to the Enterprise and Lifelong Learning Committee, at its meeting on 8 May 2001, allows one to calculate that the average level of funding per full-time student equivalent provided by SFEFC is about £2900, while the average figure provided by SHEFC is about £3900. These differentials contribute to the widespread view within the FE sector that the level of funding they are receiving for HE level work is much lower than that provided to the HEIs, and this makes it difficult to provide a similar quality of educational experience for their students. However, given the different range of courses offered in the two sectors (with HEIs having higher costs in areas such as medicine), and the responsibility for research in the HEI sector, some differences in funding levels can be expected. On the other hand, investigation undertaken in England suggests that the additional costs associated with widening access can be from 25–40 per cent (DfES, 2003). Given that the FECs in Scotland have a very high proportion of students from areas of social deprivation it has been argued that the costs associated with this should be more clearly recognised in the funding model. The Scottish Executive has now merged SHEFC and SFEFC, and created a joint tertiary education funding council. In this new context it will be interesting to see how these issues associated with funding are addressed.

It has also been noted that the emergence of the FE sector in Scotland as an important provider of short-cycle HE, and a provider of opportunities for transfer to HEIs, has been a gradual evolutionary process rather than a planned development which is designed to create a unified tertiary structure in Scotland. This has the advantage that we now have two sectors which make distinctive contributions. However, there are also important disadvantages associated with this. The first is that in a number of cases there is not a good match between the HNC/D programmes and the degrees to which students may wish to progress. These differences partly reflect differences in the original purposes of HN and degree programmes. The role of HNs as vocational programmes has already been commented on, and we now have two rather different types of HE programme in the FEC and HEI sectors. As a result there are differences in both structure and content between HN and degree programmes, and these differences can contribute to the difficulties in the matching of these programmes. In this context a number of HE admissions tutors argue that students lack the necessary underpinning knowledge to successfully enter a degree programme with credit which will give advanced standing. A second but related set of issues is associated with the culture and ethos of the different institutions, approaches to teaching and learning and associated study skills, and methods of assessment (Gallacher *et al.*, 1997; Maclennan *et al.*, 2000). There are considerable differences between the experiences of students on HN programmes in FE colleges and students on degree programmes in HEIs. These are associated with: the scale of the institutions; the size of teaching groups (groups in FE colleges tend to be relatively small); teaching methods; and assessment methods (Maclennan *et al.*, 2000; Sharp and Gallacher, 1996). These differences can create difficulties for students when making the transition from FE colleges to HEIs. These difficulties have also contributed to a situation in which a number of staff in HEIs feel that students from FE colleges are not adequately prepared for entry into degree programmes. This can confirm their uncertainties about the value of establishing agreements with colleges which enable students to enter degrees with advanced standing (Maclennan *et al.*, 2000).

There is therefore a need to consider how the differences between these types of programmes can be recognised and addressed, and the two sectors can work more closely together, to ensure that the needs of students are met more effectively. In doing this there is a need to look more closely at development in other parts of the world, and the other chapters in this collection may contribute to this process. For example, experience within the community colleges systems in the USA could help inform thinking on this issue (Bonham, this volume). In various states the need to improve articulation policies between community colleges and universities has been recognised if the needs of 'transfer' students are to be met more effectively. This has led to a number of state-wide initiatives to facilitate the transfer of students from community college to university degree programmes. One of the most interesting recent developments of this kind has been the Illinois Articulation Initiative, within which a core curriculum has been developed to facilitate transfer (Rifkin, 1998). A number of states also have community college transfer centres to provide information and support for students, which will facilitate their transfer to university.

Within Scotland there are a number of initiatives through which these issues are already being addressed, or which create the opportunity for them to be addressed. A Mapping, Tracking and Bridging Project has been established with funding from SHEFC. This is designed to map the opportunities which exist for transfer from HN programmes to degrees, and to track transfer students, so that more systematic information is available about the extent of transfer, and the experiences of transfer students. It is also addressing issues associated with the transition of students from HN programmes to degrees through developing bridging programmes. A second development is the review of HN programmes which SQA is currently undertaking. This creates the opportunity to consider the content and structure of these programmes and how they can be developed to most effectively meet the needs of students who enrol on them. A third initiative is the establishment of the Scottish Credit and Qualifications Framework (SCQF). The aim of SCQF is to establish a national unified framework through which learning of all types can be recognised and the relationships between qualifications can be clarified. One of the goals which has been identified for the framework is to 'build more credit links between the different types of qualifications to enhance flexibility and enable the accumulation and transfer of credit from different routes. This will enable learners to carry forward credit for previous learning, while recognising that the Framework creates no mandatory system of credit transfer' (SCQF, 2003, p. 16). This again creates a context in which the issues associated with articulation and transfer can be recognised and addressed. However, SCQF is still at an early stage of its implementation, and its impact remains uncertain at this point. A further initiative has been the establishment by SHEFC/SFEFC of regional fora which bring together the HEIs and FECs in the various regions within Scotland to work together to develop more effective links. These bodies have established a range of projects to develop FE/HE links; however, their impact in creating a more unified system has been limited at this point.

A further issue which has been identified above is that the patterns of articulation relationships between the FE colleges and the different HEI sectors differ greatly. Opportunities for students to progress to degree level study are far more common in the post-'92 universities than in the 'ancient' or even in the 1960s universities. Given that a disproportionately high percentage of students from areas of social deprivation study on HN programmes in the FE colleges when compared with universities (Raab, 1998; Raab and Small, 2003), and that progression opportunities are concentrated in the post-'92 universities, rather than the more elite 'ancient' universities, a number of commentators have suggested that there is a danger of a ghetto being created for students from these backgrounds, where opportunities for study and progression in HE are limited (Field, 2004). It must of course be recognised that in circumstances where post-'92 universities do more to provide for the particular needs of students making this transition from FEC to HEI, many students make a positive choice to enter these institutions. Nevertheless, it is argued that it is important that choice is not artificially limited if an equitable system is to be established. Some of the initiatives identified previously, including the Mapping. Tracking and Bridging Project and the establishment of the regional fora, are designed to tackle these problems. However, uneven distribution of articulation arrangements and opportunities for transfer remain an enduring aspect of the Scottish tertiary education system. There is again a need for a strong strategic initiative, and it remains to be seen if the merging of the funding councils will provide an opportunity to address these issues.

Overall, then, a number of challenges exist in developing links between the FEC and HEI sectors. While a number of initiatives have been taken there is a need for strategic direction, and it remains to be seen if the merging of the funding councils will provide the opportunity for development of this kind.

Notes

[1] The Age Participation Index is calculated by the Scottish Executive as 'the number of young Scots aged under 21 who enter higher education in a given year as a percentage of the population in Scotland for the relevant age group' (Scottish Executive, 2003b).

[2] However, it must be noted that this is only a headcount figure, and many of these students are part-time students, some of whom are doing only one or two HN units, rather than a full programme.

[3] Scottish Enterprise is the agency responsible for economic development and training in Scotland. It operates through a network of local enterprise companies (LECs).

References

Alexander, H., Gallacher, J., Leahy, J. and Yule, W. (1995) 'Changing patterns of higher education in Scotland: a study of links between further education colleges and higher education institutions', *Scottish Journal of Adult and Continuing Education*, 2, pp. 25–54.

Callender, C. (2003) 'Student financial support in higher education: Access and exclusion', in: M. Tight (ed.) *Access and Exclusion Volume 2*. Elsevier Science Ltd.

Davies P., Osborne M. and Williams, J. (2002) *For Me or Not For Me? That is the Question. A Study of Mature Students' Decision Making in Higher Education*. Research Report RR 297. London: Department for Education and Skills.

Field, J. (2004) 'Articulation and credit transfer in Scotland: Taking the academic highroad or sideways step into a ghetto?', *Journal of Access Policy and Practice*, 1(2), pp. 85–99.

Forsyth, A. and Furlong, A. (2004) 'Counting access: problems and puzzles', in: M. Osborne, J. Gallacher and B. Crossan (eds) *Researching Widening Access to Lifelong Learning: Issues and Approaches in International Research*. London: Routledge Falmer.

Fryer, R. H. (1997) *Learning for the Twenty-first Century*. First report of the National Advisory Group for Continuing Education and Lifelong Learning. London: Department for Education and Employment.

Gallacher, J. Leahy, J. and MacFarlane, K. (1997) *The FE/HE Route: New Pathways into Higher Education*. Research Report for SOEID, Glasgow Caledonian University.

Gallacher, J. *et al.* (2000) *Education for All? FE, Social Inclusion and Widening Access*. Final Report for Scottish Executive. Glasgow Caledonian University, Centre for Research in Lifelong Learning.

HEFCE (Higher Education Funding Council for England) (2002) *Performance Indicators in Higher Education in the UK*. Online at www.hefce.ac.uk/pi

Kennedy, H. (1997) *Learning Works: Widening Participation in Further Education*. Coventry: The Further Education Funding Council.

Maclennan, A., Musselbrook, K. and Dundas, M. (2000) *Credit Transfer at the FE/HE Interface*. Edinburgh, Scottish Higher Education Funding Council/Scottish Further Education Funding Council.

National Committee of Inquiry into Higher Education (NCIHE) (1997a) *Higher Education in the Learning Society. Main Report*. London: NCIHE.

National Committee of Inquiry into Higher Education (NCIHE) (1997b) *Higher Education in the Learning Society. Report of the Scottish Committee*. London: NCIHE.

Osborne, M., Cloonan, M., Morgan-Klein, B. and Loots, C. (2000) 'Mix and match? Further and higher education links in Scotland', *International Journal of Lifelong Education*, 19(3).

Osborne, M. *et al.* (2001) *For Me or Not For Me in Scotland: A Study of Mature Students' Participation in Higher Education*. Report for Scottish Executive, University of Stirling, Centre for Research in Lifelong Learning.

Osborne, M. and McLaurin, I. (2002) 'Data on transfer from FECs in Scotland to HEIs in Scotland', in: M. Osborne, J. Gallacher and M. Murphy (2002) *A Research Review of FE/HE Links: Report to Scottish Executive*. Stirling: Centre for Research in Lifelong Learning/Scottish Executive.

Raab, G. (1998) *Participation in Higher Education in Scotland*. Edinburgh: SHEFC.

Raab, G. and Small, G. (2003) *Widening Access to Higher Education in Scotland: Evidence for Change from 1996–1997 to 2000–01*. Edinburgh: SHEFC.

Rifkin, T. (1998) *Improving Articulation Policy to Increase Transfer*, Policy Paper. Denver: Education Commission of the States.

The Scottish Credit and Qualifications Framework (SCQF) (2003) *An Introduction to the Scottish Credit and Qualifications Framework. 2nd Edition*. SCQF.

Scottish Executive (2003a) *Life Through Learning Through Life: The Lifelong Learning Strategy for Scotland*. Edinburgh: Scottish Executive.

Scottish Executive (2003b) *Standard Tables on Higher and Further Education In Scotland 2001–2002*. Edinburgh: Scottish Executive.

Scottish Executive (2004) *First Destinations of HNC & HND Holders in Scotland 2000–01*. Data prepared for the Centre for Research in Lifelong Learning by the Scottish Executive.

Scottish Further Education Funding Council (SFEFC) (2001) *Further Education Statistics*. Edinburgh: SFEFC.

Scottish Further Education Funding Council (SFEFC) (2002) *Further Education Statistics*. SFEFC Infact Database. Online at: http://www.sfefc.ac.uk/infact/

Scottish Further Education Funding Council (SFEFC) (2003) *Examination Results and First Destination Statistics*. Unpublished data.

Scottish Higher Education Funding Council (SHEFC) (2002) *Statistical Bulletin 2/2002 Higher Education Institutions: Students and Staff 1999–2000*. Edinburgh: SHEFC.

Scottish Office (1991) *Access and Opportunity*. Edinburgh: HMSO.

Scottish Office (1998) *Opportunity Scotland*. Edinburgh: HMSO.

Scottish Office (1999) *Opportunity for Everyone: A Strategic Framework for FE*. Edinburgh: HMSO.

Scottish Office Education and Industry Department (SOEID) (1998) *Further Education Statistics 1996–97*. Edinburgh: Scottish Office.

Scottish Parliament (2002) *Enterprise and Lifelong Learning Committee: 9th Report. Final Report on Lifelong Learning*. SP Paper 679. Edinburgh: The Stationery Office.

Scottish Qualifications Authority (SQA) (2002) *Annual Statistical Report, 2001*. Glasgow: Scottish Qualifications Authority.

Sharp, N. and Gallacher, J. (1996) 'Working together: Aspects of FE/HE links in Scotland', in: M. Abrahamson, J. Bird, and A. Stennet (eds) *Further and Higher Education Partnerships: The Future for Collaboration*. London: Society for Research into Higher Education (SRHE) and Open University Press.

Ticklin, T. and Raffe, D. (1999) *Scottish School Leavers Entering Higher Education*, Scottish School Leavers Survey Special Report. Edinburgh: Scottish Executive.

UCAS (1999) *Statistical Bulletin on Widening Participation*. Cheltenham: UCAS.

Educational mobility in the USA through the community college transfer function

Barbara S. Bonham

Introduction

When the first community colleges in the USA began in 1901 their central mission was to prepare students to transfer to four-year institutions. Is that still a major mission of community colleges? How is this accomplished? Are they successful? This chapter will address those questions by looking at four major aspects of the relationship between community colleges and the four-year institutions in the USA. First, a brief overview is provided on the development of the community colleges in the USA and their evolving mission. Second, the differing types of articulation agreements between the two institutions are discussed. The third section investigates how successful community colleges and four-year colleges have been with their transfer students. In the last section a summary of the research is presented on the obstacles to the transfer process and those components and services which facilitate the process.

Historical development of community colleges

The American Association of Community Colleges recognised the 100th anniversary of community colleges in the USA in 2001. The public junior college was the original name for these institutions. The history of these public two-year colleges in the USA clearly reflects the linkage to four-year colleges. Ideas popular in the country during this period fostered the growth of these new colleges. These included an increased need for workers' training, desire for individual advancement through the acquisition of new skills, belief in upward mobility through education, and great expansion in the number of programmes to prepare individuals for a broad variety of occupations. Cohen and Brawer (1989) identified a belief prevalent during this period which they considered to be a major impetus to the growth of two-year colleges: 'Whatever the social or personal problems, schools were supposed to solve it' (p. 3). During this time, secondary enrolments were also growing rapidly in the USA, thus further increasing the demand for access to college.

The interest of the universities in the development of public two-year colleges accompanied by the increase in the number of high school graduates desiring to enter the university were major forces contributing to the development of the two-year colleges. The universities wanted these colleges to teach basic learning and thinking skills to prepare students for the rigours of university life (Phillippe, 1997). It was hoped that these new colleges could fill the gap between high school and university and prepare students for transfer. Completion of the first two years was originally certified by the Associate of Arts degree (AA) or the more specialised Associate of Science (AS) degree (Townsend, 2001). Cohen and Brawer (1989) state that these degrees have always been viewed as preparatory.

During the 1950s and 1960s, the term community college emerged as the term describing the emerging more comprehensive, publicly supported institutions. Cohen and Brawer (1989) provide a definition for community colleges which encompasses the comprehensive two-year colleges as well as many of the technical institutes which were developed during this period of time: '... the community college is any institution accredited to award the Associate of Arts or the Associate of Science as its highest degree' (Cohen and Brawer, 1989, p. 5). With this expansion of programmes and services also came a much more diverse mission. Despite the many changes occurring in the community colleges as well as among the students they serve, the transfer role still exists as a major mission.

There was a dramatic increase in the growth of community colleges throughout the 1960s. Reports (Phillippe, 1997; Phillippe and Patton, 1999) indicate that 'between 1960 and 1970, the number of community colleges increased two and one-half times, opening at a rate of nearly one a week' (p. 7). Today there are more than 1200 community and technical colleges across the USA.

Walker (2001) notes that their mission has 'expanded from a singular focus on university transfer to include technical and vocational education, adult education, workforce development, and remedial education' (p. 18). This has resulted in part from the dynamic change in job requirements. McCabe (2003) notes, 'Revolutionary changes will take place as new jobs require markedly different and higher competencies ... businesses report that their workforce is underskilled ... and each year one in four students who enter higher education are underprepared' (pp. 14–15). The need for some postsecondary education has increased dramatically in the USA. McCabe adds, 'The countries with the highest overall literacy rates and a strong bottom third of its population will remain competitive in the 21st Century' (p. 15). Community colleges play an important role in American society in meeting these challenges. They provide educational opportunity to all, even those least likely to succeed. The community colleges in the USA continue to evolve into more comprehensive institutions offering a greater variety of programmes and services to meet the needs of American society. Many are partners with baccalaureate institutions and research universities.

They are conveniently located and have open admissions. Community colleges provide the opportunities to make lifelong learning a reality for many Americans. Community colleges in some states such as North Carolina and Vermont bring higher education (HE) to within a 30-minute commute of all citizens. North Carolina, for example, has a 58-campus system, which 800,000 people used in 1997–98 (Phillippe and Patton, 1999). The College of Vermont (CCV) has 12 centres in this very rural state. Of their 4500 students, nearly half take courses with the intent of transferring to a four-year institution. This is consistent with a recent national study (US Department of Education, NCES, 2003) which reports that one-half of the undergraduates who start at public two-year colleges with the intention of obtaining a four-year degree and about one-fourth of those who start with an associate degree as a goal transfer to a four-year institution within six years. What types of articulation agreements exist between the community colleges and four-year colleges that enable students to transfer into a baccalaureate degree programme?

Types of articulation

According to Cohen and Brawer (1989), 'programme articulation refers to the movement of students, or more precisely, the students' academic credits – from one school to another' (p. 190). Kintzer (1996), in his work on the 90-year history of published material on articulation and transfer in the USA, further elaborates on the definition of articulation. He states, 'It is the totality of services for students transferring throughout higher education, and transfer depicts the formulas developed to exchange credits, courses, and curriculums' (p. 3). Whichever definition one chooses to use, the reality is that there is a need for agreements between institutions which enable students to move from a community college to a four-year college degree programme. The research reveals a variety of co-operative arrangements which facilitate the transfer of students.

Three types of articulation operate in the states, according to Cohen and Brawer (1989). These are: 'formal and legal policies; state-system policies, in which the state is the controlling agency; and voluntary agreements among institutions ...' (p. 191). Ignash and Townsend (2000) conducted a national study investigating state-wide articulation agreements that facilitate the transfer between two- and four-year colleges. Their results reveal that 34 states had established a state-wide articulation agreement but that the transfer process still needs much work in a number of states. Many of the policies only cover graduates with the AA and AS degrees. Those graduates with the Associate in Applied Science (AAS degree), which is a degree granted in technical or occupational type programmes, are frequently uncertain as to how their degrees will be interpreted. Cohen and Brawer (1989) have suggested that up to half of all community college students who transfer to four-year institutions come from occupational or technical programmes. This is an area which still needs some work to make the transition smoother for students.

In the 1970s there was very little state involvement in transfer and articulation. By the 1990s, however, the responsibility for transfer and articulation had shifted from the local level to the state. Knoell (1990), based on findings from a Ford Foundation study, reports that all 50 states have a HE co-ordinating authority. They also have activities such as specialised services for transfer students, governance structures to co-ordinate transfer and articulation, technological networks to support the administrative procedures necessary for the transfer system, and so on (Robertson and Frier, 1996). Yet not all of these work as effectively or efficiently as they could. Transfer and articulation in colleges and universities continue to be top priorities in HE policy.

Accrediting agencies also play a role in the transfer process. Accrediting agencies have taken on a large share of the responsibility in facilitating transfer agreements that treat community college students fairly. In 1980, the Council on Postsecondary Education recognised 39 specialised accreditation or approval bodies (Kells and Paris, 1986).

Prather and Carlson (1993) identify five general types of co-operative arrangements between two- and four-year institutions. Their discussion of these agreements provides a good overview on the partnerships and how they are implemented. Type one is referred to as articulation and co-ordination agreements. In this type, the academic programmes as well as services are co-ordinated between the colleges and the course contents are similar. However, each college maintains a separate administrative process. In the second type of arrangement the four-year college offers courses at the two-year college campus. This type is referred to as the on-site upper division course offering. Type three is called on-site degree programmes. It represents co-operative arrangements in which buildings on the two-year college campus are constructed or designated specifically for four-year degree programme offerings. The fourth type of arrangement is called the satellite campus. This satellite campus of the four-year college is established on the two-year campus. Lastly, and perhaps the most comprehensive, is the satellite university/university college. A consortium agreement is developed between the four-year college and one or more two-year colleges. This approach involves uniform application and financial aid processes.

Despite the many attempts to define and formalise the articulation agreements and streamline the transfer process, there are still many institutions and therefore students who experience numerous challenges and problems upon transferring. Some authors such as Ignash (1992) note that 'four-year institutions dominate the decisions about transfer ... This may suppress the use of inventive methods and innovative courses at the community college level' (p. 2). But even with institutional support, transfer students' success academically, socially, and personally has been an important issue for many community colleges. In the next section, the topic of how successful transfer students are in American four-year colleges and universities is explored.

Participation and success rates

There are many reasons why students choose to attend the community college and then transfer to a four-year institution to continue their education. The transfer function of community colleges is a major access route to HE for many students. These are students who may have been ineligible for admission to a four-year college or university, who may have been unable to afford the financial costs of a four-year college or university, who wanted or needed to remain near their home, who did not want to leave their jobs to earn a degree full time, and so on.

In a 13-state study Palmer, Ludwig and Stapleton (1994) reveal some important information about community college transfer students. These are given below.

- 75 percent of the students remained at a community college long enough to earn at least 49 sh or 1.5 years of full-time study.
- 37 percent earned the associate degree before transferring, and students transferring to doctoral institutions were less likely to have earned the associate's degree.
- The median number of credits earned at the community college was 63 and the median number accepted for transfer was 60.
- Students who transfer successfully to baccalaureate granting institutions have relatively high levels of academic ability and are as competent as students who began their degree at these institutions (p. 8).

Cohen (1994b) notes that, 'the collegiate function of community colleges is intact and that around 130,000 of the 1.25 million who enter community colleges annually transfer within four years' (p. 101). But do these students achieve their educational goals?

Using data from a national cross-sectional survey of undergraduate students, the National Center for Education Statistics published a report entitled *Transfer Behavior Among Beginning Postsecondary Students: 1989–1994* (McCormick and Carroll, 1997). Highlights from their study, as described by Laanan (2001), are listed below.

- One out of four community college students indicated in 1989–90 that they were working toward a bachelor's degree (prospective transfers). Of this group, 39 percent transferred directly to four-year institutions by 1999.
- Among community college students identified as prospective transfers, those who enrolled full-time in their first year were about twice as likely as those who enrolled part-time to transfer to a four-year institution within five years – that is, 50 percent of full-timers transferred, compared with 26 percent of part-timers.
- Among community college beginners who transferred to a four-year institution, 65 percent transferred without a degree. About one out of 3 completed an associate's degree before transferring.
- On average, community college beginners who transferred to a

four-year institution spent about twenty months at the first institution.

- While one out of four community college transfers had received a bachelor's degree by 1994, another 44 percent were still enrolled at a four-year institution, an overall persistence rate of 70 percent. This is comparable to those who began at four-year institutions.
- The bachelor's degree attainment rate was much higher among the minority of community college transfers who completed associate degrees before transferring: 43 percent of associate's degree completers had received a bachelor's degree by 1994, compared with 17 percent who transferred without any credential. (pp. 6–7)

Studies looking at the academic success rate of students who transfer have been the focus of numerous state-wide, system-wide, as well as institutional approaches to determine the effectiveness of transfer programmes. An example of this is Laanan's (2001) report on a national study which was described above.

There has been much written about the need for models to calculate transfer rates to provide consistency in the data for comparison purposes. In 1989, the Transfer Assembly project funded by the Ford Foundation was initiated by the Center for the Study of Community Colleges to determine the contribution of community colleges to students' progress towards baccalaureate degrees (Cohen and Sanchez, 1997). The Transfer Assembly project developed a systematic approach for the collection of data across the states. For an in-depth discussion of the procedures and definitions used to calculate the transfer rate, see the report by Cohen and Sanchez (1997).

Simply stated, the transfer rate is the ratio of students who transfer (numerator) to the potential number of transfer students (denominator). The data on transfer rate provided a benchmark for comparing the state's transfer rate with other indicators of college accomplishment, the effects of various interventions, and so on. Cohen and Sanchez (1997) report that over the eight years of its existence, the Transfer Assembly has contributed significantly to consistent findings about the community college transfer rate. During this period they found that approximately one-fifth of community college students transfer to four-year institutions.

The need for a valid and reliable indicator of student outcomes was met by the derived transfer rate developed in the Transfer Assembly project. This was an important accomplishment and has inspired research and programme changes as a result of its consistent findings. However, there is still debate and discussion over what constitutes *a potential transfer student* (Spicer and Armstrong, 1996). This, you might recall from the discussion earlier is the denominator in the calculation of the transfer rate. It can range from a college's total number of students to those students completing a certain number of units, to those enrolled in certain programmes, and so on. But as states move to using transfer rates as an accountability indicator, uniformity in calculation becomes a critical state issue.

Cohen and Brawer (1996) examine the between-state differences in transfer rates. They explain that this difference occurs in part due to the state-system structures which are not all the same. In some states where the two-year colleges are organised as branch campuses the rate is higher than in states with colleges organised as technical institutes. Mabry (1995) notes that the priorities of two-year colleges are also contributing factors. If their focus is more comprehensive than emphasising technical programmes, the transfer rates were higher. But in some states where both structures exist, i.e. community colleges and technical institutes, the forces influencing the disparity in transfer rates can be traced to local conditions, such as the college's proximity to a university, local employment or economic conditions, and so on. The expanding mission of community/technical colleges in the USA also contributes to the complexity of this issue. It is difficult to determine which students are potential transfer students. Community colleges today provide a variety of educational options to a very diverse clientele.

Despite the differences in the ways of defining potential transfers, studies reveal little impact on transfer rates. A large study conducted for the National Center for Education Statistics (Bradburn, Hurst and Peng, 2001) shows that even using the most restrictive definitions the rate is not that dramatically different than the consistent rate reported by the Transfer Assembly project, which is about 20 per cent.

One of the lessons to be learned from the USA experience in attempts to define transfer rates and develop a consistent model for uniform data collection across the states is the importance of definitions, consistency of terminology, and a national systematic approach to defining these terms, transfer rates, and so on. This enables the colleges to provide data on transfer students and their progress and outcomes in a consistent manner, as well as to use it for comparative purposes.

A related and important topic addressed in the research on transfer rates is the movement of minorities through the educational pipeline from two-year to four-year institutions. According to Cohen (1994a) numerous studies reveal different rates for different ethnic groups, ranging from 4 to 40 per cent with an average gap of 29 per cent in the same state. Studies (Barrera and Angel, 1991; Hirose, 1994) reveal that minority students are not transferring as often as white students even at high-transfer-rate colleges. Cohen, summarising findings from national level studies (American Council on Education, 1990), adds, 'the overall transfer rate is 23 percent, it is 25 percent for white and Asian students and 16 percent for black and Hispanic students' (p. 102). Others (Dougherty, 1992; Grubb, 1991; Pincus and Archer, 1989; Velez, 1985) report similar findings for white students compared with black and Hispanic students, noting not only lower transfer rates for black and Hispanic students but that the results also suggest that they are less likely to earn baccalaureate degrees. Just as there is concern over the differing transfer rates of minority and non-minority students, there is also concern that the degree attainment is low.

Grubb (1991) explains, 'Just as the propensity to transfer has declined for all groups of students, so too is the likelihood of receiving a B.A. degree among these students who succeed in transferring ...' (p. 209). Studies (Laanan, 2001; Pascarella and Terrenzini, 1991; Velez, 1985) reveal that students who begin their college degree at a community college and transfer to a four-year college are less likely to complete their degree than students initially enrolled in a four-year institution. Nora (1993) states that, 'the majority of studies that have examined the degree attainment of minorities transferring from community colleges have found that degree attainment diminishes when students first enroll in community colleges' (p. 218). Basically, the message she is conveying is that by beginning their college experience at a community college, minorities are immediately at risk, and are less likely to transfer and successfully attain the baccalaureate degree.

In an ongoing institutional research report, Belcheir (2000) checked the graduation rates at four, six, and ten years for transfer and non-transfer students. She identified that 'the most important variables in predicting graduation for transfer and non-transfer students were continuous enrollment, mainly full-time enrollment, and first semester GPA' (p. 3). She added that for 'transfer students, mainly full-time enrollment boosted the odds of graduating by a factor of 3.8 after four years, 4.6 after six years and 5.1 after ten years' (p. 13). What other factors contribute to an easier as well as successful transfer to a four-year institution?

Components or services that support student transfer

Numerous studies have investigated community college students and factors or strategies that support their transfer and academic success. In one of the largest of these studies, Brawer (1995) examined the transfer rates of 395 community colleges using three different survey instruments as well as site visits. Her data reveals some interesting findings. Each of these is discussed in the following section, with the inclusion of related studies.

Brawer (1995) noted that clear articulation agreements were found to facilitate transfer but only marginally influenced transfer rates. Rifkin (1998) and Helm and Cohen (2001) identify strong articulation agreements as critical aspects of transfer.

Coupled with or frequently a part of the articulation agreement is faculty collaboration, which also increases transfer rates (Brawer, 1995; Palmer, 1996; Rifkin, 1998). Eaton (1994) describes this collaboration as an example of an academic model which 'assumes that faculty are central to transfer success ... Central to the strategy is academic collaboration among two- and four-year faculty at the departmental, disciplinary, and programme levels in the development of curriculum content and expectations for students success' (pp. 1–2). Cuseo (1998), Palmer (1996), and Rhine, Milligan and Nelson (2000) provide a number of excellent suggestions for faculty to engage in collaboration regarding transfer students, courses, and programmes, such as the use of faculty mentors for transfer students.

But faculty are not the only ones who can influence transfer rates. The active endorsement and encouragement of college transfer by administrators has also been found to increase transfer rates (Brawer, 1995; Christian, 2000). Institutions with high transfer rates had key administrators who gave high priority to the transfer mission. Helm and Cohen (2001) clearly describe how presidents can accomplish this. 'They need to set clear expectations, invest in research, examine policies and practice, build relationships and programmes, and provide visibility ... These expectations need to permeate the advising and admissions processes and faculty roles' (p. 99).

Perceptions were identified as a major contributing factor towards higher transfer rates. The perceptions of the community – high school faculty, advisers, parents, and so on – can influence the number of transfers. If the community sees the community college as an appropriate alternative place to start pursuing a baccalaureate degree, then the transfer rates are higher. Helm and Cohen (2001) note that changing perceptions is not easy but it is certainly a necessary step towards increasing transfers.

Although there is not much research to back-up the impact of support services on student transfer rates, there is literature describing the types of services which exist. The support services include transfer centres (Valencia, 1993); academic advising and counselling (Bernhardt, 1997; Cohen and Brawer, 1987; King, 1992; Palmer, 1987); and assistance with financial aid and registration (St Clair, 1993). What kind of obstacles do students face when trying to transfer to a four-year institution?

Obstacles to transfer

A number of studies investigated the barriers to successful transfer and smooth transition to four-year institutions (Cuseo, 1998; King, 1992; McDonough, 1997; Wechsler, 1989; Zamani, 2001). Some of the categories included in these studies are: financial, curricular, academic, and inadequate support systems and Cuseo (1998), King (1992) and McDonough (1997) identify financial barriers to transfer students' success. A few examples in this category are high cost of a four-year college, limited financial aid for students transferring from one institution to another, low number of grants or scholarships specifically for transfer students, and transfer students who receive acceptance letters after financial aid application deadlines. Stewart (1988) and Wechsler (1989) contend that transfer students coming from low socio-economic backgrounds find it difficult if not impossible to afford the tuition costs at the four-year colleges.

The curricular barriers identified by Cuseo (1998) included confusion and difficulty with regards to transfer due to multiple missions of community colleges. They offer many different programmes and courses, many of which may be non-transferable to four-year institutions. Dougherty (1992) identifies problems experienced with the transferability of career and vocational courses. Yet, Dougherty (1992) and Hunter and Sheldon (1980) report that nearly three-quarters of the students enrolled in vocational and technical programmes desire a baccalaureate degree. Striplin (1999) adds a similar concern in her discussion of the challenges faced by first generation college students.

Other curricular issues which create obstacles for students noted by

Cuseo (1998) include: 'no identifiable transfer articulation officer; the acceptance of transfer courses for elective credit only; and inter-institutional agreements not adhered to by some college deans or department chairs at four-year institutions' (p. 7).

King (1992) and Hirose (1994) identify geographical barriers as an obstacle. For some potential transfer students, the four-year colleges in the USA are located quite a distance from the area in which they live. As Hirose (1994) points out, 'the ubiquity of community colleges is not matched by the availability of public universities' (p. 103). Adult students with families and other responsibilities sometimes find it difficult to transfer to institutions that are located at such a distance from their home. Hirose (1994) adds, 'if there is no state university within a hundred miles of that community, few students will progress beyond the community college. Isolation is an inhibitor to transfer and it affects students in every ethnicity and socioeconomic level' (p. 103). Advisers can certainly be helpful in these situations by advising students to find appropriate programmes such as external degree programmes, online programmes, and so on.

Poor academic advising for transfer students and inadequate support systems are critical impediments to the transfer students' success (Bauer and Bauer, 1994; King, 1992). Bauer and Bauer (1994) identify in their surveys the presence of major academic and social concerns of transfer students as impediments to their success. Although most community colleges in the USA have mandatory testing, students still reported academic skills problems. Bauer and Bauer (1994) state, 'Study skills emerges as the major academic concern again at the four-year colleges as it did when students were enrolled at the community college' (p. 120). Forster, Swallow and Fodor (1999) found positive effects on transfer students' grade point average (GPA) using a study skills course specifically designed for these students at a four-year college.

Dougherty (1994) contends that one reason for the ineffectiveness of the transfer function is the large number of underprepared students who enter community colleges. The success of developmental education pro-grammes at the community college level is critical to these students. But some institutions do not have mandatory assessment and placement in developmental courses. McCabe (2000) states that 'mandatory assess-ment and placement are at the core of effective remedial programmes' (p. 44). He also explains that despite the importance of developmental education as an 'essential bridge' to many educational opportunities, some community colleges do not provide adequate priority or support for these programmes.

Phillippe and Patton (1999) explain that historically community colleges have admitted underprepared students but 'they must complete all prerequisites and requisites to earn a degree. Open admissions remains a tenet of community colleges, but decisions about remedial education threaten to erode these policies' (p. 7). Limited public funds and tight budgets are two reasons cited for the concern about the large number of entering students needing basic academic skills instruction.

Glass and Bunn (1998) explain that transfer students 'once resembled their university counterparts in age and full-time enrolment patterns, but now more closely resemble their peers in community college vocational programmes' (p. 2). They describes the transfer student of today as generally older, a part-time student, and less actively involved in the college life (Glass and Bunn, 1998).

The challenges faced by transfer students before and after transfer are great. The impact on the student academically is written about frequently and is referred to as transfer shock. This term has been used 'to characterize the temporary dip in transfer students academic performance (or grade point average – GPA) in the first and second semester after transferring' (Laanan, 2001, p. 5). Diaz (1992) reveals in a meta-analysis of 62 transfer shock reports that 79 per cent of the studies report that students do experience transfer shock. He adds that the magnitude of the GPA change was one-half of a grade point or less, and that over two-thirds of the students do recover from transfer shock.

Conclusion

This review of the literature and research on the transfer of students from community colleges to four-year colleges in the US includes a discussion of reports and studies conducted by a number of national agencies and projects. These represent an attempt to provide co-ordination and uniformity to the transfer process in American community colleges.

Because of these efforts comparison data is available not only between institutions but across states for the purpose of improving transfer services to students. These studies also provide community colleges and four-year institutions with some of the information needed to promote transfer and the academic success of these students.

Phillippe and Patton (1999) describe the present situation and challenge community colleges face today: 'With increased competition from for-profit colleges and distance education providers, administrators who want their community colleges to be around for another century need to know what they are doing right and what they need to improve' (p. 9). The presence of data such as that reported here allows community colleges to evaluate their efforts and benchmark these efforts against other institutions and states. This, in turn, enables them to make data-based decisions designed to improve the extent to which USA students make the transition to baccalaureate programmes.

References

American Council on Education (1990) *Minorities in Higher Education: Ninth Annual Status Report*. Washington, DC: American Council on Education.

Barrera, A. and Angel, D. (1991) 'Rekindling minority enrollment', *New Directions for Community Colleges*, 74, pp. 7–14.

Bauer, P. and Bauer, K. (1994) 'The community college as an academic bridge: Academic and personal concerns of community college students before and after transferring to a four-year institution', *Colleges and Universities*, 69, pp. 116–22.

Belcheir, M. J. (2000) *Predicting the Probability of Graduating after Four, Six, and Ten Years*. Boise, ID: Boise State University Office of Institutional Assessment.

Bernhardt, J. J. (1997) 'Integrated, intrusive, comprehensive academic advising as a method to increase student retention, graduation, and transfer in postsecondary TRIO programmes', *Journal of Educational Opportunity*, 16(2), pp. 17–27.

Bradburn, E., Hurst, D. and Peng, S. (2001) *Community College Transfer Rates to 4-year Institutions Using Alternative Definitions of Transfer*. Washington, DC: National Center for Education Statistics.

Brawer, F. B. (1995) *Policies and Programmes that Affect Transfer*. Los Angeles, CA: Center for the Study of Community Colleges.

Christian, M. E. (2000) 'The community college function: A study of its success in higher education', Master of Science paper at Northwestern State University, OK, USA.

Cohen, A. (1994a) 'Analyzing community college student transfer rates', in: A. Cohen (ed.) Relating Curriculum and Transfer, *New Directions for Community Colleges*, 86, pp. 71–9.

Cohen, A. (1994b) 'Conclusion: The future for curriculum and transfer', in: A. Cohen (ed.) Relating Curriculum and Transfer, *New Directions for Community Colleges*, 86, pp. 101–5.

Cohen, A. and Brawer, F. (1989) *The American Community College*, 2nd edn. San Francisco, CA: Jossey-Bass.

Cohen, A. and Brawer, F. (1996) *The American Community College*, 3rd edn. San Francisco, CA: Jossey-Bass.

Cohen, A. and Sanchez, J. (1997) *The Transfer Rate: A Model of Consistency*. Los Angeles, CA: Center for Study of Community Colleges.

Cuseo, J. B. (1998) *The Transfer Transition: Summary of Key Issues, Target Areas, and Tactics for Reform*. Washington, DC: US Department of Education, Office of Educational Research and Improvement.

Diaz, P. (1992) 'Effects of transfer on academic performance of community college students at the four-year institution', *Community College Journal of Research and Practice*, 16, pp. 279–91.

Dougherty, K. J. (1992) 'Community colleges and baccalaureate attainment', *Journal of Higher Education*, 63, pp. 188–214.

Dougherty, K. J. (1994) *The Contradictory College: The Conflicting Origins, Impacts, and Future of the Community College*. Albany, NY: State University of New York Press.

Eaton, J. S. (ed.) (1994) *Strengthening Transfer Through Academic Partnerships*. National Center for Academic Achievement and Transfer. Washington, DC: American Council on Education.

Forster, B., Swallow, C. and Fodor, J. H. (1999) 'Effects of college study skills courses on a-risk first year students', *NASPA Journal*, 36(2), pp. 120–32.

Glass, J. C. and Bunn, C. E. (1998) 'Length of time required to graduate for community college students transferring to senior institutions', *Community College Journal of Research and Practice*, 22(3), pp. 239–61.

Grubb, N. (1991) 'The decline of community college transfer rates', *Journal of Higher Education*, 62, pp. 194–222.

Helm, P. and Cohen, A.(2001) 'Leadership perspectives on preparing transfer students', in: F. S. Laanan (ed.) Transfer Students: Trends and Issues. *New Directions for Community Colleges,* 114, pp. 87–98. San Francisco, CA: Jossey-Bass.

Hirose, S. (1994) 'Curriculum and minority students', in: A. Cohen (ed.) Relating Curriculum and Transfer, *New Directions for Community Colleges*, 86, pp. 71–9.

Hunter, R. and Sheldon, M. S. (1980) *Statewide Longitudinal Study: Report on Academic Year 1979–1980, Part 3*. Woodland Hills, CA: Los Angeles Pierce College.

Ignash, J. (1992) *In the Shadow of Baccalaureate Institutions*. Loss Angeles, CA: ERIC Clearinghouse for Junior Colleges. (ERIC Document Reproduction Service No. ED 348 129).

Ignash, J. and Townsend, B. (2000) 'Evaluating state-level articulation agreements according to good practice', *Community College Review*, 28(3), pp. 1–21.

Kells, H. and Paris, R. (1986) *Trends in the Accreditation Relationships of U.S. Post-secondary Institutions 1978–1985*. Washington, DC: Council on Postsecondary Accreditation.

King, M. C. (1992) 'Academic advising, retention, and transfer'. *New Directions for Community Colleges*, 21(2), pp. 21–31.

Kintzer, F. (1996) 'A historical and futuristic perspective on articulation and transfer in the United States, in: T. Rifkin (ed.) Transfer and Articulation: Improving Policies to Meet New Needs, *New Directions for Community Colleges*, 96, pp. 3–13.

Knoell, D. (1990) *Transfer, Articulation, and Collaboration: 25 Years Later*. Washington, DC: American Association of Community Colleges.

Laanan, F. (2001) 'Transfer student adjustment', in F. S. Laanan (ed.) Transfer Students: Trends and Issues, *New Directions for Community Colleges*, 114, pp. 5–13.

Mabry, T. (1995) 'A study of differences in transfer rates between community colleges and four-year colleges in fifteen states'. Unpublished dissertation, Graduate School of Education and Information Studies, University of California, Los Angeles.

McCabe. R. (2000) *No One to Waste: A Report to Public Decision Makers and Community College Leaders*. Washington, DC: Community College Press.

McCabe, R. (2003) *Yes, We Can! A Community College Guide for Developing America's Underprepared*. Washington, DC: American Association of Community Colleges and League for Innovation in the Community Colleges.

McCormick, A. C. and Carroll, C. D. (1997) *Transfer Behavior Among Beginning Postsecondary Students, 1989–1994*. Washington, DC: US Department of Education.

McDonough, P. M. (1997) *Choosing Colleges: How Social Class and Schools Structure Opportunity*. Albany, NY: State University of New York Press.

Nora, A. (1993) 'Two-year colleges and minority students' educational aspirations: Help or hindrance?', in: J. Smart (ed.) *Higher Education: Handbook of Theory and Research*, vol. IX. New York, NY: Agathon Press.

Palmer, J. C. (1987) 'Bolstering the community college transfer function', *Community College Review*, 14(3), pp. 55–63.

Palmer, J. C. (1996) 'Transfer as a function of interinstitutional faculty deliberations', in: T. Rifkin (ed.) Transfer and Articulation: Improving Policies to Meet New Needs, *New Directions for Community Colleges*, 96, pp. 3–13.

Palmer, J. C., Ludwig, M. and Stapleton, L. (1994) *At What Point do Community College Students Transfer to a Baccalaureate Granting Institution?* National Center for Academic Achievement and Transfer, Washington, DC: American Council on Education.

Pascarella, E. T. and Terrenzini, P. T. (1991) *How College Affects Students: Findings and Insights from 20 Years of Research*. San Francisco, CA: Jossey-Bass.

Phillippe, K. (1997) *National Profile of Community Colleges: Trends & Statistics 1997–1998*. Washington, DC: Community College Press, American Association of Community Colleges.

Phillippe, K. and Patton, M. (1999) *National Profile of Community Colleges: Trends & Statistics, 3rd edition*. Washington, DC: Community College Press, American Association of Community Colleges.

Pincus, F. and Archer, E. (1989) *Bridges to Opportunity: Are Community Colleges Meeting the Transfer Needs of Minority Students?* New York: Academy for Educational Development and College Entrance Examination Board.

Prather, J. and Carlson, C. (1993) 'When four-year and community colleges collide: Studies for enrollment maximization.' Paper presented at the Annual Forum of the Association for Institutional Research, Chicago, IL.

Rhine, T. J., Milligan, D. M. and Nelson, L. R. (2000) 'Alleviating transfer shock: creating an environment for more successful transfer students', *Community College Journal of Research and Practice*, 24(6), pp. 443–53.

Rifkin, T. (1998) *Issues Surrounding the Community College Collegiate Function: A Synthesis of the Literature*. Washington, DC: Office of Educational Research and Improvement.

Robertson, P. and Frier, T. (1996) 'The role of the state in transfer and articulation', in: T. Rifkin (ed.) Transfer and Articulation: Improving Policies to Meet New Needs, *New Directions for Community Colleges*, 96, pp. 15–24.

Spicer, S. and Armstrong, W. (1996) 'Transfer: The elusive denominator', in: T. Rifkin (ed.) Transfer and Articulation: Improving Policies to Meet New Needs, *New Directions for Community Colleges*, 96, pp. 45–54.

St Clair, K. (1993) 'Community college transfer effectiveness: Rethinking enhancement efforts', *Community College Review*, 21(2), pp. 14–22.

Striplin, J. J. (1999) *Facilitating Transfer for First-Generation Community College Students*. Washington, DC: Office of Educational Research and Improvement.

Stewart, D. M. (1988) 'Overcoming the barriers to successful participation by minorities', *Review of Higher Education*, 11, 329–36.

Townsend, B. (2001) 'Redefining the community college mission', *Community College Review*, 29(2), pp. 29–42.

U.S. Department of Education, National Center for Education Statistics (2003) *The Condition of Education*, NCES 2003–067. Washington, DC.

Valencia, R. (1993) 'Student services that promote transfer: The transfer center'. Paper presented at Annual Transfer Assembly of the Center for the Study of Community Colleges, Chicago, IL.

Velez, W. (1985) 'Finishing college: The effects of college type', *Sociology of Education*, 58, pp. 191–200.

Walker, K. (2001) 'Opening the door to the baccalaureate degree', *Community College Review*, 29(2), pp. 18–28.

Wechsler, H. (1989) *The Transfer Challenge: Removing Barriers, Maintaining Commitment*. Washington, DC: Association of American Colleges.

Zamani, E. (2001) 'Institutional responses to barriers to the transfer process', in: F.S. Laanan (ed.) Transfer Students: Trends and Issues, *New Directions for Community Colleges*, 114, pp. 15–24.

The role of short-cycle higher education in the changing landscape of mass higher education: Issues for consideration

Jim Gallacher and Michael Osborne

Introduction

The focus of this book has been on what we have referred to as short-cycle higher education (HE), and the links between these forms of HE and degree-level provision in the universities.[1] Short-cycle HE refers to provision at the undergraduate level which will be completed in one or two years of full-time study, or longer if completed through a part-time mode. It will normally be completed in institutions other than universities and lead to qualifications at levels lower than the Bachelor's degree (see Osborne's introduction to this book for a fuller discussion of these issues). The chapters which are included in this book, and the wider literature referred to by the authors of these chapters, have made clear that short-cycle HE is an increasingly important feature of the systems of mass HE which now exist in many societies. Much of this provision of education and training has traditionally been relatively low status and even residual in many societies. However, with its increasingly important role in mass HE it has become much more central to the policy debate, and has grown in both scale and status. These developments have, of course, not been even across all societies. In this concluding chapter we will draw together issues which have emerged in the earlier country-based chapters, and identify some of the key questions which they raise for the development of policy, practice, and research in the changing landscape of mass HE. In doing this we will endeavour to draw out key aspects of the distinctive contribution of short-cycle HE, and the nature of its links to other forms of undergraduate education. The international dimension of these contributions will enable us to identify both issues which are similar across different societies, and differences which reflect history and tradition. However, a number of contributors to this book have drawn attention to the relatively limited amount of good systematic research which has been undertaken in this field. As a result, in a number of places we can only raise issues which require consideration or further research, rather than draw firm conclusions.

The role of short-cycle HE

In considering the role of short-cycle HE in contemporary societies it can be seen that three main functions have now emerged. The first, and traditional function for many systems of short-cycle HE, is the provision of vocational education and training (VET). This can be observed in almost all societies, but is most clearly defined in societies such as Germany, which still have a clearly differentiated VET system. Coughlan (2005) also reports that the relatively recent emergence of the further education (FE) sector as an important part of the Irish educational system has been associated with its key role in developing VET. The second function, which has become increasingly important, is to increase the number of participants in HE. This is often linked to the first function in that the expansion of this type of provision is designed not only to increase the numbers participating in HE, but also to ensure that it is more vocationally relevant, and is more closely linked to the needs of employers and business. The development of foundation degrees in England is an interesting example of a recent policy initiative to use short-cycle HE in this way. The third function is to widen participation through providing increased opportunities for participation for groups who have been traditionally under-represented in HE. This is a function which has become increasingly important in a number of societies in the context of the development of systems of mass HE. Examples of this include the community colleges in USA and Canada, and the changing role of the FE colleges in Scotland. The chapters in this volume have indicated the varying ways in which short-cycle HE is fulfilling these functions. In this concluding chapter we will consider some of the key issues which this raises for the development of policy, provision, practice, and research.

Short-cycle HE and VET

The first issue that we must consider in this context is the function of short-cycle HE in providing vocationally relevant education and training. As we have noted above this has been the traditional function of a great deal of short-cycle HE in many societies.[2] This is exemplified most clearly in the countries considered in this volume by the case of Germany in which the divisions between VET and the academic HE system are for the most part clearly defined (Deissinger, 2005). It continues to have a HE system in which there is still a clear binary divide between the universities and the more vocational institutions such as the *fachhochschulen*. It also continues to have a system of VET which has been build around a dual system of work-based apprenticeship and part-time vocational schools. Wheelahan and Moodie also comment in their chapter on the fact that Australia still has a formally divided system with a unified university system alongside a VET system in which institutes of technical and further education (TAFEs) have a central role (Wheelahan and Moodie, 2005). However, even in societies in which the boundaries between the vocational and the academic have become more blurred, such as Scotland, the vocational origins of short-cycle HE are still very clear. Thus it has been noted in Gallacher's chapter that the higher national certificates and diplomas (HNC/Ds) on which short-cycle HE is based have very clear vocational origins, and when the most popular HN programmes are considered, their vocational orientation is evident (Gallacher, 2005). Similarly, an explicit aim behind the introduction of the foundation degrees which are now being developed and implemented in England has been to close the 'skills gap' at the associate professional and higher technician level (Parry, 2005).

When the role of short-cycle HE within systems of mass HE is being considered, the emphasis is increasingly placed on its role as an alternative way into and through HE, and on its links with the universities and similar institutions of HE. While these issues are very important, and have rightly been the focus of a great deal of the discussion in the book, it must also be remembered that many providers of short-cycle HE, and many students on these programmes, see them as ends in themselves, and not just as preparations for transfer to degree-level courses. Attention to these issues can help avoid a misunderstanding of the place of short-cycle HE in many societies.

The distinctive characteristics of short-cycle HE

A second set of issues that emerges from the study of short-cycle HE across a range of countries is the extent to which there are distinctive characteristics that distinguish it from undergraduate provision in the universities. In this respect it can noted that while short-cycle HE has distinctive characteristics, there are important variations both between societies and within societies.

The first area which can be identified as being of significance is the set of issues associated with the extent to which these courses are work related or work based. We have already noted how some countries have much more clearly differentiated VET systems, and this has an impact on these issues. Thus Deissinger (2005) has noted that in Germany, with its clearly defined system of VET, the apprenticeship system is based on work-based learning, and the curricula found in the *fachhochschulen* are much more vocationally oriented than those in the universities. In Australia, Wheelahan and Moodie (2005) also report that there is a national VET system which involves competency-based training packages delivered in the TAFEs and other similar institutions. However, it is not only in countries with highly differentiated VET systems that an emphasis on work-based or work-related HE is found. Thus in England, where the development of foundation degrees usually involves collaboration between the FE colleges and universities, there is also a strong emphasis on work-based learning as a key aspect of this development. A related issue is the greater emphasis on flexibility in many systems of short-cycle HE. Almost all of the countries included in this study refer to relatively high levels of part-time provision and to other forms of flexible provision.

It has also been noted that that the learning experience for students in the institutions that offer short-cycle HE is generally quite different from that which students experience in universities or other HEIs. Parry suggests that 'claims for the distinctiveness of higher education in further education rest less on separate types of courses or qualifications and more on the character of teaching and learning in college environments. A further education tradition of student-centredness and "personal pedagogy", along with the smaller scale and greater intimacy of teaching groups, serve as before to distinguish the college from the mass university' (Parry, 2005). Gallacher has also noted similar differences in the approaches to teaching, learning, and assessment in the FE colleges in Scotland (Gallacher, 2003). In Australia, Wheelahan and Moodie (2005) have noted that the 'learning environment in TAFE is quite different to that in HE'. They suggest that this is associated with smaller classes, higher contact hours, more supportive teaching and curriculum and assessment which is competence based. There is evidence from all of these countries that this distinctive cultural ethos is one which many students find supportive; however, it can also lead to problems for those who transfer from short-cycle to degree-level programmes, an issue to which we will return below.

The heterogeneity of the student group in short-cycle HE

The third set of issues which emerges from these international perspectives on short-cycle HE are ones associated with the heterogeneity of the student groups who participate in these programmes, and the relative success of this type of provision in widening access to HE. Gallacher has pointed to the fact that many of these students are older when compared with undergraduates in HEIs. He also provides evidence, drawing on the work of Raab and her associates, which shows that a much higher proportion of these students come from areas of social and economic deprivation when compared with university students (Raab and Small, 2003). Bonham (2005) also comments on the role of community colleges in making lifelong learning a reality for many Americans. In both Scotland and the USA this is associated with the geographical spread of FE and community colleges, which helps overcome problems of access associated with residential location which can be of particular significance for many adult students (Raab and Davidson, 1999). In Scotland this geographical proximity has been further enhanced by the provision of community outreach facilities that many FE colleges now provide, and that help provide cultural as well as geographical access (Gallacher *et al.* 2000). It is also reported that a more open admissions policy contributes to widening access, many of whom do not have the qualifications traditionally required for entry to HE. A related issue in widening access is the role of this type of provision in tackling problems associated with the under-representation of First Nations or Aboriginal people in post-compulsory education in both Canada and New Zealand. In Canada, Burtch (2005) reports on an number of special initiatives which have been taken within the community college sector to tackle this problem, and he reports a 30 per cent increase in Aboriginal students in colleges and universities between 1986 and 1992 (Baker, 1995). A similar range of issues to those that have emerged in Scotland and USA are identified as contributing to this success. These include: location, preparation, community linkages, peer support, cultural support, family and childcare services, and a 'culturally hospitable environment' (Baker, 1995). In New Zealand, Anderson (2005) reports that the Wānangas, which have been established to provide tertiary education for the Māori people have had considerable success in increasing participation in sub-degree-level education. At this level Māoris now participate above their population proportion (Scott, 2003). However, it is also reported that while evidence on retention is limited, it appears that attrition rates for Māoris are significantly higher than Asians and Pakehas (European New Zealanders) (Anderson). In Australia, the pattern that emerges is more complex. While VET students are more broadly representative of the whole population than HE students, the characteristics of VET students on HE-level diploma and advanced diplomas are more similar to HE students than to the rest of the VET population. They are younger, more urban, have higher school level attainment, are less likely to come from a low socio-economic background, or to be of Aboriginal or Torres Strait Island background (Karmel and Nguyen, 2003). This may reflect the fact that this provision is part of the mainstream of VET.

The research reported in this volume would therefore indicate that short-cycle HE has had considerable success in recruiting students for traditionally under-represented groups in many societies. However, it would appear that this has often been associated with community oriented flexible provision, or other initiatives which recognises the special needs of non-traditional students. Further research could help identify the factors that contribute to success of this kind, and the forms of provision that can most effectively contribute to widened participation. A further important issue which will be explored below are the opportunities for these students to progress to degree-level study.

The links between short-cycle HE and undergraduate degree-level provision

The fourth issue for consideration is the nature and extent of the links between short-cycle HE and undergraduate degree-level provision in the universities, and similar HEIs. This has been a major focus for many of the chapters in this book, and is an issue of considerable importance for the development of mass HE. The chapters in this book report on a wide range of different forms of linkage, with considerable variation both within and between societies and, in some societies, such as Germany and Ireland, the extent of the links and opportunities for transfer seem limited (Deissinger, 2005; Coughlan, 2005). However, there are also a number of common themes that emerge which will be discussed later.

The most common form of linkage is some form of articulation agreement which enables students to transfer from a college course to a university course with credit. However, the form that these articulation agreements take varies widely, both within countries and between countries. There does not seem to be any example of a country that has a nationwide scheme governing articulation. However, state-wide agreements do exist in a number of cases. Bonham (2005) reports a study in the USA which revealed that 34 states have state-wide articulation agreements (Ignash and Townsend, 2000). Burtch (2005) also reports agreements in a number of provinces in Canada which have province-wide agreements, most notably British Columbia where the British Columbia Council on Admissions and Transfer (BCCAT) facilitates and co-ordinates credit transfer among post-secondary institutions. Wheelahan and Moodie (2005) also report developments at a state level in Australia. The Victoria State Government has introduced a 'credit matrix' to facilitate credit transfer, articulation and student transfer, and this is seen as an interesting innovation that may influence other states. Below these state-wide agreements a wide variety of different forms of articulation agreement, or pathways, have been established at course or programme level. These include formal agreements that recognise a course as being equivalent in level to the first or second level of a university degree course, and may also include the guarantee of a certain number of places within a degree programme. Forms of this type of agreement can be found in the USA, Canada, Scotland, and Australia. In other cases the agreements will be more informal and depend on links between the staff and students involved.

A second common form of linkage involves franchising a programme from a university to a college or similar institution. This has been commonly used in England, where many universities, particularly the post-1992 universities (the former polytechnics that were established as universities under the terms of the 1992 Further and Higher Education Act) have franchised part of a degree programme to an FE college. This principle has been continued in England with the development of the foundation degrees. In the recent White Paper it has been made clear that it is expected that these will be developed on a franchised basis, or through consortia of FE colleges and universities. This is seen as a way of maintaining the quality of provision (DfES, 2003). Similar agreements exist in a number of states in the USA, and to a more limited extent in Canada.

A third form of linkage is at an institutional level, and a wide variety of these exist in different societies. In the USA there are a number of 'satellite campuses' established by four-year colleges on the campuses of two-year institutions. There are also 'satellite universities/university colleges' in which a consortium is established between four-year colleges and one or more two-year colleges (Prather and Carlson, 1993). British Columbia also now has a number of university colleges, while in Australia there are a number of dual sector institutions that combine a TAFE and university within the one institution. There are also co-located campuses that can comprise a secondary school, TAFE, and an HE campus. These are emerging as an important model for providing comprehensive access to post-compulsory education in more remote areas where separate institutions do not exist. In other societies that do not have such established forms of institutional linkage, other more limited arrangements exist, such as the memoranda of agreement which link a number of FE colleges and universities in Scotland.

The existence of all of these different forms of linkage reflects the extent to which short-cycle HE is now an important feature of mass HE and that this has resulted in a desire to create avenues for progression from these courses to degree-level qualifications. The desire for these forms of progression has come from students who wish to progress, from institutions who see these links as being advantageous to them, and from policy at a national, state, or province level. The influence of these drivers varies considerably both within and between countries. However, when the nature of these links and their impact is considered a number of issues emerge.

Differential of power and status in the links

Firstly, it is clear that in almost all countries there is a considerable power differential between the providers of short-cycle HE and the universities or similar HEIs. The universities have enjoyed much higher status than institutions such as FE colleges or TAFEs. This has been associated with the higher status traditionally given to academic institutions when compared with those that have their origins in the more vocational sector.

Within the university sector there are also clear differences in status, with, for example, the older universities in England and Scotland continuing to enjoy higher status than the former polytechnics. These power differentials have had a considerable impact on the nature of the links that have been established, and on the distribution of these links. This is most clearly observable in countries such as England where the system of links is based on the franchising of programmes from the universities to the FE colleges, or the establishment of consortia in which universities have a dominant role. Within these relationships funding will usually flow through the universities, and the share of funding which FE colleges receive can vary greatly depending on the agreement between the institutions involved. Quality assurance arrangements are also centred on the universities. Colleges can thus be placed in a relatively junior and disadvantaged role (Parry, 2005). In countries where articulation is the more dominant mode, such as Scotland, USA, Canada, or Australia, while colleges retain more control over their own programmes, over funding, and quality assurance, they still often have limited control over the types of articulation agreements that are established, and the extent to which credit is awarded to transferring students. Universities will commonly agree to articulation agreements when they wish to recruit students to programmes which are relatively under-subscribed, but be less inclusive when they can recruit traditionally qualified students without any difficulties (Maclennan *et al.*, 2000).

Differential access to universities

Associated with these power and status differentials is evidence that articulation agreements, and similar links, are unevenly distributed within national systems. In particular, access to the higher-status, more elite institutions is limited in many countries. Wheelahan and Moodie (2005) note that access to the elite universities in Australia is limited, while Gallacher (2003) has shown that only 3 per cent of entrants to the 'ancient' universities in Scotland, the oldest and most prestigious institutions, had an HNC or HND as their highest entry qualification, compared with 25 per cent of the entrants to the post-1992 universities. This leads Wheelan and Moodie (2005) to suggest that transfer rates can be higher in more formally stratified systems, such as some USA states, than in the apparently more unified systems which are found in Australia and Scotland. While there is certainly some evidence for this, it should also be noted that Bonham (2005) suggests that many of the state-wide agreements within the USA only cover graduates with the Associates of Arts (AA) degrees and Associate of Science (AS) degrees. Graduates with Associate in Applied Science (AAS) degrees, which is a degree granted in technical or occupational programmes, are frequently uncertain about how their degree will be interpreted. It has been suggested that these differences in patterns of access to the more elite universities in countries such as Scotland are associated with the fact that these are 'selecting' universities, who select suitable candidates from a wide range of well-qualified applicants, while some of the less prestigious institutions have to recruit students in the context of a mass HE system, where it can be difficult to fill student places in some of the less popular subject areas (Maclennan *et al.*, 2000). It should of course be noted that there can be considerable differences within as well as between institutions, with some subject areas greatly over-subscribed, while others are under-subscribed.

Initiatives to facilitate collaboration and transfer

The recognition of the uneven pattern of linkage between institutions leads on to a consideration of initiatives that have been taken or are emerging to address these issues, and it can be noted that improving articulation arrangements is increasingly being recognised in many societies as a problem that should be addressed.

The most formal responses to this issue are the state-wide articulation agreements which are now in place in many states across the USA, and it has been noted above that 34 states now have an agreement of this kind in place. A number of these, such as the California Master Plan, have spelled out clearly the relationship between the institutions in the different sectors, and the responsibilities of the four-year colleges, including the elite campuses of the University of California such as Berkley and Davis, to accept a certain number of community college graduates each year (Trow, 2000). Another approach can be observed in the Illinois Articulation Initiative, within which a core curriculum has been developed to facilitate transfer (Rifkin, 1998).

A second development, which, it has been hoped, would have a positive impact on establishing more effective articulation links and pathways between sectors, has been the establishment of national qualifications frameworks, or credit and qualifications frameworks.

These vary considerably in their nature, extent and ambitions, but they are becoming an increasingly important feature of many societies. In the countries represented in this volume it can be observed that Australia, Ireland, New Zealand, and Scotland already have frameworks of various kinds in place, while steps are now being taken to establish a framework in England. The Scottish Credit and Qualifications Framework (SCQF) is in many respects one of the most ambitious, in that it aims to include all qualifications from 'access' level (basic education) to doctoral level, and ultimately to include work-based, community-based and experiential learning, as well as learning in the more formal institutional contexts. It has been developed through a partnership of key stakeholder groups, which have included representatives of the HE sector, and the universities have been generally supportive of its development. It is hoped by those associated with developing SCQF that this will facilitate the transfer of students from FE colleges to universities with credit. However, given that the recognition of credit for transfer purposes is still something entirely controlled by each university and staff within these institutions at a local level, and that the implementation stage of SCQF is still at a relatively early stage, it is not yet clear what impact this ambitious framework will have in facilitating the transfer of students from FE colleges to HEIs, or in creating new opportunities for transfer. The Irish framework is a complex and inclusive one, but it is also at an early stage of implementation (Coughlan, 2005). The Australian model is a somewhat different one. The Australian Qualifications Framework (AQF) was created in 1995 but, unlike the SCQF, has no accreditation or recognition function. It designates which qualifications are offered in each sector, and the descriptors that accompany each. These are designed, at least in part, to facilitate the recognition of equivalence of level of qualifications and, in this way, facilitate learning pathways and credit transfer. With this in mind, credit transfer guidelines have been promulgated. However, Wheelehan and Moodie (2005) suggest that sectoral differentiation has remained a key aspect of the framework, and while this has helped maintain sectoral peace, it has been at the expense of facilitating the seamless movement of students and credit between sectors. Despite this limited progress at a national level, Wheelahan and Moodie (2005) also report the development of a 'credit matrix' by the Victorian State Government. They suggest that this has been influenced by development elsewhere, including the SCQF, and has achieved a high level of support, including the involvement of the universities. However, the impact of this relatively new initiative remains to be seen.

Overall, then, it can be seen that qualifications or credit and qualifications frameworks are emerging as an increasingly important aspect of policy and provision in many societies. As yet their impact on articulation routes and credit transfer pathways has not been systematically investigated, in part because many of these frameworks are only in the process of implementation. However, the autonomy of universities with respect to the recognition of entry requirements may well create a situation where their impact is uneven.

A third set of issues are associated with the initiatives at national, state, or institutional level, which are designed to build closer links between institutions and facilitate the transfer of students. One of the clearest examples of a national initiative has been the establishment in Scotland of four regional wider access forums. These now include all of the FE colleges and universities, and an important function is to encourage them to work together at a regional level to widen access to education. A Mapping, Tracking and Bridging project has also been established to provide more systematic information and support for students and institutions in the transitional arrangements for movement from FE to HEIs. In the USA, the growing involvement of state-level organisations in facilitating links between community colleges and four-year colleges has been noted. Bonham notes evidence from Knoell (1990) that all 50 states now have a HE co-ordinating authority, and many have community college transfer centres to provide information and support for students which will facilitate their transfer to university (Rifkin, 1998). While developments are more limited in Canada, with quite different patterns across the provinces, Burtch reports that the British Columbia Council on Admissions and Transfer (BCCAT) is now responsible for facilitating and co-ordinating credit among post-secondary institutions, which includes in-house research, funding articulation meetings, and producing a handbook.

At an institutional level a number of factors have emerged from research in different countries. First of all, Bonham quotes Rifkin (1998) and Helm and Cohen (2001) as identifying strong articulation agreements as critical aspects of transfer. Alexander *et al.* in Scotland have also noted the concentration of articulation agreements in the post-1992 university sector, and we have earlier noted that students are much more likely to transfer into universities in this sector than to the older universities. Bonham also quotes research that emphasises the role of staff, both faculty based and at an administrative or managerial level, in contributing to high transfer rates. The importance of transfer centres and other support services is also noted in this research. Wheelahan and Moodie, in the rather different context of Australia where, as we have noted, articulation and transfer arrangements are less fully developed, have also observed that outcomes are most successful when staff from the different sectors have established good collaborative and trusting relationships. In this respect they refer to the interesting concept of the 'boudary spanner' that has been developed to describe staff that have a designated role in developing links between sectors, and the key role that these staff can have in achieving successful outcomes (Sommerlad *et al.*, 1998).

The experience of transferring students

The final set of issues to be discussed concerns the experience of students in transferring from short-cycle to degree-level HE. The first point that must be noted here is the problem of attempting to assess the proportion of students who transfer. We have noted above the limited access to degree-level study in some institutions and subject areas, but it is not clear whether this actually restricts access for potential students who would want to transfer to these institutions or subject areas. There is a problem of a lack of good data in almost all countries on this issue, and this is further complicated by a problem of defining who the potential transfer students are. For example, in studying transfer from community colleges in the USA are the potential transfer students all community college students, or are they only ones on particular courses? Despite these difficulties, Bonham reports that the Transfer Assembly project in the USA indicates a transfer rate of about 20 per cent (Cohen and Sanchez, 1997). In Scotland, similar difficulties with data and definitions are reported by Gallacher; however, it seems that if one considers all students who successfully complete HNCs or HNDs and would be eligible for transfer, the figure would be around 28 per cent. Nevertheless, it should be noted that a number of these eligible students will be part-time students who are in employment, and have no intention of transferring to a degree, while a significant number of the HNC students will progress to HNDs before moving on to degree-level study. On this basis the transfer rate for those who have completed a qualification may be considerably higher. This, however, is a fairly restrictive definition of potential transferring students, and it is clear that more research is needed on this topic. There are also important questions regarding the rate of transfer for students from traditionally disadvantaged groups, and evidence from both the USA and Australia indicates that transfer rates are lower for ethnic minority and Aboriginal groups than for white students.

The second point for consideration under this heading is the experience of students at the point of transfer and after entry to degree-level programmes. The differences between the approaches to teaching, learning, and assessment, and the general cultural ethos of colleges when compared with universities, has been referred to above. This can result in what has been referred to as 'transfer shock' (Laanan, 2001), a problem that has been noted in many societies. This can result in a temporary dip in performance, or in some cases to longer-term problems for some students, which can result in lower completion rates. Data on completion rates is patchy and inconsistent. Completion rates are associated with the social and educational background of students, and the type of preparation they have had before entry to their degree programme. At this time it is not really possible to provide any clear summary of data on this issue, but it is again a question that should be more fully investigated. There is certainly evidence from a growing number of countries of special provision to assist students with transition. In the USA developmental educational programmes are well established in many states, and McCabe refers to these programmes as an essential bridge for many students. Reference has also been made to the 'bridging' programmes in Scotland, and Anderson refers to the growing importance of bridging programmes in New Zealand. All of this points to the need to investigate further the issues associated with providing effective support for transfer students.

Conclusions

It is clear from all the research reported in the chapters in this volume that short-cycle HE is now an increasingly important part of the mass systems of HE that have emerged in many societies. While this form of HE continues to be distinctive, it is clear that the boundaries between it and the more traditional degree-based HE are becoming increasingly blurred, even in countries such as Germany where there is still a more clearly differentiated VET system. It is also clear that many of the institutions that provide short-cycle HE have had considerable success in widening access to this type of HE. However, opportunities for progression from short-cycle to degree-level education are still unevenly distributed in many societies, students often find it difficult to transfer from one sector to another with credit, and they can experience a range of problems during and after transfer. These are all challenging issues for research, policy, and practice, as different societies throughout the world attempt to develop mass systems of HE that are differentiated, but equitable for all participants.

Notes

[1] This distinction between short-cycle and degree-level education can also be referred to as the distinction between the level V type A and level V type B levels of undergraduate provision as defined by the International Standard Classification of Education (ISCED). Level V type A are academic programmes of a largely theoretical nature, while those with an occupational orientation are classified as level V type B.

[2] Although it must be noted that the original function of the community colleges in the USA was the one of preparing students for transfer to four year institutions, which has widened out to include other functions including technical and vocational education (Walker, 2001)

References

Alexander, H., Gallacher, J., Leahy, J. and Yule, W. (1995) 'Changing patterns of higher education in Scotland: A study of links between further education colleges and higher education institutions', *Scottish Journal of Adult and Continuing Education*, 2, pp. 25–54.

Anderson, H. (2005) 'New Zealand tertiary education: Patterns and pathways', in: J. Gallacher and M. Osborne (eds) *A Contested Landscape: International Perspectives on Diversity in Mass Higher Education*. Leicester: NIACE.

Baker, D. (1995) 'Aboriginal education in community colleges', in: J. Dennison (ed.) *Challenge and Opportunity: Canada's Community Colleges at the Crossroads*. Vancouver: University of British Columbia Press, pp. 208–19.

Bonham, B. (2005) 'Educational mobility in the USA through the community college transfer function', in: J. Gallacher and M. Osborne (eds) *A Contested Landscape: International Perspectives on Diversity in Mass Higher Education*. Leicester: NIACE.

Burtch, B. (2005) 'Review of further education/higher education links in Canada', in: J. Gallacher and M. Osborne (eds) *A Contested Landscape: International Perspectives on Diversity in Mass Higher Education*. Leicester: NIACE.

Cohen, A. and Sanchez, J. (1997) *The Transfer Rate: A Model of Consistency*. Los Angeles, CA: Center for Study of Community Colleges.

Coughlan, D. (2005) 'The further education system in Ireland', in: J. Gallacher and M. Osborne (eds) *A Contested Landscape: International Perspectives on Diversity in Mass Higher Education*. Leicester: NIACE.

Deissinger, T. (2005) 'Links between vocational education and training (VET) and higher education: The case of Germany', in: J. Gallacher and M. Osborne (eds) *A Contested Landscape: International Perspectives on Diversity in Mass Higher Education*. Leicester: NIACE.

Department for Education and Skills (DfES) (2003) *The Future of Higher Education*, Cm 5735. London: The Stationery Office.

Gallacher, J. (2003) *Higher Education in Further Education Colleges: The Scottish Experience*. London: The Council for Industry and Higher Education.

Gallacher, J. (2005) 'Complementarity or differentiation: The roles of further education colleges and higher education institutions in Scotland's higher education system', in: J. Gallacher and M. Osborne (eds) *A Contested Landscape: International Perspectives on Diversity in Mass Higher Education*. Leicester: NIACE.

Gallacher, J. *et al*. (2000) *Education for All? FE, Social Inclusion and Widening Access*, Final Report for Scottish Executive. Glasgow Caledonian University, Centre for Research in Lifelong Learning.

Helm, P. and Cohen, A. (2001) 'Leadership perspectives on preparing transfer students', in F. S. Laanan (ed.) Transfer Students: Trends and Issues, *New Directions for Community Colleges*, 114, pp. 87–98. San Francisco, CA: Jossey-Bass.

Ignash, J. and Townsend, B. (2000) 'Evaluating state-level articulation agreements according to good practice', *Community College Review*, 28(3), pp. 1–21.

Karmel, T. and Nguyen, N. (2003) *Australia's Tertiary Education Sector*. Centre for the Economics of Education and Training 7th National Conference, Melbourne.

Knoell, D. (1990) *Transfer, Articulation, and Collaboration: 25 Years Later*. Washington, DC: American Association of Community Colleges.

Laanan, F. (2001) 'Transfer student adjustment', in: F. S. Laanan (ed.) Transfer Students: Trends and Issues, *New Directions for Community Colleges*, 114, pp. 5–13.

Maclennan, A., Musselbrook, K. and Dundas, M. (2000) *Credit Transfer at the FE/HE Interface*. Edinburgh: Scottish Higher Education Funding Council/Scottish Further Education Funding Council.

Osborne, M. (2005) 'Introduction', in: J. Gallacher and M. Osborne (eds) *A Contested Landscape: International Perspectives on Diversity in Mass Higher Education*. Leicester: NIACE.

Parry, G. (2005) 'Higher education in the learning and skills sector: England', in: J. Gallacher and M. Osborne (eds) *A Contested Landscape: International Perspectives on Diversity in Mass Higher Education*. Leicester: NIACE.

Prather, J. and Carlson, C. (1993) 'When four-year and community colleges collide: Studies for enrollment maximization', Paper presented at the Annual Forum of the Association for Institutional Research, Chicago, IL.

Raab, G. and Davidson, K. (1999) *Distribution of FE Provision in Scotland*. Edinburgh, SOEID.

Raab, G. and Small, G. (2003) *Widening Access to Higher Education in Scotland: Evidence for Change from 1996–1997 to 2000–01*. Edinburgh: SHEFC.

Rifkin, T. (1998) *Improving Articulation Policy to Increase Transfer*, Policy Paper. Denver: Education Commission of the States.

Scott, D. (2003) *Participation in Tertiary Education*. NZ: Ministry of Education.

Sommerlad, E., Duke, C. and McDonald, R. (1998) *Universities and TAFE: Collaboration in the Emerging World of 'Universal Higher Education'*. Canberra: Higher Education Council. Online at: http://www.deetya.gov.au/nbeet/publications/hec/overview.html

Trow, M. (2000) 'From mass higher education to universal access: The American advantage', *Minerva*, 37, pp. 1–26.

Walker, K. (2001) 'Opening the door to the baccalaureate degree', *Community College Review*, 29(2), pp. 18–28.

Wheelahan, L. and Moodie, G. (2005) 'Separate post-compulsory education sectors within a liberal market economy: Interesting models generated by the Australian anomaly', in: J. Gallacher and M. Osborne (eds) *A Contested Landscape: International Perspectives on Diversity in Mass Higher Education*. Leicester: NIACE.

Contributors

Jim Gallacher, Professor of Lifelong Learning and Co-director for the Centre for Research in Lifelong Learning, Glasgow Caledonian University, has been responsible for managing a large number of externally funded research and development projects in the area of lifelong learning. His current research interests include mass higher education, the role of further education colleges and the transition from further to higher education. He was an adviser to the Scottish Parliament for their Inquiry into Lifelong Learning, and is a member of the National Forum on Lifelong Learning.

Michael Osborne is Professor of Lifelong Learning and Deputy Head of the Institute of Education at the University of Stirling, where he is also Co-director of the PASCAL Observatory and the Centre for Research in Lifelong Learning (CRLL) His particular areas of interest are: the participation of adults in learning, including in vocational and work-based learning, and in further and higher education; and the development of learning regions. He has conducted and coordinated many research and development projects at a national and European level. His current projects include the development of audit tools for stakeholders within Learning Regions, and an Economic and Social Research Council, Teaching and Learning Research programme project on the 'Social and Organisation Mediation of University Learning'.

Helen Anderson is currently the national manager for the New Zealand Curriculum Alignment Project, a lecturer in Education for The University of Auckland at Manukau Programme, and a researcher and a senior manager at Manukau Institute of Technology. A recurring theme in her work has been developing strategies for quality participation for all students in the New Zealand tertiary education system. This has included work in bridging and foundation education, the establishment of curriculum pathways for local schools and private training enterprises into tertiary institutes, the development and evaluation of the Special Supplementary Grant (Māori and Pasifika), managing The University of Auckland at Manukau programme's support and pathways, and work on the development of self-access centres.

Barbara S. Bonham is the Coordinator of the Higher Education Graduate Programs and Professor in the Department of Leadership and Educational Studies at Appalachian State University, Boone, NC, USA. She serves as Senior Researcher for the National Center for Developmental Education and is a faculty member for the Kellogg Institute. She has over 30 years teaching experience and has served as consultant to numerous colleges and universities, the US Department of Education (Council of Educational Opportunity), state boards of higher education, and to business and industry. Her publications, presentations and areas of research interest include planning educational programmes for adult learners, assessment and evaluation, designing inclusive learning environments and teaching community college students, characteristics of the developmental mathematics student, access opportunities to higher education, and learning styles.

Brian Burtch is a Full Professor in the School of Criminology, an associate member in Simon Fraser University's (SFU) Department of Women's Studies, and academic director of SFU's Integrated Studies Program which is designed for mid-career students. His key interests are sociology of law, gender and law, midwifery and the state, critical criminology, penal abolition, and efforts to support non-traditional postsecondary students. Other interests include teaching with online technology and cohort-based education, such as the integrated studies programme and SFU Criminology's undergraduate Honours programme. His publications include *Trials of Labour: The Re-emergence of Midwifery* (McGill-Queen's University Press, 1994), *The Sociology of Law* (2nd edition, Nelson Thomson Canada, 2003), and a co-authored reader with Nick Larsen, *Law in Society: Canadian Perspectives* (1999), the second edition of which will be published in September 2005 by Nelson Thomson Canada. He chaired the Ad Hoc Committee on Lifelong Learning at SFU.

Dermot Coughlan is Director of Lifelong Learning and Outreach at the University of Limerick in Ireland. He was appointed to this position in 2000 when the University of Limerick established a Department of

Lifelong Learning. Prior to assuming this position he worked in human resources management for almost 30 years. He has a keen interest in work-based learning, the accreditation of prior learning and in the issue of quality.

Thomas Deissinger, born in 1958, studied at the University of Mannheim (Baden-Württemberg/Germany) where he also took his Ph.D. in 1991. He became Professor of Business Education (Wirtschaftspädagogik) at the University of Konstanz (Baden-Württemberg/Germany) in 1998. His duties outside the university system include lectures and seminars with the German Foundation of International Development (DSE), now InWEnt GmbH, in Mannheim, in the field of VET in developing countries. He has specialised in vocational training policy and comparative research activities in the area of VET. Research interests also include didactical issues and the history of VET as well as school-based VET and practice firms in vocational schools. Several among his publications are devoted to the nature and development of the VET systems in the UK and Australia from a comparative perspective.

Gavin Moodie is principal policy adviser at Griffith University, Australia. He has published over 40 refereed papers and chapters on higher education and on the relations between higher education and vocational education in Aotearoa New Zealand, Australia, Canada, the UK and the US, which is the subject of his doctoral thesis. He was joint editor of the *Journal of Higher Education Policy and Management* for a decade and is currently the reviews editor and a regular referee for that journal. He is a regular correspondent for *The Australian*'s higher education supplement.

Gareth Parry is Professor of Education at the University of Sheffield. He was a consultant to the Dearing inquiry into higher education in the United Kingdom (1996–97) and the Foster review of further education colleges in England (2004–05). He is a Fellow of the Society for Research into Higher Education and Co-Editor of *Higher Education Quarterly*.

Leesa Wheelahan is a senior lecturer in the School of Vocational, Technology and Arts Education at Griffith University, Australia. Her research and publications focus on cross-sectoral relations between the sectors of post-compulsory education and training. In 2002–03 she led a project for the Australian Qualifications Framework Advisory Board to develop recognition of prior learning principles and guidelines for all sectors of post-compulsory education and training in Australia. She is a regular correspondent for *Campus Review* on relations between the vocational education and training and higher education sectors, and on VET policy.

Index

A

AA (Associate of Arts) degree – USA 179, 181

AAS (Associate of Applied Science) degree – USA 181

Abitur – Germany 102

access programmes – Australia 31–2

adult and community education – New Zealand 149

American Association of Community Colleges 178

Andres, L. 52–3

ANTA (Australian National Training Authority) 20, 24

apprenticeships – Germany 92–7, 107–8

AQF (Australian Qualifications Framework) 22–5, 205
credit transfer guidelines 32

AS (Associate of Science) degree – USA 179, 181

Association of Canadian Community Colleges 53, 55

Australia 18–46, 197
access programmes 31–2
ANTA (Australian National Training Authority) 20, 24
AQF (Australian Qualifications Framework) 22–5, 32, 205

AVCC (Australian Vice-Chancellors' Committee) 24, 26
co-located institutions 35, 36, 202
credit transfer 30–1, 32–4, 35–6, 38
dual-sector awards 37, 38
dual-sector institutions 34–5
Kangan Committee 38
nested awards 37
TAFE (technical and further education) 20, 21, 30–1, 33, 38–9
VET (vocational education and training) 20–1, 24–5, 27, 28–9, 38–40
Victorian Qualifications Authority 33

AVCC (Australian Vice-Chancellors' Committee) 24, 26

B

Baden-Württemburg 99, 101
vocational academies (*Berufsakademien*) 102–7

Bauer, P. and Bauer, K. 189

BC (British Columbia)
community colleges 48
credit transfer 50–1

G

H

I